A Journey in FAITH

Facilitator Guide

Bobby H. Welch and Doug Williams

with David Apple

LifeWay Press®

Nashville, Tennessee

Credits/Acknowledgments

Special thanks to the congregation of First Baptist Church, Daytona Beach, Florida. With graciousness and patience, you have opened your doors and facilities so that many might be trained.

For modeling what it means to be a Great Commission church, intentionally opening your hearts so that more people might be reached with God's saving message, we are especially grateful.

Editor
Sharon Roberts

Graphic Design Specialist
Dale Royalty

Illustration, *A Step of Faith*
Stephen S. Sawyer

Cover Design
Steve Diggs & Friends
Marketing Communications
A Division of The Franklin Group

© Copyright 1998 LifeWay Press
Revised © February 2002
All rights reserved

No part of this work may be reproduced or transmitted in any form or by any means, electronic or mechanical, including photocopying and recording, or by any information storage or retrieval system, except as may be expressly permitted in writing by the publisher. Requests for permission should be addressed to LifeWay Press; One LifeWay Plaza; Nashville, TN 37234-0175.

ISBN: 0-7673-9857-2

Dewey Decimal Classification: 269.2
Subject Heading: EVANGELISTIC WORK IN THE SUNDAY SCHOOL

The FAITH Sunday School Evangelism Strategy® is an evangelistic ministry of LifeWay Christian Resources and is endorsed by the North American Mission Board.
FAITH Sunday School Evangelism Strategy® is a registered trademark of LifeWay Christian Resources of the Southern Baptist Convention.

Scripture quotations marked NIV are from the *Holy Bible, New International Version,* copyright © 1973, 1978, 1984 by International Bible Society.

The *New King James Version* is the text for Scripture memory in the FAITH gospel presentation. Scripture quotations marked NKJV are from the *New King James Version.* Copyright © 1979, 1980, 1982, Thomas Nelson, Inc., Publishers.
To order additional copies of this resource, write to LifeWay Church Resources Customer Service; One LifeWay Plaza; Nashville, TN 37234-0113; fax (615) 251-5933; phone (800) 458-2772; or e-mail *customerservice@lifeway.com.*

Printed in the United States of America

Leadership and Adult Publishing
LifeWay Church Resources
One LifeWay Plaza
Nashville, TN 37234-0175

Dedication

To Jimmy Draper, Gene Mims, Ted Warren, Bill Taylor,
and others at LifeWay Christian Resources of
the Southern Baptist Convention

To the North American Mission Board, for partnering with
LifeWay Christian Resources in evangelism

To all those who had the courage and honesty to face our desperate
need to do better at winning and discipling our world in our lifetime
and who boldly assumed accountability to provide a way—
the FAITH Sunday School Evangelism Strategy®

To all the individuals who have committed or will commit themselves to
do the last thing Christ told us to do: "Therefore go and make disciples of
all nations, baptizing them in the name of the Father and of the Son
and of the Holy Spirit, and teaching them to obey everything I
have commanded you. And surely I am with you always,
to the very end of the age"
(Matt. 28:19-20, NIV).

Contents

Foreword

Sunday School As It Was Intended to Be

What an incredible opportunity the FAITH Sunday School Evangelism Strategy has placed before Southern Baptists! This is Sunday School as it was intended to be . . . with a focus on ministry and evangelism.

FAITH offers a simple way to present the gospel to the lost—and the mechanics to make Sunday School groups effective and dynamic. FAITH Originator Churches, where FAITH was launched, report significant revitalization of their Sunday Schools and dramatic increases in professions of faith.

This clear, simple, straightforward means of incorporating Sunday School and evangelism together is the way God will use to lead us to our greatest years of growth in Bible study and evangelism. Thank God for this strategic partnership with the North American Mission Board. Not only does it maximize the resources of both agencies, it also clarifies options for local churches and strengthens our focus on reaching the unsaved for salvation and Christians for greater growth and maturity through Sunday School.

James T. Draper, Jr.

JAMES T. DRAPER, JR., PRESIDENT
LIFEWAY CHRISTIAN RESOURCES

Baptists Do Best What Baptists Do Together

Although the Southern Baptist Convention has primarily entrusted the North American Mission Board with evangelistic strategies, the North American Mission Board is proud to partner with LifeWay Christian Resources in the development of the FAITH strategy. Along with Dr. Jimmy Draper and the LifeWay Christian Resources leadership team, I believe that evangelism is a crucial heart beat for Sunday School.

In 1945 J. N. Barnette said that "where evangelism has been the heart of the message and the work of Sunday schools, church buildings have been crowded, people have been baptized, and money has been given. . . . Sunday schools grow fastest when the fires of evangelism burn the hottest."[1]

In addition to servicing multi-pronged evangelism strategies, the North American Mission Board stands strong with our partners at LifeWay Christian Resources. We pray that God will use FAITH as a major tool to see Southern Baptists baptize 500,000 in one year and then move to the significant goal of baptizing 1 million people in one year.

This partnership shows that Baptists do best what Baptists do together.

BOB RECCORD, PRESIDENT
NORTH AMERICAN MISSION BOARD

[1]J. N. Barnette, *The Place of the Sunday School in Evangelism* (Nashville: The Sunday School Board of the Southern Baptist Convention, 1945), 43. Out of print.

Foreword

Preface

Following is one church's journey of intentionally reaching out and witnessing through Sunday School ministry.

An Extraordinary Journey Awaits You

FAITH is the story of what is about to happen in your life and in your church. It is the journey of faith in which God led a congregation of believers—much like yours—into a most extraordinary life-changing adventure. This adventure characterized us individually and collectively, locally and globally. It all occurred because of the Lord's blessings on a very ordinary pastor, staff, and church. Their deep and only desire was to see members become committed Great Commission Christians and to actually begin using an intentional strategy to win and disciple their world in their lifetime.

The results have been revolutionary in individuals and in the church as a whole. The evidences are experienced and seen in a multitude of ways through the lives of people just like you. You will read the details of our journey on pages 73-77 of *Evangelism Through the Sunday School: A Journey of FAITH.*

Individually, members have been brought to an exceptional level of soul consciousness for the world around them. Also, they have come to a place of unusual commitment to equip themselves to do something about their world. People of FAITH have become believers "on the grow" as well as "on the go." They have come to correctly believe and expect that, if they are in FAITH, something good and spiritual will happen in their lives and in the lives of their friends and families. And it does!

Congregationally, over the past 12-plus years, there has been the ever-recurring belief and expectation that "Something is happening in our church; something exciting is going on!" We call this belief in our church the "Book of Acts" atmosphere. It accounts for the fact that in those years more than 1,400 people have participated in evangelism training—approximately 65 percent of the adults who are eligible for such training. Some adult classes have 75 percent of their class experiencing the "grow and go" of FAITH. This did not happen in one year, but it all began right where you are now.

FAITH Teams come and go, month by month, with an intentional strategy to win and disciple their world in their lifetime. Such experiences cannot be kept within one church, but should move out into other cities, counties, countries, and continents.

Oh, the unspeakable thrill of being in a 21st-century church and Sunday School ministry that has first-century excitement for souls! Welcome to the extraordinary journey of FAITH!

These Experiences Can Be Yours

FAITH is making lasting and meaningful "heart prints" on churches and individuals. Following are comments from some churches that are experiencing FAITH:

- "FAITH has put the passion for people back into my (a pastor's) heart."
- "One of our FAITH Teams went to a stranger's door, introduced themselves, and then introduced her to the Savior. That stranger is now a faithful friend, a beloved sister in Christ, a servant of Jesus. If we are faithful to go and tell, God will transform the stranger into a faithful friend and a fellow servant."
- "Our entire Sunday School and congregation has had a fire lit within it, a fire of 'soul consciousness' through FAITH."
- "We sent a Median Adult Team out for a ministry visit to a member who had missed three consecutive Sundays. As they approached the house, they could see there were no lights on in the house. They proceeded to go to the door and, sure enough, no one answered. A Team member encouraged the Team to pray for the couple who lived at the house. They prayed and then went toward the car. As they did, they could see the approaching headlights of a car coming down the road, so they waited.

  "The husband turned into his driveway, got out of his car, and said, 'I really needed to see someone from my church tonight.' They had an incredible ministry visit. During Celebration Time, the rest of the Teams could see the awesome power of prayer."
- "FAITH is how I led my husband and son to the Lord."
- "Twenty middle-schoolers and five leaders are consistently involved in Student FAITH each week," in addition to the adult Teams.
- "I've never seen anything change a church as quickly as FAITH has. We're in revival."
- "We have had someone saved each week as we have been going out."
- "FAITH is responsible for our having more people involved in visitation than we have had in years."
- "My entire family is in church because of FAITH."
- "FAITH is allowing our church and Sunday School ministry to be 'another chapter' in the Book of Acts."

Preface

Yet to be written is *your* testimony.

Prayerfully begin FAITH expecting God to do great things in you and your church.

- "A lady who helps her husband teach a Young Married class went to the home of a couple and led a young mother to Christ. She was so excited because she had been praying for this young lady for several weeks, and now was able to lead her to Christ. She had visited this couple several times but was never able to share her faith; now she felt equipped to share her faith, and God gave her the victory."

- "Until now, I have never as pastor had 20 people involved in outreach visitation in one week. I have never heard any of my members say, 'You mean we have to wait a week to go out and do this again?' The prayer team is impatient because they want to be trained to go out too. I have never had that 'problem' before. I thought you might enjoy a FAITH testimony from a once-small, flat-lined church in the Northwest. We don't fit that description anymore."

- (Says the pastor) "I have watched people who are shy and bashful turn into warriors for Christ, sharing the gospel every chance they get. These are people who never would have considered visitation, much less evangelism.

  "The only way I know to describe the change is that they now have a new heart, a broken heart; a broken heart for people who are living and are struggling without Jesus as Lord and Savior."

- "A Christian is called to keep the faith, but not to himself" (Student FAITH participant).

Overview of Materials

This resource will help you as FAITH Facilitator to train a group of Learners in their foundational semester of training (FAITH Basic). Your FAITH Director or pastor received *A Journey in FAITH: Training Pack for Sunday School Evangelism Strategy* when your church participated in a FAITH Training Clinic. The items—an Administrative Guide, sample of Learner materials, a Facilitator Guide, overhead transparencies, videotapes, audiocassette, and computer presentation—will help you teach the first 16 sessions of FAITH and your director to administer the FAITH process.

Your main teaching resource is *A Journey in FAITH: Facilitator Guide*. As you familiarize yourself with the Guide, you will find these features:

• *Lesson material is provided for Teaching Time and assignments are given for home study.*—The commentary in the center (wide) columns of pages x and xi is an example of how all session content is presented. You have the same information Learners have in *A Journey in FAITH: Journal.* Learners will be on the same page with you throughout the study.

• *A step-by-step teaching plan is in the margins of the Facilitator Guide.*—Each session plan gives you specific sequential steps organized around these main activities in Teaching Time: HEAR IT, SEE IT, SAY IT, and STUDY IT. HEAR IT describes possible lecture content; SEE IT refers to opportunities to view a new segment of the FAITH Visit Outline on video or as role play; SAY IT indicates opportunities to practice new information with a partner; and STUDY IT is the time to overview Home Study Assignments. Review each week's material in advance.

Each session includes 45 minutes of Teaching Time, except for Session 1 (Orientation); Session 12, a practice session; and Session 16, a final check-up. Highlight (and encourage Team Leaders to do the same) items that will appear on the Session 16 written review.

A Journey in Faith Begins

Welcome to a journey of faith, a journey leading you to learn to celebrate and share your faith in Christ with others. This resource is designed to help you participate in and eventually take the lead in making evangelistic and ministry visits to persons assigned to your Sunday School. The very nature of a journal is reflective, interactive, and dynamic. Commit yourself to use this resource and process for these kinds of results.

FAITH can change your life! Since you will focus on doing the work of a Great Commission Christian, let's reflect again on some key words in Matthew 28:18-20 (NIV).

ALL AUTHORITY . . .

FAITH will help you:

- focus on ways Jesus is working in your life as a believer;
- identify ways Jesus is working in the lives of nonbelievers; and
- realize how evangelism and ministry are the heartbeat of our faith.

GO . . .

FAITH will help you:

- replace the fear and apprehension of "going" with excitement and zeal;
- be trained in a simple but direct visitation outline;
- learn how to share your faith in a wide variety of situations;
- visit prospects and members from your Sunday School class each week, as a Team; and
- learn to be sensitive to visits as divine appointments.

TEACHING . . .

FAITH will help you:

- be trained by someone who already has been trained in and is practicing FAITH; and
- learn how to teach other believers to share their faith.

BAPTIZING . . .

FAITH will help you:

- learn a wonderfully simple but meaningful gospel presentation;
- realize that people will get saved because of your obedience;
- experience the joy of seeing people pray to receive Christ as Savior;
- rejoice as these persons publicly acknowledge faith in Christ; and
- experience the thrill of helping people grow in their faith.

I AM WITH YOU ALWAYS . . .

FAITH will help you:

- observe dynamic ways in which Christ is working in your life;
- witness the life-changing power of God as you are available and obedient to Him; and
- receive blessings and joy that can come only from God.

FAITH can change the lives of people you encounter! Many will receive joy because they are praying with and for you. Several will hear the good news of the gospel for the first time. Many will start considering the life-changing implications of the gospel for their life. Some will commit to a renewed relationship with the Lord. Several will be saved. Many will be blessed by the Holy Spirit because you cared enough to go and share.

Others will be encouraged to begin witnessing and ministering because of your faithfulness. Many in your church will focus on the joys of their own faith in Christ and will grow in boldness and commitment.

Your primary responsibility in this training is to learn to conduct a FAITH visit. Memorize and be prepared to recite the FAITH Visit Outline as overviewed. The outline is segmented so that each session deals with a specific section of the visit. Assignments will be given in each session to help you understand and relate to that specific aspect.

You will begin making visits with your Team in Session 2. Be prepared to participate in the evangelistic and ministry visits and in the Celebration Time that follows.

A Word About Your Journal

Features of this resource are designed to help you throughout training:

- Material for taking notes, fill-in-the-blank activities, and practice exercises;
- Session material enhanced with a creative videotape that models that portion of the FAITH visit;
- Each week's new memory work in the FAITH Visit Outline;
- Home Study Assignments with reading, memorizing, and writing opportunities to help reinforce and enhance what it means to share your faith;
- Space for journaling your own personal growth and for recording prayer requests and answers to prayer throughout FAITH training;
- Team Leader Supplement pages, to help you identify how to deal with specific situations during a visit at the time you need the information.

This resource and process will help you understand the scope of growing as a committed Great Commission Christian and of being prepared to lead someone to accept Jesus as Savior and Lord.

- *In the Learner's Journal, the narrow side columns are left blank for notes.*
- *Fill-in-the-blank words and phrases help Learners understand significant concepts in FAITH training.* Use visuals (four-color overhead cels or computer presentation slides) to display the words and phrases to be filled in or emphasized. Leave them on screen as long as Learners need, and comment accordingly.

Some sessions have additional computer presentation frames to enhance your teaching session. Generally, that information is highlighted in the "In Advance" section of the Facilitator Guide (first page of each session). Whatever media is used, preview the presentation in its entirety before Orientation.

- *Icons in the teaching plan column highlight times projected visuals may be used.*

Icons Indicate Use of

Overhead Cels or Computer Presentation Slides

Training Videotape

Also in the Training Pack is an audiocassette with the FAITH Visit Outline. Make memorization easy for Learners by duplicating the cassette and giving them a copy. *FAITH Visit Outline Cards* are another option.

A FAITH Visit Role Play (p. 72 in the Administrative Guide) is an option to the Training Video (has closed captioning).

The forms needed for FAITH are described in the Administrative Guide. The forms themselves are available as products, which can be ordered through Customer Service in the quantities needed for your church. Forms not available as products or which need customization for different uses are provided as bonus text files on your Training Pack CD-ROM.

Supplemental items (shirts, pencils, certificates, and so forth) are described in the FAITH Catalog that comes to every FAITH church.

Key leaders

My FAITH Director ____________________

FAITH Facilitator ____________________

Assistant Facilitator ____________________

My Group Leader ____________________

My Team Leader ____________________

Assistant Team Leader (if appropriate)

____

Other Learners:

____

____

Key actions in sessions

Session 2	Sunday School testimony due
Session 5	Written evangelistic testimony due
Sessions 10-12	Heavy levels of memory work; increasing role in visits
Session 12	FAITH Visit Outline memorized
Session 16	Written and verbal reviews

Glossary/What's Ahead

FAITH Director: Leader who oversees FAITH in our church

Facilitator: Person designated to lead a training group in a 16-week semester of FAITH training using *A Journey in FAITH: Journal*

Group Leader: Leader already trained in FAITH who coordinates work of several FAITH Teams and is a Team Leader

Team Leader: Individual who guides two Learners from the same Sunday School class/department to learn the FAITH Visit Outline and to take the lead in visits

Learner: Your role in the first semester of FAITH; goal is to learn the FAITH Visit Outline and to take the lead in evangelistic visits

FAITH Visit Outline: Sequence to learn throughout FAITH training; it not only suggests points of contact and conversation with a prospect, but also ways to assess whether and how to continue with a specific gospel presentation based on the word *FAITH*

Session 1 overviews the process of FAITH training, familiarizes you with resources, and suggests ways your Sunday School testimony can be used in a visit.

Session 2 begins with 15 minutes of Team Time CHECK IT activities. Teaching Time helps you identify specific things to do to begin a visit. You will begin making visits/returning for Celebration Time during this session.

Session 3 focuses on elements in your evangelistic testimony. You have two weeks to practice writing your evangelistic testimony.

Session 4 highlights how to make a Sunday School ministry visit.

Session 5 overviews the gospel presentation beginning with the Key Question.

Session 6 helps you focus on FORGIVENESS in the gospel presentation.

Session 7 adds the elements, AVAILABLE FOR ALL and BUT NOT AUTOMATIC, to the outline.

Session 8 directs your attention to IMPOSSIBLE, or why it is impossible for God to allow sin into heaven.

Session 9 explains what it means to TURN from sin and self to Christ only.

Session 10 focuses on HEAVEN—both now and in eternity—and HOW you can help someone know God's forgiveness is possible for him/her.

Session 11 helps you learn how to invite someone to saving faith in Christ using *A Step of Faith* and how to lead the person to make commitments for growth.

Session 12 is for additional practice of the outline, with no Teaching Time.

Session 13 overviews ways to share FAITH in everyday experiences.

Session 14 suggests how to handle difficulties and distractions in a visit.

Session 15 highlights involvements in future FAITH training opportunities.

Session 16 is a time of written and verbal reviews.

FAITH Participation Card

Name ______________________ Semester dates __________

Address ______________________ Phone __________

Sunday School class/department ______________ Teacher __________

Other Team members ______________________

Check one: ❑ FAITH Team Leader ❑ FAITH Assistant Team Leader ❑ FAITH Team Learner

	1	2	3	4	5	6	7	8	9	10	11	12	13	14	15	16	Totals
Class Participation *Place a check to indicate completion for the appropriate session.*																	
Present																	
Home study done																	
Outline recited																	
Visitation *Indicate a number for the following areas.*																	
Number of tries																	
Number of visits																	
Number of people talked with																	
Type of Visit *(Assignments)*																	
Evangelistic																	
Ministry																	
Baptism																	
Follow-up																	
Opinion Poll																	
Gospel Presented																	
Profession																	
Assurance																	
No decision																	
For practice																	
Gospel Not Presented																	
Already Christian																	
No admission																	
Sunday School Enrollment																	
Attempted																	
Enrolled																	
Baptism Explained																	
Committed																	
No decision																	
Life Witness																	
Profession																	
Assurance																	
No decision																	

Expression of Commitment

A Journey in FAITH

I commit myself to **FAITH** Sunday School evangelism training in my church. I recognize **FAITH** training as a way to help my church, to grow as a Great Commission Christian, and to obey God's command to be an active witness.

Signed ______________________________

Address ______________________________

City ____________________ State ________ ZIP __________

Phone number (home) ______________ (business) ______________

E-mail ____________________ Fax ______________

I will faithfully attend and participate in this 16-week semester of **FAITH** training as: ❑ a Team Leader ❑ an Assistant Team Leader ❑ a Team Learner

My Team members ______________________________

My Sunday School department/class ______________________________

Dates of my *A Journey in FAITH* training ______________________________

SESSION 1

Orientation to FAITH *Training*

In this session you will

HEAR IT: discover how FAITH training can help you become a Great Commission Christian, who is obedient to God's command to be a witness; overview the schedule, processes, and materials for FAITH training; and learn how to write your Sunday School testimony;

SEE IT: view video modeling of entire FAITH Visit Outline, including the gospel presentation; meet the video character George and think about what also might happen to *you* through FAITH;

STUDY IT: overview the purposes of Home Study Assignments and specific assignments for Session 1.

In Advance

- Pray for Learners, people who will be visited during FAITH, and FAITH training.
- Familiarize yourself with all session material. Prepare carefully for Orientation (Session 1). Also overview Part 1 of *FAITH Sunday School Evangelism Strategy: FAITH Director's Administrative Guide* to include other key points about FAITH, as your group needs.

  Note: The Administrative Video (has closed captioning) in your Training Pack highlights the philosophy and purposes of FAITH. If your Learners have not seen this video in FAITH enlistment efforts, consider showing all or part with Step 3, "Sunday School and Evangelism Work Together." Extend the total training time for Orientation and have this video ready after using Part 1 of the Training Video.
- Have sufficient Journals to distribute to Learners as they arrive.
- Gather all media needed. Decide whether to use Session 1 overhead cels (#1-15) or the computer presentation slides (note *additional slides* for this session). Reserve appropriate equipment.
- Cue the Training Video to "A Journey of FAITH: The Story of George—Part 1." Part 2 follows with the entire visit. If the role play is preferred for modeling a FAITH visit, duplicate parts from the Administrative Guide (pp 72-81); enlist individuals for the roles; and practice in advance.
- Schedule a break at a time most convenient for your group.

Teaching Time

HEAR IT

STEP 1 (10 min.) **Distribute Journals as Learners arrive. Welcome the group and pray. Overview "Welcome to an Exciting Journey in Faith!" content using cels or computer presentation slides to illustrate the lecture.**

Suggest Learners turn in their Bibles to the Scripture passages referred to (or read them later during home study).

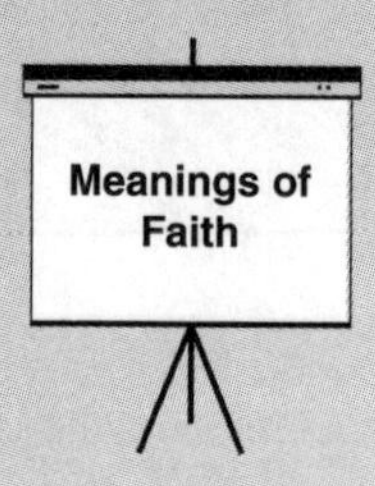

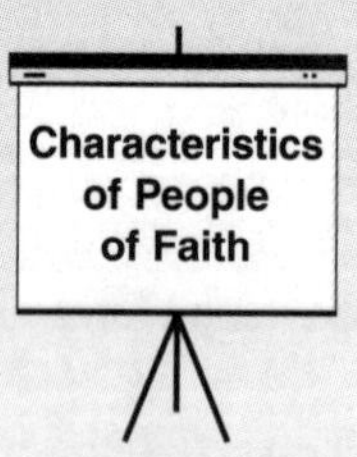

Welcome to an Exciting Journey in Faith!

What comes to your mind when you hear the word *faith?* Did you think about responses similar to these?

MEANINGS OF FAITH

- Belief in Jesus Christ
- A relationship with God through Jesus
- Life in the spiritual dimension
- Trusting Christ to take control of your life
- Taking God at His word and doing what He says, even when you do not understand all the implications
- A journey that begins upon accepting Jesus and that continues until you see Him face-to-face in heaven

Faith is all of these! One of the most intriguing passages in Scripture is Hebrews 11. "Faith is being sure of what we hope for and certain of what we do not see" (Heb. 11:1, NIV).

You are a Christian today because of the sacrificial death of Jesus in payment for your sins. You did nothing, nor can you do anything, to earn that salvation. Somewhere along the way, someone shared with you the good news of Jesus. Once you accepted Jesus as your Savior, you entered into a personal journey of faith. This journey not only includes being salt and light through your life (Matt 5:13-14), but also being His witness in our world (Acts 1:8).

In looking at Hebrews 11 in its entirety, some people of faith become evident: Abraham, Moses, Noah, among others. Do you see in this chapter some characteristics of people of faith? Do you see some ways your journey of faith parallels theirs?

CHARACTERISTICS OF PEOPLE OF FAITH

- People of faith take God at His word. *Our journey of faith* shows us times when we are led by God to go to places we have never been and to people we have never seen.
- People of faith believe God's promises. *Our journey of faith* is filled with a growing awareness of His promises.

• People of faith make themselves available to God. *Our journey of faith* is filled with times when God asks, "Whom shall I send? And who will go for us?" (Isa. 6:8, NIV).

• People of faith allow themselves to be used in extraordinary ways. We are gathered as a group of rather ordinary believers, in ordinary circumstances. In *our journey of faith,* God is saying to us, "Come, follow Me."

One purpose of FAITH training is to help you become a Great Commission Christian, who shares his/her faith with joy and effectiveness.

How Do We Do FAITH? Sunday School and Evangelism Work Together

During the next 16 weeks you will learn to make evangelistic and ministry visits to prospects and members of your class or department. In many cases, the prospects you visit will have some connection to our church from attending Sunday School or worship services. In some cases, you will visit members who have become inactive or who need a contact. The people we visit are targeted for Bible teaching, ministry, and evangelism.

In our Sunday School:

• believers gather for Bible study, prayer, and fellowship;

• nonbelievers can (and are urged to) join Sunday School;

• members reach people and are involved in evangelism;

• every person discovered "belongs" to a specific class, department, or Bible study group; and

• Bible study resources help believers grow and encourage nonbelievers to investigate (and hopefully accept) the claims of Christ on their lives.

Over the next few weeks, notice how Sunday School helps you "connect" with people you visit and how individuals you encounter often make significant decisions—to begin attending Sunday School or church after being inactive; to accept Christ; to bring their entire family to church. What better place to help them grow than through our Sunday School?

Also notice how, through Sunday School classes and departments, we pray for, plan for, and follow up on persons we visit. We *do* FAITH through Sunday School because Sunday School is our foundational strategy.

During FAITH notice how you may begin to model 2 Timothy 2:1-2 to grow in grace and equip someone else, thus multiplying our ministry.

SEE IT

STEP 2 (5 min.) **After concluding your overview with the comment about becoming a Great Commission Christian, say:**

Being obedient to God's command to be a witness does not mean you are without fears. Are you anxious about making a visit? Are you nervous about what you might encounter? Meet George, who also had concerns.

Show training video segment "A Journey of FAITH: The Story of George—Part 1." ***(Part 1 is a cliff-hanger and will be resolved in Part 2.)***

HEAR IT

Explain the relationships of FAITH to Sunday School using "How Do We Do FAITH? Sunday School and Evangelism Work Together" content, computer presentation slides or cel, and FAITH Administrative Guide or administrative video.

Option: **If more information is needed by your group and enough time has been allowed, show segments of the FAITH Administrative Video to highlight the important connection between FAITH training and Sunday School. If using this video, you may not need the cel.**

Make sure the relationship between FAITH training and 2 Timothy 2:1-2 is highlighted; it will be a question on the final written review.

STEP 4 (10 min.) Explain the purposes of FAITH training based on "What Are We Learning? FAITH Visit Outline" content and computer presentation slide or cel.

Say: You will learn a specific outline called the *FAITH Visit Outline.* This outline describes the sequence of a visit and possible areas of conversation. It also includes a specific gospel presentation based on the word *FAITH.*

You will be using this outline in actual visits after you have learned it and watched your Team Leader model it. Key words and sentences will become a part of your thinking and can help you know what to discuss next. You will receive help throughout FAITH training to handle different situations that can come up.

To get us started, let's look at the *basic outline.* Each week we will "expand" this outline with subpoints and training about those points.

(If used by your church) FAITH Visit Outline Cards, containing key points of the outline, may be kept in purses or wallets to aid learning.

STEP 5 (15 min.) Overview FAITH materials:

• *A Journey in FAITH: Journal*—Sign Expression of Commitment *(p. 1;* remind of 16-week commitment; point out such Journal features as fill-in-the-blank activities.)

• *Evangelism Through the Sunday School: A Journey of FAITH*—Write your name inside.

• FAITH Participation Card—One copy is in your Journal; another is your name placard and Team summary each week. Write your name, address, phone number, and Sunday School class on the table copy. Your Team Leader will help you complete this card each week.

What Are We Learning? FAITH Visit Outline

FAITH VISIT OUTLINE (Basic)

Preparation

INTRODUCTION
INTERESTS
INVOLVEMENT
INQUIRY

Presentation

F (FORGIVENESS)
A (AVAILABLE)
I (IMPOSSIBLE)
T (TURN)
H (HEAVEN)

Invitation

INQUIRE
INVITE
INSURE

What Are We Using? Schedule, Expectations, and Resources

Familiarize yourself with your Journal. Notice that there is room to take notes during Teaching Time. Each session of Teaching Time—primarily through fill-in-the blank activities—helps you focus on key concepts. Sessions build on each other so that by Session 16, you should feel comfortable taking the lead in a visit—and ready to lead a Team through FAITH!

Throughout the sessions, this symbol highlights important new information to be memorized in the FAITH Visit Outline. At the end of each session are Home Study Assignments. The section called A Journey in Faith gives you space to record your personal "growth-in-faith" experiences.

FAITH is a complete experience characterized each week by *time* to grow closer as a Team (TEAM TIME); *time* to learn together (TEACHING TIME); *time* to reach out and intentionally share the gospel with others (VISITATION TIME); and *time* to share victories (CELEBRATION TIME).

OUR FAITH TRAINING SCHEDULE

_____ (date) to ______ (date)

Team Time begins: ___________________ (time and dates)
(CHECK IT activities)

Teaching Time begins: ___________________
(HEAR IT, SEE IT, SAY IT, STUDY IT class activities)

Visitation Time *(DO IT through visits)* begins: __________

Celebration Time *(SHARE IT through reports)* begins:
____

FAITH training concludes: _________________________ (date).

FAITH Festival takes place: __________________ (date/time).

EXPECTATIONS OF ALL PARTICIPANTS

• Learn a specific visitation outline and sequence called the FAITH Visit Outline. Within that outline, learn how to share a gospel presentation based on letters in the word *FAITH.*

• Participate fully in all training sessions according to the guidelines set by the church (policy for absences, being on time, and so forth). Each session builds on the preceding one to help you learn the FAITH Visit Outline.

• Complete all Home Study Assignments before the next session. Be prepared to ask/answer questions about the previous week's session and to recite to your Team Leader that week's portion of the FAITH Visit Outline.

• Successfully complete a written review in Session 16. You will receive recognition after completing FAITH training (and certification after serving as a Team Leader and leading a Team through training).

• Faithfully attend/participate in Sunday School; help meet evangelism and ministry needs; and follow up on opportunities to enroll nonmembers.

• If as a FAITH participant you also are an elected Sunday School leader, attend weekly Sunday School leadership meetings.

MY CHURCH'S EXPECTATIONS

____
____
____
____

STEP 6 (10 min.) **Using "What Are We Using? Schedule, Expectations, and Resources" content, lead Learners to fill in the blanks. Use cels or computer presentation slides to help them.**

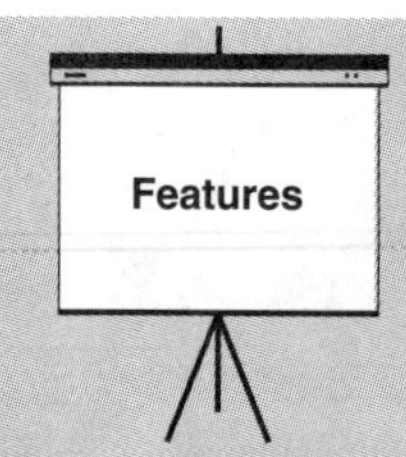

Help Learners find an example from Session 1 of:

- **Highlighted material (✹)—Throughout each session to indicate new memory content for outline**
- **FAITH Tip—"Evangelism Through Sunday School Ministry" *(p. 17)***
- **Home Study Assignments—Follows the session content each week *(pp. 14-20)***
- **Your Journey in Faith—Last section of each week's Home Study Assignment *(pp. 19-20)***
- **Team Leader Supplement pages—Back of Journal, directed to your Team Leader *(pp. 249-270)***

STEP 7 (5 min.) **Highlight roles and responsibilities using "Team Positions and Team Responsibilities" content (and Administrative Guide content as needed).**

FEATURES OF *A JOURNEY IN FAITH: JOURNAL*

- New material highlighted by a FAITH logo (✹) indicates new material to be memorized in FAITH __________ Outline .
- ____________ ________ are articles that enhance your skills or understandings in a selected aspect of FAITH training. *(Session 1, p. 17)*
- __________ __________ ______________________ reinforce one week's content and prepare you for the next week's session by providing memory work, practice opportunities, and reading/writing assignments. *(Session 1, pp. 14-20)*
- _________ ______________ ____ _________ section helps you highlight your spiritual growth throughout FAITH *(Session 1, pp. 19-20)*
- __________ ___________ ____________________ pages help your Team Leader guide you in FAITH. *(pp. 249-270)* Hopefully, you will use these pages in the future as you become a Team Leader and agree to mentor two other Learners! You can refer to them now, too.

Team Positions and Team Responsibilities

FAITH Teams are comprised of a FAITH Team Leader and two FAITH Learners. Many of you already know one another from being in the same Sunday School class or department. Other issues affect the makeup of a FAITH Team—for example, the need for each Team to include both male and female members.

As a result, your attendance each week is very important. Here are some reasons:

- If a male Team member is absent, the remaining man and woman should not visit together unless they are married. The reason is to protect the ministry and the individuals from any perception of improper behavior. Other reasons are for the safety of visitors and for the comfort level of the person(s) being visited.
- Two men can visit together. However, recognize that when visiting a woman whose husband is not at home, in most cases they will not be invited inside. If a woman is on the Team, members usually are invited into the house.

RESPONSIBILITIES OF FAITH TEAM LEADER

- Lead Team Time CHECK IT activities (hear Learners recite the FAITH Visit Outline, review Home Study Assignments, ask/answer questions, provide practice opportunities, and offer help to strengthen visits).
- Train two FAITH Learners to learn the FAITH Visit Outline and to be able to share it in actual visitation settings. Help them handle situations for which they are not yet prepared.
- Involve Learners in practice opportunities during Team Time and Visitation Time.
- Lead the Team to report during Celebration Time.
- Be accountable to your FAITH Group Leader for training Learners.
- Participate in weekly Sunday School leadership meetings.
- Pray for opportunities during the week to share your faith.

RESPONSIBILITIES OF FAITH LEARNERS

- Learn and practice the FAITH Visit Outline. Each week present the appropriate portion to your Team Leader for approval. Begin to share what you have learned in actual visits, as prompted by your Team Leader.
- Be responsible for other Home Study Assignments.
- As appropriate during early visits, share your Sunday School testimony and/or evangelistic testimony. Always be prepared to invite someone to participate in and enroll in Sunday School.
- Faithfully attend Sunday School and worship.
- Pray for opportunities throughout the week to build bridges to unbelievers.

Sunday School Testimony: a Key Element in a FAITH *Visit*

A key part of a FAITH Visit is the Sunday School testimony.

Sunday School Testimony

Tell general benefits of Sunday School.

Tell a current personal experience.

You will be learning to share both general benefits of Sunday School and a current personal experience reflecting benefits you have received. As you make visits and continue in FAITH training, you will learn not only how to share personal benefits of Sunday School, but also those benefits that might be needed by the person(s) being visited. Your Team Leader will be able to discern needs in the home and to ask the appropriate Team member to share his or her Sunday School testimony.

Present "Sunday School Testimony: A Key Element" content. Use the cel or computer presentation slide to help Learners fill in the blanks with benefits of Sunday School. Help Learners understand how these benefits might appeal to people they visit.

If time allows, share your own Sunday School testimony.

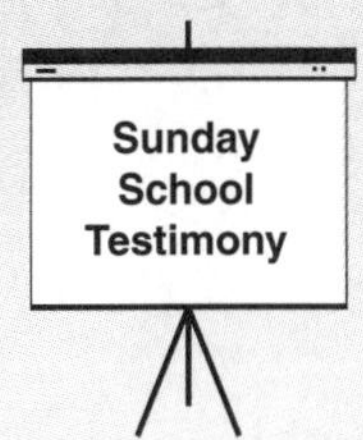

Help Learners who *work* in Sunday School to see unique ways their Sunday School testimony might be developed or shared.

Meet Anne, a young mother new to town and without friends. Three women from church visited Anne in her home and responded in these ways to her expressions of loneliness.

"Through Sunday School we have made so many friends, and they are our age with the same needs and problems. We share and pray for one another. We keep praying all week long. On Sundays we share answered prayers and other prayer needs.

"Sometimes we get phone calls and notes from our teacher or other members during the week. We do fun things with our Sunday School class all the time—ladies' Bible studies, dinner or lunch together, once-a-month fellowships, baby showers, and all kinds of church activities.

"In fact, this Saturday is a ladies' luncheon. We'll come pick you up if you can go with us. And we'll meet you in the parking lot on Sunday morning and take you to our Sunday School class."

Anne joined these women on Saturday for the luncheon. On Sunday they met her and her children in the parking lot, taking her children to the Preschool Department and Anne to their class. They sat together in the worship service, walked down the aisle with Anne when she made public her profession of faith, met her Sunday night to view a film on baptism, and sat with her in church. They followed up the next week and are continuing to enjoy times of fellowship together. Anne has new friends, a new faith, and a new church family.

BENEFITS OF A SUNDAY SCHOOL TESTIMONY

In general, the following benefits are most likely to reflect your Sunday School testimony. Relate the benefit that most applies to you; you are not trying to share all of them. Remember, your Sunday School testimony is dynamic, so it may reflect different benefits at different times.

- __________/__________ : Give a specific example of support you receive and friendships (new or long-term) you have developed through your class/department.

- ______ ___ _______ ____ _______: Tell about an experience in which Sunday School members assisted you in a crisis.

- ________________ ___ _________ _____ _________ ______'_ _______: Describe benefits of Bible study through the class.

- __________ ____ ___ _____________: Tell about ways you have grown as a Christian through experiences in or through the Sunday School.

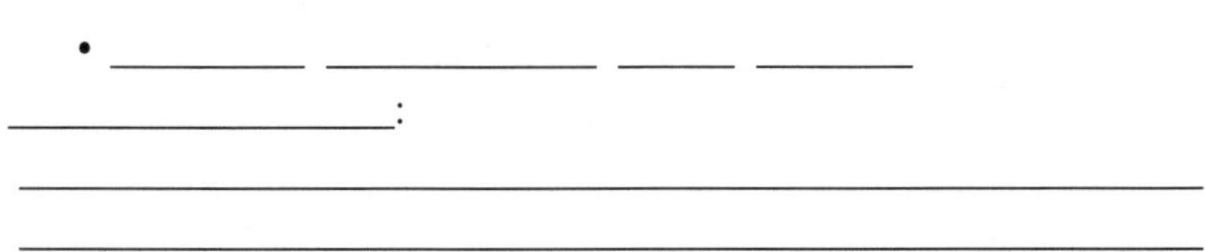

As part of this week's Home Study Assignments, you will write your Sunday School testimony. This testimony is dynamic, reflecting different experiences you have had. It can help you "connect" with a person in unique ways.

Begin to share current benefits and experiences in actual visits, as your Team Leader prompts.

Who Will We Visit? Good Question!

This question will be answered during Team Time and Teaching Time, but most clearly as you make visits. These are the kinds of experiences you can expect in the important visits we will make each week during Visitation Time. Begin now to pray for the persons you will be visiting beginning next week.

PEOPLE WE WILL VISIT

We will visit persons who:

- already have some relationship to our church through Sunday School and/or worship services;
- have no contact with our church or anyone's church;
- have shown interest by attending some special event of our church;
- are prospects for Bible study;
- could benefit from a ministry contact from our Sunday School;
- need to be invited to accept Jesus or who need/want reassurance of their faith in Him;
- already have accepted Christ (As we encounter believers, we will seek to celebrate and to encourage them in the Lord.); and
- have completed an Opinion Poll.

In general, we will make evangelistic *prospect visits* (to nonmembers) and Sunday School *ministry visits* (to members).

Highlight "Who Will We Visit? Good Question!" content to indicate the kind of visits Learners can expect.

In general, we will make evangelistic *prospect visits* (nonmembers) and Sunday School *ministry visits* (members), as well as follow-up visits to people who make decisions to accept Christ.

STEP 10 (10 min.) Point out each visitation folder. Describe purposes based on "Visitation Folder: One of Your Most Important Tools" content. Allow time for Learners to examine items.

• Customized/church items—Specify any additional church items beyond ones indicated; explain use(s)

• *A Step of FAITH*

• Visit Assignment Cards

• FAITH Participation Card

• *Exploring Faith*

• Opinion Poll—Used when additional prospects are needed

• FAITH Evaluation Card.—Distribute a card to each person each week, to be completed before Team members leave. Team Leaders review the information and Group Leaders collect/make further use. The Facilitator and FAITH Director identify areas where improvement is needed. Note follow-up actions.

(A master is in the FAITH Director's Administrative Guide, p. 258 of this resource, and on the Training Pack CD-ROM.)

Visitation Folder: One of Your Most Important Tools

INFORMATION ABOUT OUR CHURCH/SUNDAY SCHOOL:

- Room locations/map showing Sunday School classes
- Department printouts
- Information about baptism and church membership
- Church brochure(s)
- Appropriate Bible study member/leisure-reading/devotional resources
- Containers for brochures/visitation materials
- *Believe,* a devotional magazine to help new believers become grounded in their faith (available from LifeWay Christian Resources)

FAITH RESOURCES

• *A Step of Faith:* Leaflet we use as we conclude the gospel presentation; it may be left with the person and includes a card to indicate various decisions, including Sunday School enrollment

• Visit Assignment Card: Your church's preferred way to make prospect assignments; basis for receiving your weekly prospect, ministry, and/or follow-up visitation assignment and for recording results of each visit; samples are provided in the Administrative Guide

• FAITH Participation Card: Record of individual participation and basis of Team's summary report (parallels Celebration Report Board or cel)

• *Exploring Faith:* Tract we can leave when no one is at home; also is helpful if the individual needs more time to consider a decision for Christ;

• Opinion Poll for Ministry Development: Nonthreatening survey to get a person's opinion about the role of our church in the community and his or her openness to church ministries

FAITH EVALUATION CARD (p. 258)

You will be asked to complete an Evaluation Card for each session of FAITH training. Turn in Session 1 Evaluation Card before leaving.

The Journey Begins

Each person who by faith receives Jesus as Savior and Lord also receives a new identity in Him. This is the beginning of a journey of spiritual transformation. Spiritual transformation is *God's work* of changing a believer into the likeness of Jesus by creating a new identity in Christ and by empowering a lifelong relationship of love, trust, and obedience which glorifies Him.

As your own identity becomes more closely identified with Christ, you will want to see others come to know Him. As a FAITH participant, you will have the privilege of seeing many people receive Him and begin their journey of faith for the first time. You will have the privilege of nurturing them as they grow through our Sunday School ministry.

You are a FAITH participant but you also are a Sunday School member or leader. We purposely do FAITH through Sunday School because of new ways of thinking about Sunday School: *Sunday School is the foundational strategy in a local church for leading people to faith in the Lord Jesus Christ and for building Great Commission Christians through Bible study groups that engage people in evangelism, discipleship, fellowship, ministry, and worship.*

Enter FAITH training expecting God to transform your life through FAITH training, for He will. Approach FAITH expecting God to transform our Sunday School ministry, for He will. Begin FAITH expecting God to use you to change others, for He will.

You will find that FAITH is not the end, but the beginning of your obedience to be a more effective Great Commission Christian. Let these expectations be our prayer for one another as, together, we begin an important journey of faith.

STUDY IT

STEP 11 (10 min.)

Point out areas of work for home study. Overview specific assignments for Session 1. Say: You may want to read session notes once blanks have been filled in from Teaching Time. A good time is before home study each week. This week:

- **Memorize—Assigned portion of the FAITH Visit Outline; *bold* indicates new information to be learned each week**
- **Write—Your Sunday School testimony**
- **Read—*Evangelism Through the Sunday School* assignments, FAITH Tips: "Evangelism Through Sunday School Ministry," "At the Beginning of a Visit"**
- **Journal—Your Journey in Faith**

Say (if appropriate): As you come in next week, locate your name placard at a table. This will be your location throughout training.

SEE IT

STEP 12 (25 min.)

Say: Many of you may still be asking, *What is this experience going to be like for me?* Earlier we met George, who wasn't quite sure whether he wanted to get into FAITH. We left George at the prospect's door, frightened and uncertain. Let's watch Part 2 of our Training Video to find out what happened to George—and what can happen to you.

(Show training video segment "A Journey of FAITH: The Story of George—Part 2." Or use the role play of the entire visit if preferred.)

Close by relating George's experience to what can happen to the group using "The Journey Begins." Pray for one another. Dismiss.

Home Study Assignments

You may want to read your session notes again once blanks have been filled in from Teaching Time. A good time to review your notes is before doing Home Study Assignments each week.

Memorize the following points of the FAITH Visit Outline. Be prepared to recite them to your Team Leader during Session 2 Team Time.

FAITH VISIT OUTLINE

Preparation

INTRODUCTION
INTERESTS
INVOLVEMENT
Church Experience/Background
Ask about the person's church background.
Listen for clues about the person's spiritual involvement.
Sunday School Testimony
Tell general benefits of Sunday School.
Tell a current personal experience.
INQUIRY

Presentation

F (FORGIVENESS)
A (AVAILABLE)
I (IMPOSSIBLE)
T (TURN)
H (HEAVEN)

Invitation

INQUIRE
INVITE
INSURE

In the space provided, write your Sunday School testimony based on current experiences/benefits that apply to you and information presented in the session.

On a separate sheet of paper, write another copy of your Sunday School testimony to turn in to your Team Leader next session. It may be part of future promotion for FAITH training, with your permission.

Share your Sunday School testimony with one person in your class/department.

In *Evangelism Through the Sunday School: A Journey of FAITH* by Bobby Welch read:

"What Is FAITH?" (pp. 20-56);

"The Training Understanding" (pp. 129-130)

Also read the testimonies on pages 21, 55, and 69.

Did you find yourself in "The Local Church," one of the nine key ingredients of FAITH? The church is "the group that God expects to win the world!" (p. 37). And in thinking about the Great Commission, recall with gratitude: "We do indeed have a great God who demonstrated a great love, gave us a great Savior, and provided us a great honor by choosing us to carry out His Great Commission" (p. 37).

Read and make appropriate responses to the following FAITH Tips: "Evangelism Through Sunday School Ministry" and "At the Beginning of a Visit."

Evangelism Through Sunday School Ministry

Read the following verses and write in the note-taking space important truth(s) you understand to be common in each verse: **Matthew 28:18-20; Mark 16:15; Luke 24:47-48; John 20:21; Acts 1:8.**

____

____

____

____

A passage that further describes the purpose and intended process for believers is 2 Timothy 2:1-2. Read these verses and describe, based on the following phrases, what you understand to be your purposes as a Christian:

Be strong in grace: ______________________________

Teach others: ______________________________

So they can teach: ______________________________

Over the past decades, many Sunday Schools have lost their focus on reaching spiritually lost people. And many believers have lost their focus on accomplishing the commands God gave to each believer, not only to know and do what God's Word says, but also to share what God is doing in their lives and to train others to do so.

Perhaps it is time to think and do things differently. Consider this way of thinking about and doing Sunday School ministry: *Sunday School is the foundational strategy in a local church for leading people to faith in the Lord Jesus Christ and for building Great Commission Christians through Bible study groups that engage people in evangelism, discipleship, fellowship, ministry, and worship.* FAITH will help us focus more strategically on people and on our purposes, as participants from other FAITH churches can affirm.

Look at this definition again, and also consider these characteristics that can help us do evangelism through our Sunday School. Underline key words/phrases that highlight the importance of a strategic Sunday School ministry focused on evangelism:

- Believers gather for Bible study, prayer, and fellowship and learn how to live out their faith seven days a week, in daily relationships.
- Bible study groups remain open, and non-Christians are urged to join Sunday School whereas they cannot join the church without accepting Jesus as Savior and being baptized.
- There is a place for everyone in a strategically organized Sunday School ministry. Every class should have at least one person (or team) to lead the class to discover, nurture, reach, and assimilate nonbelievers into the class.
- Any person discovered (believer or non-Christian) fits in somewhere in our Sunday School. No one is eliminated from being assigned to a specific class or department.
- Bible study resources not only help believers to grow in the context of personal and family relationships, they also encourage nonbelievers to investigate (and hopefully accept) the claims of Christ on their lives.
- Sunday School gives us a vital and natural opportunity to equip believers to accomplish (apply) the scriptural instructions and relate God's Word to their lives.

At the Beginning of a Visit

Here are some suggestions for making a home visit. They can be adapted to an office, school, or other setting.

Arriving for the Visit

Be alert as you arrive and, if possible, park at the curb; do not block access to the driveway or garage. Use the walkway; do not walk on the grass. Watch for points of interest in conversation (toys, out-of-state license tags, a boat in the driveway, and so forth). Quietly move up the sidewalk to the house without talking and laughing so as not to alarm those inside. After ringing the doorbell, step back from the door.

At the Door

Usually it is best if the woman on the Team is the first person to be seen when someone opens the door. Once the door is opened, quickly identify yourself. "Hello, I am ___________ *(your name)*. This is _________ *(partner's name)*. We are from _________ *(name of church)*. Mr. (or Mrs.) _________. *(Call the name of the person you are visiting, if you know it.)* If not, ask, "And your name is _________?" *(Give opportunity for the person inside to answer.)*

Then state, "We wanted to come by and visit with you for a few minutes." Pause. Usually the person will invite you in. If it appears that you are intruding or the person does not invite you inside, share for a few moments at the door.

Beginning the Conversation

When invited inside, take a seat near the person. Begin the conversation by getting acquainted. Be ready to listen.

People enjoy talking about things that interest them. Ask nonthreatening questions about family, occupation, hobbies, and other points of interest, such as: Will you tell me about your family? How many children do you have? Where did you grow up? What kind of work do you do? Such questions open the door to meaningful conversation. Your Team Leader will suggest specific involvements you may have, such as sharing your Sunday School or evangelistic testimony.

Some Practical Tips

- Depend on the Lord. Let Him lead.
- Practice 1 Corinthians 13. Christian love is never out of place.
- Be neat, tactful, and kind.
- Be a good listener.
- Show concern for the other person and his or her needs.
- Prepare spiritually; prayer is the key to spiritual preparation.
- Make personal preparation for the visit. Dress appropriately. Use breath freshener or breath mints.
- Take appropriate Bible study material (including follow-up material for new Christians), church brochures, and a small Bible.

Adapted from "Making a Visit to Share the Gospel" by Darrell Robinson in *Going . . . One on One: A Comprehensive Guide for Making Personal Visits* (Nashville: Convention Press, 1994), 43-50. Out of print.

Your Journey in Faith

How does it feel to share with someone what your Sunday School class means to you?

Describe how you decided to participate in this significant FAITH training. Write a prayer that expresses your feelings about participation in FAITH.

Dear God,

Amen.

Read Hebrews 11:7-28. List names of at least three persons who have been significant models of faith to you. Describe what each person has done to be a model.

Each week in this section, get in the good habit of listing and of turning over to God specific prayer concerns regarding FAITH. At the same time, write down ways God is answering your prayers. Periodically look back at Your Journey in Faith to reflect on how God is working in your life and in the lives of persons for whom you are praying.

Prayer Concerns	*Answers to Prayer*

Dear Learner:

Welcome to the Lord's worldwide FAITH Team!

You have made one of the most important, life-changing commitments of your entire life! You will never be the same. Not only you, but eternity itself will be changed because you have begun your journey in FAITH!

Multiplied thousands of other people are on this learning-training journey. This is a proven training method and I promise you, from the bottom of my heart and soul, that your personal spiritual growth is about to skyrocket. The beginning focus of FAITH is to invest in your spiritual growth and development. FAITH begins at building you as a Christian. You can expect results in personal growth, confidence, joy, Christian discipline, changed lives, and more.

Your pastor, staff, and Team Leader are going all out for you to make your training experience the best possible. (Please pause now and pray for these good folks and others who are in FAITH with you.) In the course of this experience you will see people saved; you will become a witness in your daily life; your Sunday School class will care for its members in a more meaningful way.

Yes, and you'll grow in the likeness of Christ! "Let us run with endurance the race that is set before us" (Heb. 12:1, NKJV).

Don't attempt to make a commitment one week at a time to stay in FAITH. Go ahead now and make ONE COMMITMENT for the next 16 weeks and then "run with endurance the race that is set before us." I'm going to do exactly that myself, and thousands of others will also. The Lord will help you every step of the way!

A secretary who has been in this training for years said, "I would do this training—even if no one ever was saved—because of what it does for my own personal growth!" That experience awaits us all!

With You in His Certain FAITH Victory!

Bobby H. Welch

Bobby Welch

P.S. I got down on my knees and prayed for you and everyone else who reads this note:
Dear Lord, make this journey the most glorious and rewarding one ever, as You rise up in us for the glory of God and to win and disciple our world in our lifetime!

SESSION 2

Preparing for a Meaningful Visit

In this session you will

CHECK IT: engage in your first Team Time activities;

SEE IT: see video on one way to begin a visit;

HEAR IT: learn the ***Preparation*** portion of the FAITH Visit Outline; recognize the importance of a good beginning in establishing rapport and building relationships prior to sharing the gospel; begin to understand the importance of the Key Question as transition into the gospel presentation;

SAY IT: practice asking and answering the Key Question;

STUDY IT: overview Home Study Assignments for Session 2;

DO IT: make your first visit and, at your Team Leader's cue, share your Sunday School testimony;

SHARE IT: celebrate.

In Advance

- Pray for Teams who will make their first FAITH visits and for persons who will be contacted.
- Familiarize yourself with session material and your teaching suggestions.
- Prepare the room for teaching. Reserve all equipment, and check all media. Use Session 2 overhead cels (#16-22) or the computer presentation slides to support teaching.
- Work with appropriate persons to make sure each Team has visitation assignments and sufficient forms.
- Preview and cue Session 2 training video segment ("The Visitors"). If the role play is preferred, enlist persons and practice the part in which the Team gets acquainted with the prospect.

(15 min.) CHECK IT

If the computer presentation is used, display the agenda frame for Team Time, as desired. Add other points as needed.

Team Time

CHECK IT

Your Team Leader directs this important time, checking off memory work, reviewing previous sessions and completed assignments, answering questions, and providing guidance to strengthen home visits.

Agenda:

✓ FAITH Visit Outline

✓ Sunday School testimony

✓ Other Home Study Assignments

✓ Session 1 debriefing

✓ Help for strengthening a visit

❑ ***Outline memorized?—check it!***

Team Leader: In the adjacent box, check off each word as the Learner recites it correctly. In the space provided for sign-off, indicate your approval by signing your name.

FAITH VISIT OUTLINE

❑ *Preparation*

❑ **INTRODUCTION**
❑ **INTERESTS**
❑ **INVOLVEMENT**
- ❑ **Church Experience/Background**
  - ❑ **Ask about the person's church background.**
  - ❑ **Listen for clues about the person's spiritual involvement.**
- ❑ **Sunday School Testimony**
  - ❑ **Tell general benefits of Sunday School.**
  - ❑ **Tell a current personal experience.**

❑ **INQUIRY**

❑ *Presentation*

❑ **F** (FORGIVENESS)
❑ **A** (AVAILABLE)
❑ **I** (IMPOSSIBLE)
❑ **T** (TURN)
❑ **H** (HEAVEN)

❑ *Invitation*

❑ **INQUIRE**
❑ **INVITE**
❑ **INSURE**

_________________ *Team Leader Sign-off*

❑ ***Sunday School testimony turned in to your Team Leader?—check it!***

Congratulations! You have learned an important element in the FAITH Visit Outline—and so have completed an important part of FAITH training.

Team Leader: Indicate your approval in the space provided.

_________________ *Team Leader Sign-off*

❑ ***Other Home Study Assignments completed?—check it!***

Did you finish all Home Study Assignments, including A Journey in Faith? What questions do you have? Ask your Team Leader now.

Team Leader: Journal pages are private so do not read them. However, you may want to skim each Learner's Journal to make sure he or she is on track on all Home Study Assignments. Answer questions.

❑ ***Any questions from Session 1?—check it!***

What questions do you still have about Session 1? Ask your Team Leader now.

Team Leader: It is important for Learners to have a clear understanding of the information shared in Orientation, especially of roles and expectations. You may want to assess Learners' understandings of Session 1 by asking them some questions.

Especially highlight information from Session 1 that will appear on the written review in Session 16.

❑ ***Need help in strengthening a visit?—here's where you'll find it!***

Team Time is where help for strengthening a visit is provided each week. It is an opportunity to practice what you have learned, which helps you on a visit.You will be visiting in Teams for the first time this week.

Team Leader: Learners may be anxious about their first home visits. Pray together before leaving the church. Share any visitation tips needed by your Team. Make good use of travel time. Make sure Learners understand the visitation assignment form and the type of assignment they have. Help them complete their Participation Cards.

(5 min.) Transition to classrooms for instruction on content of session.

Teaching Time

SEE IT

STEP 1 (5 min.) Open by asking, What kind of visitor will *you* be? Show the training video segment "The Visitors."

Debrief: What kind of visitors were Norm and Ralph? Did they establish rapport? How open do you think this woman will be to another contact from this or any other church?

HEAR IT

STEP 2 (5 min.) Review "The Beginning Is Important." Highlight:

- Purposes
- Role of Team Leader
- Amount of time

STEP 3 (5 min.) Ask Learners to fill in the blanks while you share key points from *Preparation* portion of outline:

I. Introduction
II. Interests
III. Involvement
IV. Inquiry

Use "Make Introduction, Discuss Interests, Determine Involvement, Make Inquiry" content and media support.

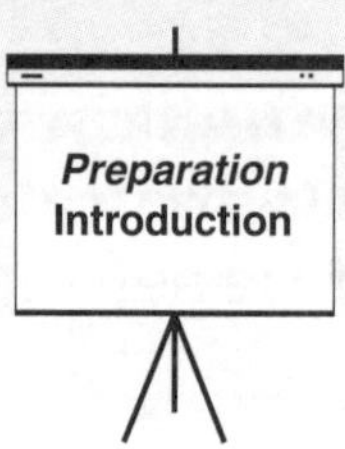

As you visit, keep in mind the purpose of your visit. And think about this question: What kind of visitor will *you* be?

The Beginning Is Important

The beginning of a visit is where you are trying to get acquainted and establish rapport. While you should not overstay your welcome, neither do you want to rush this portion of the visit.

Your Team Leader will use his or her discretion in setting the pace. The beginning easily could last from 10 to 20 minutes, depending on the situation. A good beginning to a visit may make the difference in how the rest of the visit goes.

Remember, you are visiting as a Team. All Team members participate in this part of the visit although, in early visits, your Team Leader takes the lead. Lend your support and be prepared and available to share a Sunday School testimony at your Team Leader's cue. He or she will let you know in advance how you will be involved.

Make Introduction, Discuss Interests, Determine Involvement, Make Inquiry

These points in the ***Preparation*** portion of the FAITH Visit Outline help you get a visit off to a good beginning.

Preparation

INTRODUCTION

Make the opening of a visit comfortable for everyone in these ways:

• _______________ and _____________ yourself as from our church.

• Make sure you __________ the full name of the person to whom you are speaking.

• Introduce the ________ __________ visiting with you.

• Clarify what _________________ the visit. For example, this statement might be appropriate: "You visited our church/Sunday School and we wanted to follow up."

(Since you're visiting as a Team you may preface statements or questions with *We* rather than *I: "We* wanted to follow up"; *"We'd* like to share with you how the Bible answers this question" and so forth.)

INTERESTS

Express interest in those things important to the person(s) being visited:

• Ask ________-________ ____________ (cannot be answered with a yes or no) about family, work, and hobbies (boating, fishing, and so forth).

• __________ ______________ while persons speak.

• As often as possible (and appropriate), call persons by their _________ __________.

INVOLVEMENT

Be sensitive to a person's church/spiritual background in these ways:

• Ask about *each person's* __________ background and involvement.

• Listen for clues as to each person's _______________ _______________.

• Indicate that our ____________ as a church/Sunday School class is to help people gain assurance of God's forgiveness/heaven.

• Briefly discuss our church/Sunday School ____________. This is where a Sunday School testimony is shared. Enroll the person(s) if possible.

• Share a brief personal ______________ ______________ that does not tell how you came to know the Lord.

INQUIRY

You will learn to make transition to the gospel presentation, as follows:

• Ask the ______ ___________.

• Make ______________ by asking permission to share how the Bible answers that question.

Accepting outsiders into one's home is not encouraged by society, particularly if people think we want to "sell" them something or "put them on the spot." It is important to be at ease personally and to make the individuals being visited feel comfortable. You are on someone else's "turf" and should respect every aspect of their time and territory. You may or may not be given an audience, but you want to keep the door open for future efforts.

Time spent in the ***Preparation*** portion of a visit is time well spent. You are getting acquainted and discussing mutual interests. You are assessing someone's church involvement and sharing our church's ministries and purposes.

Because it reveals overall benefits and values to you personally, a Sunday School testimony helps establish a comfort level and identifies benefits that may be desired or needed. An evangelistic testimony further helps your Team determine spiritual needs.

Since some people you visit have never considered any need for Christ in their lives, you are seeking to establish, in the beginning portion of a visit, a basis for relating to spiritual things.

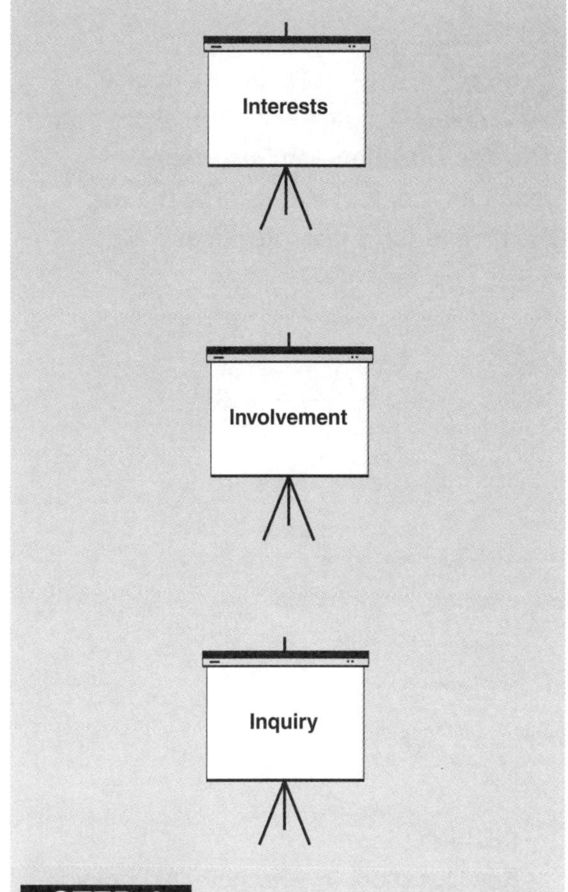

STEP 4 (5 min.) **Describe the importance of assessing spiritual needs, establishing comfort level, and providing a basis to discuss spiritual things.**

Say: As you get acquainted, don't overlook the importance of enrolling in Sunday School prospects who are not active in other churches. Evangelistic opportunities arise each week as persons study God's Word and interact with caring Christians.

After the Team shares a Sunday School testimony, say: "We have weekly Bible study opportunities for all ages in our Sunday School. You'd be in our class; we'd love to enroll you right now, with your permission. We can enroll your family, too."

Use *A Step of Faith* to record information. Leave age-appropriate Bible study material in the home.

STEP 5 (5 min.) **Direct Learners to take notes while you share from "The Key Question—an Important Transition" content and to write the Key Question in the space provided.**

INQUIRY

Key Question: In your personal opinion, what do you understand it takes for a person to go to heaven?

STEP 6 (10 min.) **Direct Learners to fill in the blanks while you share content from "Their Answer, Our Response." Use overhead cels or the computer slides to help Learners easily see their answers and our possible corresponding responses.**

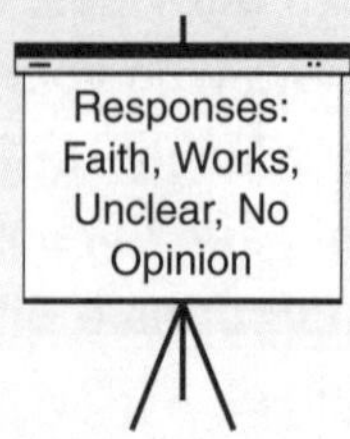

The Key Question— an Important Transition

FAITH training includes learning several important transition statements or questions. As you learn these statements or questions and rely on the Holy Spirit to sense spiritual conditions and directions to take, you should be able to move easily from one part of the conversation to another. An important transition question is the Key Question.

At this point in a visit you have established rapport by making INTRODUCTION, discussing INTERESTS, and determining church INVOLVEMENT (both theirs and yours).

Next, as appropriate, someone on your Team will set the stage for the Key Question by sharing a brief evangelistic testimony. Because of the importance of the evangelistic testimony, we will devote Session 3 to helping you develop a concise written evangelistic testimony.

What we describe as the Key Question can help you, under the Holy Spirit's guidance, open up opportunities to share the gospel with unsaved people by asking a nonthreatening personal-opinion question.

INQUIRY

Key Question

___ _______ ____________ ___________, ______ _____ _____ ____________ ___ _______ _____ ___ ________ ___ ___ ___ _________?

From this point on, we will refer to this question as the *Key Question.* When you ask this question, expect to hear and to respond to four general types of answers.

Their Answer, Our Response

Possible answers: Faith, works, unclear, no opinion

1. One answer someone may give is a ___________ answer, indicating an understanding and personal acceptance that eternity and heaven can only be experienced by trusting Jesus as Savior.

According to Titus 3:5-7:

"He saved us, not because of righteous things we had done, but because of his mercy. He saved us through the washing of rebirth and renewal by the Holy Spirit, whom he poured out on us generously through Jesus Christ our Savior, so that, having been justified by his grace, we might become heirs having the hope of eternal life" (NIV).

If someone responds with a faith answer, affirm him or her for the correct response. Ask the person to share how he/she came to know the grace of God's forgiveness. For example, you might comment: "That's right. What circumstances led you to that experience?" This can be a good place to ask about church relationships. Celebrate together as fellow Christians.

2. Another response might be a ___________ answer. Many people think that if they live a good life by doing good things, or at least avoiding serious offenses, then they will be rewarded with heaven. However, we know that no one can earn salvation.

If you detect a works answer, be particularly sensitive: You may have been given an opportunity from the Lord to share the gospel. You will learn how to ask for the privilege of sharing what the Bible has to say about how a person enters heaven. When you do, you also introduce the thought that *everything* you will share (gospel presentation) is from God's Word.

You may hear your Team Leader comment in response: "Actually, ________________ *(person's name),* that is the answer many people give." *(moving into Transition Statement)* "I'd like to share with you how the Bible answers this question, if it is all right."

3. Sometimes a person gives an ____________ answer, one that does not readily indicate his or her spiritual condition—for example, "I love God" or "I believe in God." If a response is unclear, gently ask for more explanation. For example, you might ask, "___________ *(person's name)*, I think I know what you mean, but would you tell me more?"

4. A person may say he has ____ _____________. Such a response may indicate a lack of interest or an inability to express one's thoughts.

Your response might be similar to that given for a works answer: ask for clarification and the opportunity to share from God's Word what you know to be true. Use a comment such as: "Many people answer this question by saying, 'If you live by the Golden Rule and do the best you can (be sincere), God will allow you to enter heaven'—does this express what you mean?"

Observe your Team Leader as he or she handles these various answers from persons you visit.

SAY IT

STEP 7 (5 min.) **This is the first SAY IT segment, a time of practice during Teaching Time. We also practice during Team Time. Now, with a partner, practice asking and answering the Key Question.**

Here is an easy way to remember their answers and our responses:

- **Faith - Ask**
- **Works - Share**
- **Unclear - Ask**
- **No opinion - Share**

STUDY IT

STEP 8 (5 min.) **Overview Home Study Assignments for Session 2.**

- **Memorize—Additional points of the FAITH Visit Outline**
- **Read—*Evangelism Through the Sunday School* assignments, two FAITH Tips: "Learning About Someone's Spiritual Interests and Background," "Helpful Visitation Tips"**
- **Journal—Your Journey in Faith**

(5 min.) Transition to assemble with FAITH Teams to prepare for home visits.

(110 min.) DO IT

STEP 9 (5 min.) **Instruct Learners to make at least one visit according to their visitation assignments and to return at ______ *(time)* for Celebration Time. Clarify the type of assignment if needed.**

To encourage Teams as they depart, share points from this week's FAITH Tip, "Helpful Visitation Tips" that would most help your group:

- **Carry a small New Testament.**
- **Pray together.**
- **Use travel time wisely.**
- **Allow your Team Leader to take the lead. Participate in the *Preparation* portion of the visit.**
- **Include all family members as you get acquainted.**
- **Look at the person who is speaking (rather than the prospect) if the gospel is being shared.**
- **Pray for the person sharing the gospel.**
- **If appropriate, seek to enroll someone in Sunday School.**
- **Evaluate the visit as a Team.**
- **Ask a Learner to pray for the person who heard the gospel.**

Remind Learners to make good use of travel time by:

- **talking about plans en route; and**
- **discussing what happened after the visit.**

Visitation Time

DO IT

This is when you put feet to your prayers and preparation. Your goal is to make at least one quality visit each week. Because you already have begun praying for one another and for the persons you will be visiting, you may find some visits to be "divine appointments."

Many people have significant needs or literally are waiting for someone to explain to them how they might be saved or become involved in a Bible study group. Be sensitive to God's leading you and your Team to such a person or family.

Be prepared to share your Sunday School testimony in a visit. Your Team Leader will involve you in the conversation at the appropriate time.

As you depart for your first home visits, the question remains: What kind of visitor will *you* be? Allow the Holy Spirit to guide you.

Celebration Time

SHARE IT

Celebration Time can be a time of encouragement and motivation. Your first report time should reflect excitement and victories. Celebrate not only the victories of your Team, but also those of other Teams as visit results become apparent on the Report Board. Be a part of sharing your Team's experiences as your Team Leader instructs.

Do not forget to turn in Session 2 Evaluation Card before leaving.

Your Team Leader will assist you in completing the FAITH Participation Card and in updating visitation assignments with results so appropriate follow-up can be made.

(30 min.) SHARE IT

For reporting to be most effective:

- **start on time;**
- **encourage Teams to stay on target, not to exceed 1 1/2 minutes for each report;**
- **help Teams focus by asking them to give reports on one or two visits, to indicate many times the Key Question was asked, and to note the number of professions of faith that were made;**
- **affirm *all* efforts, especially in early visits, no matter the outcomes—Teams may be planting seeds;**
- **help Teams avoid getting bogged down in trivial/negative reports (dog barked, and so forth);**
- **remind Team Leaders to collect and submit all reports;**
- **compile written summaries on the Report Board; and**
- **conclude on time. Some Teams may come in late (they won't leave in the middle of a visit), so ask for their reports next week.**

Before dismissing do make sure everyone is back and safely accounted for.

You may want to read your session notes again once blanks have been filled in from Teaching Time. A good time to review your notes is before doing Home Study Assignments each week.

Memorize the following points of the FAITH Visit Outline. Be prepared to recite them to your Team Leader during Session 3 Team Time. New information is highlighted in **bold.**

FAITH VISIT OUTLINE

Preparation

INTRODUCTION
INTERESTS
INVOLVEMENT
- Church Experience/Background
  - Ask about the person's church background.
  - Listen for clues about the person's spiritual involvement.
- Sunday School Testimony
  - Tell general benefits of Sunday School.
  - Tell a current personal experience.
- **Evangelistic Testimony**
  - **Tell a little of your pre-conversion experience.**
  - **Say: "I had a life-changing experience."**
  - **Tell recent benefits of your conversion.**

INQUIRY
Key Question
Transition Statement

Presentation

F (FORGIVENESS)
A (AVAILABLE)
I (IMPOSSIBLE)
T (TURN)
H (HEAVEN)

Invitation

INQUIRE
INVITE
INSURE

In *Evangelism Through the Sunday School: A Journey of FAITH* by Bobby Welch, read:

"But Wait! I Don't Have the Gift of Evangelism!" (pp. 108-110)
"You Can Be a Soul-Winning Discipler" (pp. 100-106)

Also read the testimonies on pages 54 and 120.

Read the FAITH Tips "Learning About Someone's Spiritual Interests and Background" and "Helpful Visitation Tips."

Learning About Someone's Spiritual Interests and Background

Every Christian has received a commission from the Lord to witness (Acts 1:8). A person does not merely learn a technique. Rather, he tells others about Jesus from the overflow of personal experience with Him. Witnessing also is sensitivity to a person's spiritual needs and interests. The underlying prerequisite is a genuine love for Jesus and for people.

The danger of any one method of visitation is this: People will memorize only to practice it mechanically and superficially. Last week's FAITH Tip identified suggestions for establishing relationships upon first contacting someone in his/her home, so valuable for establishing rapport and showing genuine love. If such INTRODUCTION is set appropriately, as the Holy Spirit leads, there may be opportunities to move the conversation toward spiritual matters. Your Team Leader will take the lead in early visits.

Just as persons respond to nonthreatening questions about family, occupation, and other interests, so are they more likely to respond to nonthreatening questions about religion. Ask such questions as the following: What is your church background? What church did you attend growing up? Where is your church home? Have you found a church home in this area? Regardless of the person's church background, use the conversation to affirm the church.

A nonthreatening involvement many people choose for themselves or their children is to participate in a Sunday School class. A Learner may be asked to share his or her Sunday School testimony at this time in the conversation. Many people are looking for friends/support, help in times of need, opportunities to learn and apply God's Word, or other benefits—all of which are elements of a Sunday School testimony. The additional benefit of growing as a Christian may be shared with someone who already has accepted Christ.

For many persons, a Bible study group or class is a means of expressing interest in spiritual things. A home visit also may be an opportunity to enroll persons in Sunday School.

Some Do's and Don'ts

- Do realize that Satan will attempt to defeat your effort with interruptions and interferences.
- *Don't* take personally any negative reaction of the person you are visiting.
- *Don't* discuss controversial issues; you are there as a witness to Jesus.
- *Don't* degrade any other church or religion.
- *Don*'t violate confidences.
- *Don't* stay too long.
- Do leave the door open to be able to return.

Adapted from "Making a Visit to Share the Gospel" by Darrell Robinson in *Going … One on One: A Comprehensive Guide for Making Personal Visits* (Nashville: Convention Press, 1994), 43–45, 47. Out of print.

Helpful Visitation Tips

We visit as a Team for reasons of safety and propriety. Another reason is for encouragement—both for one another and for the person(s) being visited. As you begin making visits with your Team, keep the following tips in mind. Refer to these reminders throughout training as needed.

✔ Carry only a small New Testament during a visit. (A large study Bible could overwhelm someone!)

✔ Pray together in the car before leaving the church parking lot (rather than in front of someone's home).

✔ Use travel time wisely; go over the "game plan" for visits.

✔ Allow your Team Leader to take the lead in visit(s) until you have learned how to make a FAITH visit.

✔ Once someone answers the door, quickly identify yourself and our church.

✔ Remember, all Team members participate in the INTRODUCTION, INTERESTS, and INVOLVEMENT parts of the visit.

✔ While they probably will not be the focus of the gospel presentation, children should be included in conversation as you get acquainted and establish rapport with the family. Do avoid taking a child into a room by yourself; rather, visit a child with another family member present. When you are talking with a child, direct your conversation to the child.

✔ During early visits, fade out of the conversation once your Team Leader begins to talk with the person about his or her church background.

✔ Once the gospel presentation begins, look at the person who is speaking rather than staring at the prospect.

✔ Pray for your Team Leader and the person(s) hearing the gospel presentation. (Don't bow your head.)

✔ If appropriate, seek to enroll the person in Sunday School before leaving.

✔ As a Team, evaluate the visit on the way back to the church.

✔ Before exiting the car for Celebration Time, make sure one Learner has assumed responsibility to pray for the person(s) who just heard the gospel presentation.

Your Journey in Faith

Describe the visit(s) you made during Visitation Time of Session 2.

Describe how you understood the Lord to be working in preparation for the visit, the actual visit, and visitation follow-up.

Describe ways you anticipate growing as a Christian by being part of FAITH training and by making visits in which the gospel will be shared.

Read Isaiah 6:1-8. Describe ways you understand God to be calling and working in your life. What are ways you will ask the Lord to use you during the coming weeks?

Prayer Concerns

Answers to Prayer

SESSION 3

Developing Your Evangelistic Testimony

In this session you will

CHECK IT: engage in Team Time activities;

SEE IT: view video in which Dr. Faith prescribes actions for an effective evangelistic testimony;

HEAR IT: learn how to share your evangelistic testimony using a three-point outline; see relationship between sharing your evangelistic testimony and asking the Key Question; learn a Transition Statement; and write a rough draft of your evangelistic testimony for evaluation;

STUDY IT: overview Home Study Assignments for Session 3;

DO IT: visit;

SHARE IT: celebrate.

In Advance

- Make prayerful preparation.
- Familiarize yourself with teaching ideas/session content.
- Be prepared to share your evangelistic testimony using the principles in this session.
- Prepare the room for teaching. Decide on media to be used, and reserve all equipment. Use Session 3 overhead transparencies (#23-27) or the computer presentation slides.
- Make sure all Teams have visitation assignments and sufficient forms and resources.
- Cue the training videotape for Session 3, “Dr. Faith: The Testimony.” Or enlist persons to do the evangelistic testimony part of the role play (pp. 74-75, Administrative Guide) if that option is preferred.

(15 MIN.) CHECK IT

If the computer presentation is used, display the agenda frame for Team Time, as desired. Add other points as needed.

Team Time

CHECK IT

Your Team Leader directs this important time, checking off memory work, reviewing previous sessions and completed assignments, answering questions, and providing guidance to strengthen home visits.

Agenda:
✓ FAITH Visit Outline
✓ Other Home Study Assignments
✓ Session 2 debriefing
✓ Help for strengthening a visit

❑ ***Outline memorized?—check it!***

Team Leader: In the adjacent box, check off each word as the Learner recites it correctly. In the space provided for sign-off, indicate your approval by signing your name.

FAITH VISIT OUTLINE

❑ *Preparation*

- ❑ **INTRODUCTION**
- ❑ **INTERESTS**
- ❑ **INVOLVEMENT**
  - ❑ **Church Experience/Background**
    - ❑ **Ask about the person's church background.**
    - ❑ **Listen for clues about the person's spiritual involvement.**
  - ❑ **Sunday School Testimony**
    - ❑ **Tell general benefits of Sunday School.**
    - ❑ **Tell a current personal experience.**
  - ❑ **Evangelistic Testimony**
    - ❑ **Tell a little of your pre-conversion experience.**
    - ❑ **Say: "I had a life-changing experience."**
    - ❑ **Tell recent benefits of your conversion.**
- ❑ **INQUIRY**
- ❑ **Key Question**
- ❑ **Transition Statement**

❑ *Presentation*

❑ **F** (FORGIVENESS)
❑ **A** (AVAILABLE)
❑ **I** (IMPOSSIBLE)
❑ **T** (TURN)
❑ **H** (HEAVEN)

❑ *Invitation*

❑ **INQUIRE**
❑ **INVITE**
❑ **INSURE**

_____________________ *Team Leader Sign-off*

❑ ***Other Home Study Assignments completed?—check it!***

Show your Team Leader these pages. Were you able to complete all assignments? Indicate any problems you had.

How are assignments in *Evangelism Through the Sunday School: A Journey of FAITH* helping you stay focused and motivated?

❑ ***Any questions from Session 2?—check it!***

You may still be uncertain about the Key Question and ways to respond to the different answers people give to it. This important content will become clearer as you participate in actual visits and see how your Team Leader handles different situations.

A person's answer gives you some important information about his or her spiritual needs. When you are sensitive to the possibilities, you can make the appropriate response.

Even though it may seem awkward, take a few moments to practice asking and answering the Key Question with another Team member.

Team Leader: As needed, review any information from Session 2 that will appear on the written review in Session 16.

❑ ***Need help in strengthening a visit?—here's how!***

Discuss general impressions from your first visit. How did you participate in the ***Preparation*** portion of a visit? What did you observe your Team Leader doing? What might have been done differently?

Team Leader: To help Learners best understand what happened in a visit, ask and answer these kinds of questions in the car immediately after the visit and as you are returning to the church for Celebration Time.

Also begin to highlight the differences in how a visit continues when it is with an evangelistic prospect and how it continues when it is with a Sunday School member. There are some important differences, which will be part of next session's Teaching Time.

(5 min.) Transition to classrooms for instruction on content of the session.

Last session we overviewed specific actions to take and things to say during the ***Preparation*** portion of a visit.

As you review this portion of the FAITH Visit Outline, notice that we are to share a short Sunday School testimony and a brief evangelistic testimony. These opportunities become springboards for assessing and discussing spiritual needs.

At the end of Session 2, we identified the following as the Key Question:

In your personal opinion, what do you understand it takes for a person to go to heaven?

This session will help you see the relationship between sharing your evangelistic testimony and asking this important question that can lead into the gospel presentation based on the letters in *FAITH.*

A Concise, Effective Evangelistic Testimony

Many of us could spend hours sharing about our faith journey. But when making a visit, we normally have a limited amount of time in which to share. It is important to know how to share only significant highlights.

You will be learning to write your evangelistic testimony in order to share it *within a maximum of three minutes.* Sharing your testimony concisely and naturally can create a desire in someone to know how to have assurance of God's forgiveness and heaven.

In general, as you develop your evangelistic testimony, try to use words ___________ ___________ _________________. You will hear me asking you to give __________ examples with the different parts of your testimony. The reason is that people relate to such events. _________ "churchy" words such as *being saved* or being *born again* to describe your experience.

The following outline can help you share highlights:

- **____ - ____________ Experience**
- **____________ Experience (Say: "I had a life-changing experience.")**
- **Recent _________ of Conversion (Includes Assurance Statement)**

Teaching Time

SEE IT

STEP 1 (5 min.) **After opening comments or review, show the video segment "Dr. Faith: The Testimony" in which Dr. Faith prescribes actions for an effective evangelistic testimony.**

HEAR IT

STEP 2 (5 min.) **Make transition from the video to the teaching content by sharing your evangelistic testimony based on the three-point outline.**

STEP 3 (20 min.) **Lead Learners to fill in the blanks while you share information from "A Concise, Effective Evangelistic Testimony." Use cels or computer slide to illustrate the lecture.**

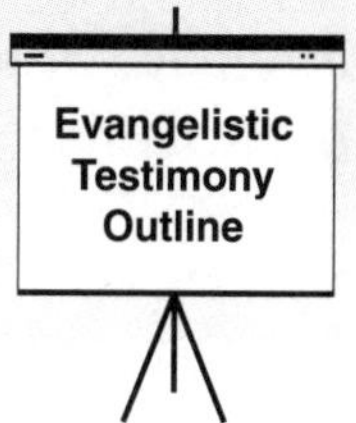

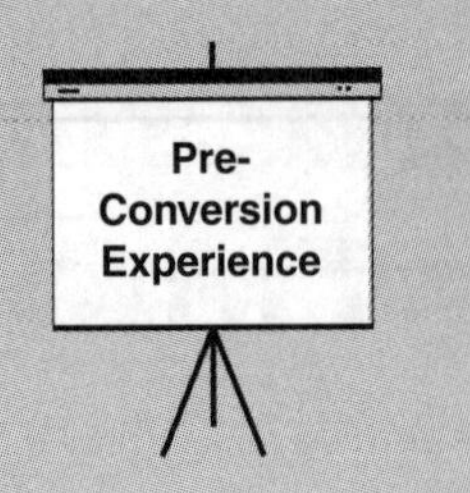

• My Pre-Conversion Experience

In the space provided, write a few words/concepts about your pre-conversion experience.

Complete this work later.

In the space provided, write: I had a life-changing experience.

• PRE-CONVERSION EXPERIENCE

Select a time in your life that illustrates what it was like __________ __________ of heaven. Many lost people can relate to experiences/feelings of loneliness, fear, guilt, lack of purpose in life. Many can relate more to these experiences than they can to words like *being saved* and *accepting Christ*. Be as specific as possible so that another person can relate to your pre-conversion experience.

This part of your testimony should not exceed _____ __________.

If you were converted as a child, you may not have a lengthy list at this point. You may be able to begin by saying: "I'm glad I know I have the forgiveness of God and the assurance I will go to heaven." Remember, your Team Leader will be helping you write your testimony.

MY PRE-CONVERSION EXPERIENCE

____

____

• CONVERSION EXPERIENCE

For each of us in this room, _________ changed our lives in very different but specific ways. Use the statement __ _____ __ _____-__________ __________ to describe a specific point in time.

This statement is helpful because it expresses the fact that your life was changed without telling, at this point, the details. Those details are shared in presenting the gospel.

Do not tell how you accepted Christ as your Savior at this time. Soon you will be asking the _____ __________, and you do not want to give away the "answer" with your testimony. If you tell someone now that you accepted Jesus as your Savior, then you are sharing the "answer" to how a person gets to heaven. The person could merely repeat your answer.

Our tendency is to "_______ _____" in our testimony. The purpose of the evangelistic testimony is to create a desire in the person to want to know how to go to heaven. Now you merely want to "_______ ________ __________"; do not tell at this time how you accepted Jesus.

This part of your testimony should not exceed _____ __________.

MY CONVERSION (STATEMENT ONLY)

____

____

- **RECENT BENEFITS OF CONVERSION**

Now share some statements and recent events that reflect ________ ______________ to you. With this point, you are sharing evidences of your ____________ of ___________.

Close your testimony with a statement of assurance, such as "I know that if I were to die tonight, I would spend eternity in heaven."

The third part of your testimony should not exceed _____ _________.

RECENT BENEFITS OF MY CONVERSION

____

____

____

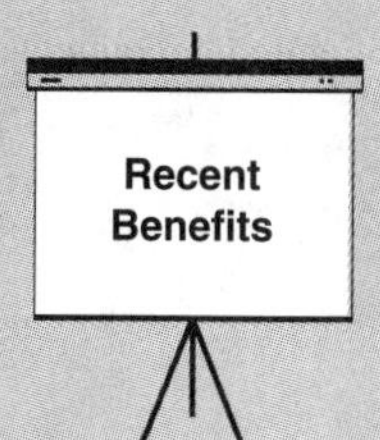

In the space provided, write words or phrases that help you remember recent experiences in your relationship with Christ. A concluding statement should express your assurance of heaven.

Complete this work later.

Make a Transition

During a visit someone on your Team may have shared a Sunday School testimony and his or her evangelistic testimony. You can further inquire about a person's spiritual background by asking the Key Question.

Remember how we talked about different answers you may get to the Key Question? That session, plus watching your Team Leader, can help you handle different situations. Hopefully, with an unsaved person, you will be able to make a transition to the gospel presentation by making this statement:

TRANSITION STATEMENT

I'd like to share with you how the Bible answers this question, if it is all right.

If the person says no, graciously thank him/her for an opportunity to share. By your response, leave the door open for future contact. See whether there is openness to being enrolled in Sunday School and to allowing you to leave some information about the church.

If the person expresses interest in knowing how the Bible answers this question, continue this way:

There is a word that can be used to answer this question: *FAITH (spell out on fingers).*

The transition into the gospel presentation becomes very natural.

STEP 4 (10 min.) **Highlight "Make a Transition" information. Discuss use of hand as a simple memory device. Demonstrate spelling out of *FAITH* on fingers of your hand.**

STUDY IT

STEP 5 (5 min.) **Overview Home Study Assignments for Session 3.**

- **Memorize—FAITH Visit Outline through the Transition Statement**
- **Write—First draft of evangelistic testimony, for Session 4 Team Time. Your Team Leader will help you. Be prepared to turn in a completed testimony in Session 5.**
- **Read—Paul's evangelistic testimony, *Evangelism Through the Sunday School* assignments, FAITH Tip: "Sharing Your Evangelistic Testimony"**
- **Journal—Your Journey in Faith**

(5 min.) Transition to assemble with FAITH Teams to prepare for home visits.

Visitation Time

(110 MIN.) DO IT

DO IT

It is amazing how the Holy Spirit works in a nonbeliever when he or she hears highlights of a Christian's genuine journey. Usually, you will share your evangelistic testimony with a nonbeliever.

However, it is very appropriate on occasion to share your evangelistic testimony with another believer. This opportunity will especially come up as you make Sunday School ministry visits to members.

As you share your evangelistic testimony with another Christian, you are celebrating together what the Lord is doing in your lives. Rather than communicating that you think the person is not saved, you may be helping him recall and/or share the joy of his salvation. You may help draw her back into meaningful church involvement. Sharing with another believer also gives you a comfortable setting in which to practice your evangelistic testimony.

Your testimony is wonderfully yours to share! Go now and share it with confidence and joy.

Celebration Time

(30 MIN.) SHARE IT

SHARE IT

- Reports and testimonies
- Session 3 Evaluation Card
- Participation Card
- Visitation forms updated with results of visits

Home Study Assignments

You may want to read your session notes again once blanks have been filled in from Teaching Time. A good time to review your notes is before doing Home Study Assignments each week.

Memorize the following points of the FAITH Visit Outline. Be prepared to recite them to your Team Leader during Session 4 Team Time.

FAITH VISIT OUTLINE

Preparation

INTRODUCTION
INTERESTS
INVOLVEMENT
- Church Experience/Background
  - Ask about the person's church background.
  - Listen for clues about the person's spiritual involvement.
- Sunday School Testimony
  - Tell general benefits of Sunday School.
  - Tell a current personal experience.
- Evangelistic Testimony
  - Tell a little of your pre-conversion experience.
  - Say: "I had a life-changing experience."
  - Tell recent benefits of your conversion.

INQUIRY
Key Question: In your personal opinion, what do you understand it takes for a person to go to heaven?

Possible answers: Faith, works, unclear, no opinion

Transition Statement: I'd like to share with you how the Bible answers this question, if it is all right. There is a word that can be used to answer this question: *FAITH (spell out on fingers).*

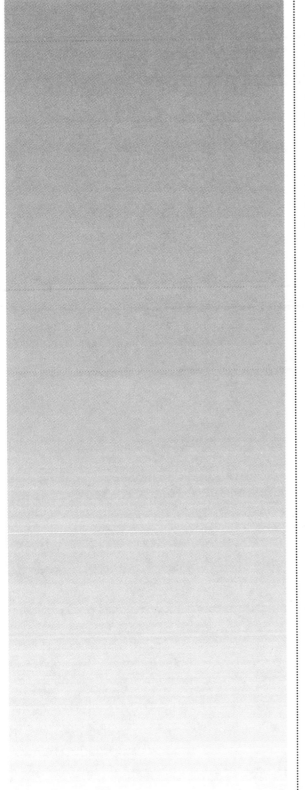

Presentation

F (FORGIVENESS)
A (AVAILABLE)
I (IMPOSSIBLE)
T (TURN)
H (HEAVEN)

Invitation

INQUIRE
INVITE
INSURE

On a separate sheet of paper, write a rough draft of your evangelistic testimony. Turn it in during Session 4 Team Time, for evaluation by your Team Leader. Use the outline as the basis of your testimony.

Evangelistic Testimony

Tell a little of your pre-conversion experience.
Say: "I had a life-changing experience."
Tell recent benefits of your conversion.

A final version of your evangelistic testimony is due Session 5 Team Time. Testimonies may be used, with your permission, in publicity for future FAITH training or to encourage others.

Read Acts 26. Think about how Paul's testimony very naturally corresponds to our three-point outline. Think about other times in the New Testament when Paul shared clear benefits of his conversion experience. Write several descriptive words in the space provided.

Paul's Pre-Conversion Experience

____

____

Paul's Conversion Experience

____

____

Paul's Conversion (Recent Benefits)

____

____

God worked in Paul's life in dynamic ways. Thank Him for the ways He is working in your life.

In *Evangelism Through the Sunday School: A Journey of FAITH* by Bobby Welch read: "The Urgency of Now" (pp. 149-154) and "Return to the Biblical Model" (pp. 84-85); and the testimonies on pages 35 and 156. Circle words or phrases in these testimonies that encourage you as a fellow believer.

Read the FAITH Tip: "Sharing Your Evangelistic Testimony."

FAITH Tip

Sharing Your Evangelistic Testimony: Just the Directions, Please

Have you ever encountered an overly eager direction-giver? You know you have one when they light up as soon as you ask for help: "I know right where that is, honey. Come around here. I'll just draw you a map. How long are you going to be staying there? There's lots to see. I have some postcards from our last trip. Isn't that spectacular? Let me tell you about that one. That was the summer. . . ."

Nice people. Accurate directions. Helpful bits of information. But you are in an awkward position. You need the directions . . . but only to a point! Just another example of Lostology Law #12: **Detailed directions add confusion**. People don't know when enough is enough.

When Jesus interacted with people, He carefully controlled the volume of truth He shared. He knew all truth; He was the Truth. Yet for those seeking spiritual answers, Jesus measured out the truth in portions that matched the individual's capacity to receive. . . . On one occasion, Jesus simply told them they were not ready for all He could tell them (John 16:12).

What sensitivity! Jesus did not tell them all He knew. He did not even tell them all they wanted to know. He told them exactly what they needed to know. He never dumptrucked truth all over people. He watched. He waited. When the time was right, He gave them more.[1]

Your evangelistic testimony should be based on the same sensitivity to people. It should create a desire for the person to want to know how you came to the assurance that you are going to heaven. Including these elements can help "whet their appetite":

- Identify at least one negative impact on your life in the pre-conversion part of your testimony.
- Be sure not to answer the Key Question. State only, "I had a life-changing experience" to explain your conversion experience.
- Identify at least one positive benefit since having your life-changing experience.
- Be sure to close your testimony with a statement of assurance. If you were saved as a child, you may share more recent benefits without commenting extensively on pre-conversion.
- You should be able to share your testimony in three minutes, preferably less.

Write your testimony and present it to your Team Leader during Session 4 Team Time. The version you write this week during home study is not to be turned in. The reason for writing your testimony is so your Team Leader can help evaluate it based on the above criteria. Do not be concerned if you are asked to rewrite it; most people are asked to do additional work. Your Team Leader will approve your revised written testimony during Session 5 Team Time. When you have done this work, you will have completed another vital requirement of FAITH training.

[1] Adapted from John Kramp, *Out of Their Faces and Into Their Shoes* (Nashville: Broadman & Holman Publishers, 1995), 85-86.

Your Journey in Faith

Read 1 Peter 1:3-9. What are similarities in your testimony and the ways in which Peter described his relationship with Christ?

List significant words or phrases from this passage that help you realize what Jesus has done for you.

What would you share about your testimony with someone you know to be a believer?

What are you learning about yourself as a believer through FAITH training?

Prayer Concerns	Answers to Prayer

SESSION 4

Making a Ministry Visit

In this session you will

CHECK IT: submit the first draft of your evangelistic testimony and practice your Sunday School testimony;

HEAR IT: work by Teams to refine your evangelistic testimony; learn how to make a Sunday School ministry visit;

SAY IT: practice your Sunday School testimony;

STUDY IT: overview Home Study Assignments for Session 4;

DO IT: visit;

SHARE IT: celebrate.

In Advance

- This session takes a purposeful detour from the FAITH Visit Outline, to describe other important visits Teams are making: Sunday School ministry visits as well as evangelistic visits.
- Make sure Teams have ministry visit assignments, and highlight these reports during Celebration Time.
- Pray for Learners, as they work to clearly write their evangelistic testimonies.
- Review teaching suggestions and all session content in this Guide. Make appropriate adjustments in Team Time and Teaching Time agendas. If time is limited, omit practicing the Sunday School testimony.
- There is no video or role play for this session. Session 4 overhead transparencies (#28-31) or computer presentation slides provide teaching support.

(15 min.) CHECK IT

If the computer presentation is used, display the agenda frame for Team Time, as desired. Add other points as needed.

Team Time

CHECK IT

Your Team Leader directs this important time, checking off memory work, reviewing previous sessions and completed assignments, answering questions, and providing guidance to strengthen home visits.

Agenda:

✓ FAITH Visit Outline

✓ Evangelistic testimony—first draft

✓ Sunday School testimony—practice

✓ Other Home Study Assignments

✓ Session 3 debriefing

✓ Help for strengthening a visit

❑ ***Outline memorized?—check it!***

Team Leader: In the adjacent box, check off each word as the Learner recites it correctly. In the space provided for sign-off, indicate your approval by signing your name.

FAITH VISIT OUTLINE

❑ *Preparation*

- ❑ **INTRODUCTION**
- ❑ **INTERESTS**
- ❑ **INVOLVEMENT**
  - ❑ **Church Experience/Background**
    - ❑ **Ask about the person's church background.**
    - ❑ **Listen for clues about the person's spiritual involvement.**
  - ❑ **Sunday School Testimony**
    - ❑ **Tell general benefits of Sunday School.**
    - ❑ **Tell a current personal experience.**
  - ❑ **Evangelistic Testimony**
    - ❑ **Tell a little of your pre-conversion experience.**
    - ❑ **Say: "I had a life-changing experience."**
    - ❑ **Tell recent benefits of your conversion.**

- ❑ **INQUIRY**
- ❑ **Key Question: In your personal opinion, what do you understand it takes for a person to go to heaven?**
  - ❑ **Possible answers: Faith, works, unclear, no opinion**
- ❑ **Transition Statement: I'd like to share with you how the Bible answers this question, if it is all right. There is a word that can be used to answer this question: *FAITH (spell out on fingers).***

❑ *Presentation*

- ❑ **F** (FORGIVENESS)
- ❑ **A** (AVAILABLE)
- ❑ **I** (IMPOSSIBLE)
- ❑ **T** (TURN)
- ❑ **H** (HEAVEN)

❑ *Invitation*

- ❑ **INQUIRE**
- ❑ **INVITE**
- ❑ **INSURE**

____________________ *Team Leader Sign-off*

❑ ***First draft of evangelistic testimony turned in?—check it!***

Turn in the first draft of your evangelistic testimony. Do not be concerned if you are asked to do additional work. If your testimony needs no revision, turn it in as the final copy. Otherwise, be prepared to turn in a final draft next week.

Team Leader: Do your best to keep a Learner's "story" intact while helping eliminate unnecessary details. As needed, help Team members use words that describe their experience clearly to an unchurched person. Use these criteria to evaluate testimonies:

- Define some specific event before (pre-conversion) and after your conversion (benefits).
- Do not answer the Key Question.
- Keep your testimony brief (three minutes or less).
- Do not give too many (unnecessary) details; instead, concisely reflect your experience.
- Conclude your testimony with the assurance that you are going to heaven.

❑ ***Sunday School testimony learned?—practice it!***

Team Leader: Time is an issue in this session. Evaluating and refining the evangelistic testimony is priority. If there is not enough time to practice the Sunday School testimony, or if practice is planned during Teaching Time, eliminate this activity.

❑ ***Any questions from Session 3?—check it!***

Most Home Study Assignments this week focused on the evangelistic testimony. Are Learners keeping up with memorization of the FAITH Visit Outline? If not, think of ways to help them.

(If ordered and used by your church), remind Learners of their FAITH Visit Outline Card, which contains key points. Placing the card in their purse or wallet can keep the presentation before Learners on a daily basis. The audiocassette also can be helpful.

Highlight information from Session 3 that will appear on the written review.

(5 min.) Transition to classrooms for instruction on the content of the session

❑ ***Need help in strengthening a visit?—here's help!***

Team Leader: Explain why you have taken different approaches in visits. Explain that ministry visits will be highlighted during Teaching Time.

A Glance Back

Earlier sessions introduced the elements of beginning a visit effectively, giving your Sunday School testimony, and sharing your evangelistic testimony.

You probably are finding it easy and comfortable to share benefits of being part of Sunday School. You also may be finding that other people want what you are experiencing. To review, people we visit need or desire:

- friends and support;
- help in times of need;
- opportunities to learn and apply God's Word;
- (if a Christian) growth as a Christian; and
- other benefits we experience on a regular basis.

Do not overlook the opportunity to give a Sunday School testimony describing general benefits and a current personal experience. As you ask someone to enroll in Sunday School, you are inviting them to experience what you have discovered.

Sunday School Testimony

Tell general benefits of Sunday School.
Tell a current personal experience.

Sunday School Ministry Visits

By now you have been a part of several types of visits. You probably have observed they fall into two basic categories: evangelistic prospect visits and Sunday School ministry visits. Our visitation assignments indicate the situation or focus of a visit.

A Sunday School ministry visit is made to someone who already is a member of Sunday School. Just as you have discovered some evangelistic visits to be divine appointments, so can Sunday School ministry visits be timely both for us and for the people we visit. It may be the point at which a member "re-connects" to Sunday School and, in some cases, back into the church.

Remember, Sunday School is *foundational*—our strategy, if you will—not only for doing the work of evangelism, but also of discipleship, fellowship, ministry, and worship. As we reinvolve Sunday School members and meet their needs, this strategy takes on another dimension and significance.

Teaching Time

HEAR IT

STEP 1 (10 min.) **Instruct Team Leaders to help Learners on an individual basis with their evangelistic testimonies. Use the criteria from Team Time and Session 3 FAITH Tip.**

SAY IT

STEP 2 (5 min.) **If not done during Team Time, allow Learners to practice their Sunday School testimonies. Use "A Glance Back" content as needed.**

HEAR IT

STEP 3 (5 min.) **Using "Sunday School Ministry Visits" content, explain a ministry visit.**

Say: This session's Teaching Time does not focus on a part of the FAITH Visit Outline, but on a significant type of visit: the Sunday School ministry visit.

Remind the group that Sunday School is foundational strategy not only for evangelism, but also for discipleship, fellowship, ministry, and worship. In using Sunday School as strategy we also visit and minister to our members.

STEP 4 (20 min.) **Lead Learners to fill in the blanks while you share the four steps in "How to Make a Sunday School Ministry Visit."**

Use media support to help Learners fill in the blanks with correct answers.

Highlight actions to take in visits to:

- **Absentees**

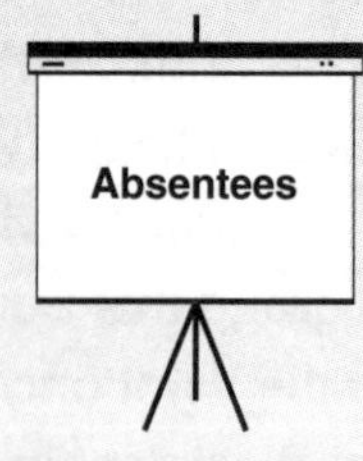

Ministry visits most often are made to:

- absentees;
- nonatttenders (people on roll but not attending); and
- members with special life needs (illness, hospitalization, death in the family, counseling need, and so forth).

Ministry needs calling for visitation assignments are discovered and communicated at *weekly Sunday School leadership meetings.* Requests for a FAITH visit are routed to the appropriate age-group Team. Of course, all age groups continue to follow up very naturally and immediately as needs surface in their Sunday School class/department.

Our primary focus is on making visits to evangelistic prospects. However, there are a number of times when it is very appropriate and beneficial to make a Sunday School ministry visit.

How to Make a Sunday School Ministry Visit

Step 1. If you do not know the person well, ____________ yourself/ your Team. In any case, even when you know the individual, explain you are visiting for the Sunday School and ask for a few minutes of time.

Step 2. This should be a relaxed, comfortable time of ____________ ____________________ about areas in common. Remember, you are under no pressure and should not appear to be pressuring the member.

Step 3. When it seems appropriate, your Team Leader will call attention to the ______________ of the visit. This may be when a Sunday School testimony is shared. Primarily you will be responding to needs reflected by three types of ministry visits:

- **ABSENTEES**

Intentionally contacting an absentee may keep that person from becoming a chronic absentee. In such a visit, address the subject of the person's absence in a ______________ manner. Say (be truthful!) how much the individual has been missed, and describe the exciting things that are happening. Take along current Bible study/leisure-reading material if the absence was on a Sunday when new material was distributed. Bring the person up-to-date on churchwide events.

Ask whether the member has problems with the class. If something ________________ is expressed, thank the person for being open and honest. State (then follow up) you will do what you can to address the concern. Don't agree with negative statements about the church/its ministry.

Commit to pray for the situation. By all means, listen politely. Close with strong encouragement to ____________ on Sunday.

• **NONATTENDERS**

Nonattenders may be on the Sunday School roll but do not attend, or they may be chronic absentees. In such a visit, the person may not know you, so introduce yourself and the Team. It would be good for Learners to give their Sunday School testimonies. Take along current Bible study material, and give a brief description of upcoming lesson topics. You will want to share a _________________ ___________ received from Bible study, including ways you have been able to apply truths in your daily life.

Be prepared for possible negative comments, which usually indicate why the person does not come to Sunday School. Listen politely but ____ ______ __________with criticisms about the church, the pastor, or any other part of the ministry.

Thank the person for being honest, and express a desire to overcome whatever has caused the nonattendance. Then seek to share the information so the situation can be remedied.

• **MEMBERS WITH SPECIAL MINISTRY NEEDS**

Contacting persons who experience some kind of special life event—surgery, hospitalization, birth of a baby, and so forth—can keep them in touch with their Sunday School class and the Sunday School class in touch with their needs. Usually Teams will know the nature of the need before arriving at the home, but sometimes needs become apparent during a visit.

After introducing yourself/Team and discussing general interests, address the purpose of your visit. Identify the ministry the Team is there to provide (for example, "We wanted to express sympathy in the death . . .").

Ask for ________________ ____________________ if more information is needed in order for Sunday School to minister effectively. If it seems appropriate, lead in a special time of prayer to take that special need to the Lord. Other Team members also should participate in prayer. If not private, ask permission to share this need with your Sunday School class.

Identify any ______________ the class could take in helping minister to this special need. Express your love and offer to stay in touch.

In all ministry visits be alert to the possibility of sharing the gospel. Such sharing needs to be a sensitive response to the Holy Spirit's leading.

Step 4. Conclude the visit. Thank the person for allowing the visit. Leave on a positive note. Ask for the privilege of praying before you leave.

• **Nonattenders**

• **Members with Special Ministry Needs**

STUDY IT

STEP 5 (5 min.) **Overview Home Study Assignments for Session 4.**

- **Memorize—Review outline, no new memory work**
- **Write—Final version of evangelistic testimony**
- **Read—*Evangelism Through the Sunday School* assignments, FAITH Tip: "Ministering to Members and Prospects," "Relationships: a Strength of Sunday School Ministry"**
- **Journal—Your Journey in Faith**

(5 min.) Transition to assemble with FAITH Teams to prepare for home visits

(110 min.) DO IT

Visitation Time

DO IT

If your visits included a Sunday School member, think about what happened: What kinds of things occurred? How did your Team Leader handle them? How were you involved? Why are Sunday School ministry visits important? How do they help us use our Sunday School as strategy?

As you visit people in their homes, you likely are becoming increasingly sensitive to needs or to follow-up opportunities. Sometimes simply interacting with someone in their home setting surfaces a need or clarifies a situation. If children or senior adults are in the home, for example, some unique opportunities or needs may exist. This is one reason complete written reports are so vital; other workers or members, age groups, or ministers in our church will follow up a FAITH visit.

Some people you visit, such as absentees, may understand the nature of your visits and visitation training. They may provide an opportunity for you to practice what you have learned thus far in FAITH.

(30 min.) SHARE IT

Celebration Time

SHARE IT

Rejoice when contact is made with someone who has not been an active part of our Sunday School! Make sure written reports include sufficient details so follow-up can be done.

- Reports and testimonies
- Session 4 Evaluation Card
- Participation Card
- Visitation forms updated with results of visits

Home Study Assignments

You may want to read your session notes again once blanks have been filled in from Teaching Time.

FAITH VISIT OUTLINE

Preparation

INTRODUCTION
INTERESTS
INVOLVEMENT
  Church Experience/Background
    Ask about the person's church background.
    Listen for clues about the person's spiritual involvement.
  Sunday School Testimony
    Tell general benefits of Sunday School.
    Tell a current personal experience.
  Evangelistic Testimony
    Tell a little of your pre-conversion experience.
    Say: "I had a life-changing experience."
    Tell recent benefits of your conversion.
INQUIRY
Key Question: In your personal opinion, what do you understand it takes for a person to go to heaven?
  Possible answers: Faith, works, unclear, no opinion
Transition Statement: I'd like to share with you how the Bible answers this question, if it is all right. There is a word that can be used to answer this question: FAITH (spell out on fingers).

Presentation

F (FORGIVENESS)
A (AVAILABLE)
I (IMPOSSIBLE)
T (TURN)
H (HEAVEN)

Invitation

INQUIRE
INVITE
INSURE

In the space provided, write the final draft of your evangelistic testimony. This will become your personal copy.

Revisions should be based on the helpful comments provided by your Team Leader. Try to write your testimony in a natural, comfortable manner—as if you were sharing it in a conversation/visit.

Once you have finalized it here as you want, write it again on a separate sheet of paper. Turn in that copy to your Team Leader.

In *Evangelism Through the Sunday School: A Journey of FAITH* by Bobby Welch, read the following information:

"Visitation—The Way It Could Be" (pp. 113-114);

"Restoring A Birthright" (pp. 82-84);

"FAITH's Advances and Advantages" (pp. 132-133).

Read the testimonies on pages 130 and 131.

Read the FAITH Tips "Ministering to Members and Prospects" and "Relationships: a Strength of Sunday School Ministry."

Ministering to Members and Prospects

As FAITH has gotten under way, our Sunday School is discovering even more opportunities to minister to believers and nonbelievers, to members and prospects. Each week as you faithfully complete your FAITH Participation Card and share results during Celebration Time, you help our Sunday School follow up on people and their needs. The visits you make each week help our classes/departments to love, care, minister, and share a personal touch. It is important that our Sunday School ministry be ready to receive and welcome new people. An atmosphere of caring and love will attract individuals and families to our church.

Toward the end of His earthly ministry, Jesus gave His disciples the following instructions: "A new commandment I give to you: Love one another. As I have loved you, so you must love one another. By this all men will know that you are my disciples, if you love one another" (John 13:34-35, NIV). How do the people we visit know that we are His disciples? What would make them begin their own faith journey or join us on ours?

How effectively do the words *love, care, minister,* and *share a personal touch* describe our Sunday School? You can help your class/department to show love by taking these actions:

Lead Your Class to Pray

Enlist a class leader or team to be responsible for ongoing prayer by the class. Encourage all class members to pray for FAITH Team members who visit and for people who need ministry and follow-up by the class.

Stress Love

A class must love one another before it can expect to have much influence in reaching others for Bible study. Did not Jesus say, "By this all will know that you are My disciples, if you have love for one another"? Plan regular ways to help the class demonstrate love.

Organize

You may be participating in FAITH to help accomplish your Sunday School outreach-evangelism responsibilities. If not, make sure your class/department is organized for outreach and ministry. Encourage members to be ready to start new units as new growth occurs.

Create a Caring Atmosphere

When a class emphasizes people and plans its activities well—including Bible study that impacts learners seven days a week—a great spirit of fellowship is evident.

What actions can *you* take to help your class/department cultivate these characteristics?

Adapted from *The Sunday School Leader: Smaller Church Edition,* January-February-March 1993, 22. Out of print.

FAITH *Tip*

Relationships: A Strength of Sunday School Ministry

In *Revitalizing the Sunday Morning Dinosaur,* Ken Hemphill identifies 7 reasons Sunday School ministry is the 21st-century church's major Great Commission tool. Reason 5—**Sunday School ministry has been vastly underutilized as an evangelistic tool—**has significant implications for FAITH Teams who represent their Sunday School class. Consider his key points:

. . . Many churches have ignored the vast potential of Sunday School ministry as an effective growth tool (Kennedy Smartt, "Evangelism Through Sunday Schools," in Roger S. Greenway, ed., *The Pastor-Evangelist* [Phillipsburg, N. J.: Presbyterian and Reformed Publishing Company, 1987], 106). First, we have ignored the basic truth that people come to a particular church primarily because they are invited by a friend or relative. Different growth authors have estimated that 79 to 86 percent of persons chose a particular church because of a personal invitation from a friend or relative. A fully-graded Sunday School provides a vast network of people who, when properly trained and motivated, can bring their friends to their small group.

Those who argue that people are attracted by the large celebrative worship service are off base. *People are attracted through relationships, not events.* Events—such as the celebrative worship service or a singing Christmas tree—may provide the opportunity for church members to invite their friends to attend with them, but it is the personal invitation that works, not the event. . . .

To me, the argument over "front door" or "side door" is a nonissue. Bring your friends to church through any door possible. Different people with different needs may enter through different doors. The fact remains that you must bring them with you through the door. The small-group structure of Sunday School provides bountiful opportunities of natural networks for bringing unsaved friends.

George Barna's research . . . reveals that Sunday School does work as an entry point for the unsaved. He discovered 13 million adult non-Christians who attend Sunday School (George Barna, *What Americans Believe* [Ventura: Regal Books, 1991], 263). We don't always know how many unsaved people attend our worship services because we have no sure method of recording their attendance. The intimacy of the small-group structure of Sunday School virtually assures that you will know the unsaved persons who are attending. Sunday School in most churches is an untapped evangelistic gold mine.

Furthermore, the intimacy of a small group like a Sunday School class is more relational than a worship service. Here friendships can be made that may become a natural bridge to presenting the gospel. . . .

The focus on evangelism through Sunday School ministry will have another positive effect. . . . The evangelistic focus will require that you create new units and keep the small groups at a manageable size.

Adapted from Ken Hemphill, *Revitalizing the Sunday Morning Dinosaur* (Nashville: Broadman and Holman Publishers), 41-42.

Your Journey in Faith

Use the space below to write a letter to God. Express your feelings about writing and sharing your evangelistic testimony.

List names of people with whom you would like an opportunity to share your evangelistic testimony. Opposite each name, write prayer concerns regarding that person and how you hope God will use you in sharing your testimony with him/her.

Names **Prayer Concerns**

Read Ephesians 2:1-10. Write about your personal life-changing experience when you accepted Jesus as your personal Savior and Lord.

Prayer Concerns	*Answers to Prayer*

SESSION 5

Overviewing the Gospel Presentation

In this session you will

CHECK IT: engage in Team Time activities—turn in written evangelistic testimony;

HEAR IT: hear and see key words, statements, and Bible verses for each letter in the FAITH gospel presentation; write key words to help you recall them;

SEE IT: view video of entire gospel presentation;

SAY IT: using notes, practice gospel presentation with a partner;

STUDY IT: overview Home Study Assignments for Session 5;

DO IT: visit;

SHARE IT: celebrate.

In Advance

- Pray for Learners as they make visits and learn the gospel presentation.
- Preview teaching suggestions and all session content. Be able to model the gospel presentation naturally and comfortably.
- Cue video to Session 5, "The Gospel Presentation." If the role play is preferred, enlist persons well in advance and practice, giving attention to all details.

Note: Session 5 overhead cels (#32-45) are available; also use appropriate ones in the session in which each letter is taught. (For example, use cel 33, F is for FORGIVENESS, in Sessions 5 and 6.) Or use the computer presentation slides if preferred.

(15 min.) CHECK IT

If the computer presentation is used, display the agenda frame for Team Time, as desired. Add other points as needed.

Team Time

CHECK IT

Your Team Leader directs this important time, checking off memory work, reviewing previous sessions and completed assignments, answering questions, and providing guidance to strengthen home visits.

Agenda:

✓ FAITH Visit Outline

✓ Final draft of evangelistic testimony due

✓ Practice Key Question/Transition Statements

✓ Other Home Study Assignments

✓ Session 4 debriefing

✓ Help for strengthening a visit

❑ ***Outline memorized?—check it!***

Team Leader: In the adjacent box, check off each word as the Learner recites it correctly. In the space provided for sign-off, indicate your approval by signing your name.

FAITH VISIT OUTLINE

❑ *Preparation*

- ❑ **INTRODUCTION**
- ❑ **INTERESTS**
- ❑ **INVOLVEMENT**
  - ❑ **Church Experience/Background**
    - ❑ **Ask about the person's church background.**
    - ❑ **Listen for clues about the person's spiritual involvement.**
  - ❑ **Sunday School Testimony**
    - ❑ **Tell general benefits of Sunday School.**
    - ❑ **Tell a current personal experience.**
  - ❑ **Evangelistic Testimony**
    - ❑ **Tell a little of your pre-conversion experience.**
    - ❑ **Say: "I had a life-changing experience."**
    - ❑ **Tell recent benefits of your conversion.**

- ❑ **INQUIRY**
- ❑ **Key Question: In your personal opinion, what do you understand it takes for a person to go to heaven?**
  - ❑ **Possible answers: Faith, works, unclear, no opinion**
- ❑ **Transition Statement: I'd like to share with you how the Bible answers this question, if it is all right. There is a word that can be used to answer this question: *FAITH (spell out on fingers).***

❑ *Presentation*

- ❑ **F** (FORGIVENESS)
- ❑ **A** (AVAILABLE)
- ❑ **I** (IMPOSSIBLE)
- ❑ **T** (TURN)
- ❑ **H** (HEAVEN)

❑ *Invitation*

- ❑ **INQUIRE**
- ❑ **INVITE**
- ❑ **INSURE**

____________________ *Team Leader Sign-off*

❑ ***Evangelistic testimony turned in to your Team Leader?—check it!***

Congratulations! You have learned an important element in the FAITH Visit Outline—and so have completed another important part of FAITH training. Your evangelistic testimony is vital to your personal journey of faith, so it is important to be able to share it concisely.

Team Leader: Sign your approval here. Call for your copies, and turn them in to the FAITH Director. Ask permission before using testimonies in any way.

____________________ *Team Leader Sign-off*

❑ ***Key Statement/Transition Statement practiced?—check it!***

If not already done, recite to your Team Leader the Key Question and the Transition Statement. As you do, try to comfortably and naturally spell out the letters of *FAITH* on the fingers of your hand.

❑ ***Other Home Study Assignments completed?—check it!***

Are you on track with your Home Study Assignments, including A Journey in Faith? What do these reflections reveal to you about your walk with the Lord?

In what ways are you experiencing visitation the way it could be?

❑ ***Any questions from Session 4?—check it!***

What questions do you have about Session 4? Ask your Team Leader now.

Team Leader: As needed, highlight any information from Session 4 that will appear on the written review (Session 16).

❑ ***Need help in strengthening a visit?—here's how!***

How have our Sunday School ministry visits included absentees, nonattenders, and members with ministry needs? What results have occurred from making these contacts?

(5 min.) Transition to classrooms for instruction on content of the session.

Your Journey of Faith Continues

You chose to participate in FAITH training in obedience to God's command to be an active, effective witness. Do you find yourself growing as a Great Commission Christian? Are you becoming active in sharing your faith? Are you becoming a person of deepening faith in Christ? Is our church growing as a Great Commission church? Is our Sunday School undergoing transformation?

This session introduces the heart of FAITH training and the FAITH Visit Outline: a specific gospel presentation based on letters in the word *FAITH.* This session will give you an overview, and the next five weeks we will focus on each letter in the word *FAITH* in more detail.

By this time in a visit, you have asked the Key Question and heard an answer that indicates it may be appropriate to share the gospel presentation.

INQUIRY
Key Question: In your personal opinion, what do you understand it takes for a person to go to heaven?
Possible answers: Faith, works, unclear, no opinion
Transition Statement: I'd like to share with you how the Bible answers this question, if it is all right. There is a word that can be used to answer this question: *FAITH (spell out on fingers).*

If in response to the Transition Statement the person expresses interest and gives permission, continue by sharing the gospel presentation. Learn to share it naturally and with sensitivity, relying on the Holy Spirit to lead you.

You'll also become more comfortable using your hand to spell out the letters. That's why Team Time and SAY IT times of practice can help ease any awkwardness. You do not want to get so caught up in the method that you lose the importance of your message.

Teaching Time

HEAR IT

Using "Your Journey of Faith Continues" and "The Gospel Presentation" content, direct Learners to fill in the blanks with key words about each letter. Use cels or computer slides to help Learners see answers easily.

Model the presentation comfortably and demonstrate the use of your hand as a memory device as you present each letter (thumb for *F*; index finger, *A*, and so forth).

Say:

Here is what you can expect to learn for each letter in FAITH:

A word defines each major concept (FORGIVENESS, AVAILABLE, IMPOSSIBLE, TURN, and HEAVEN). One or more brief sentences describe the theological truths behind each concept. A Bible verse supports each truth, emphasizing that what you share is from the Bible.

- This session overviews the entire gospel presentation.
- The next five weeks highlight each letter. Next week's focus is on letter *F.*
- Begin memorizing each word, statement, and verse.
- Learn to share the gospel presentation naturally and comfortably.

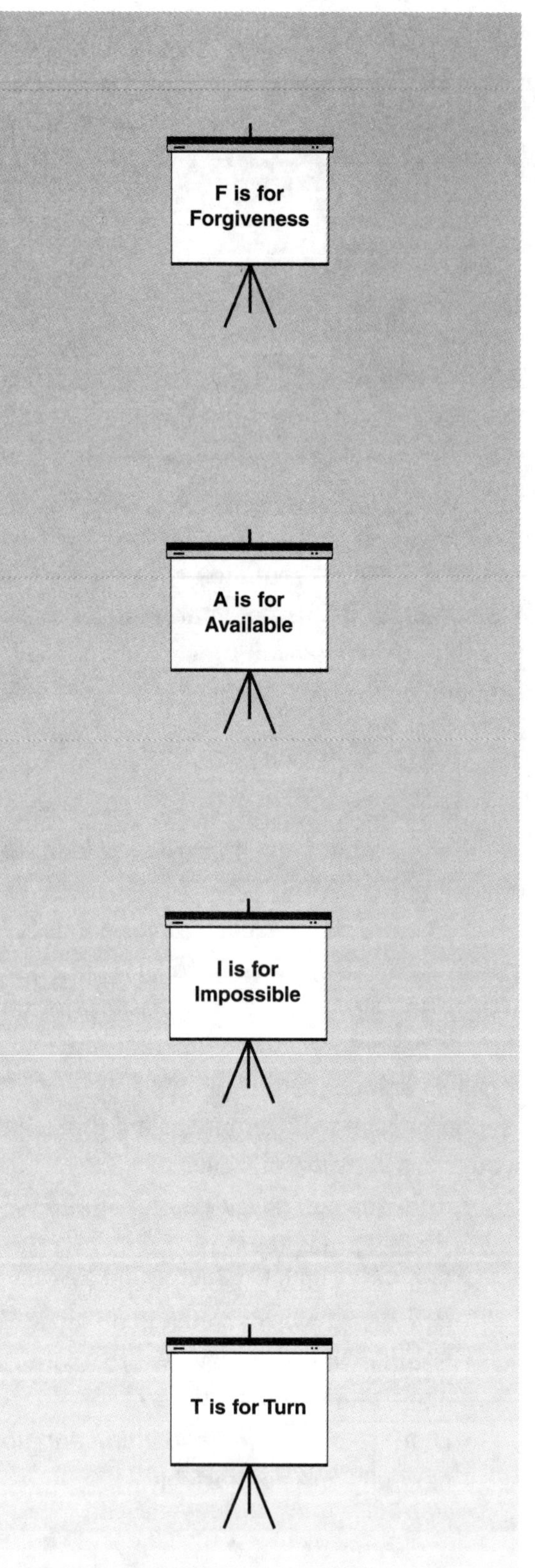

The Gospel Presentation

F is for ________________

We cannot have ____________ ______ ______ ____________ without God's forgiveness.

"In Him [meaning Jesus] we have redemption through His blood, the forgiveness of sins"—Ephesians 1:7a, NKJV.

A is for ________________.

____________________ is available. It is—

____________________ ______ ______

"For God so loved the world that He gave His only begotten Son, that whoever believes in Him should not perish but have everlasting life"—John 3:16, NKJV.

________ ______ ____________________

"Not everyone who says to Me, 'Lord, Lord,' shall enter the kingdom of heaven"—Matthew 7:21a, NKJV.

I is for ____________________.

It is impossible for God to allow ______ into heaven.

________ ___—

- ________

John 3:16, NKJV

- ________

"For judgment is without mercy"—James 2:13a, NKJV.

________ ___ ____________

"For all have sinned and fall short of the glory of God"—Romans 3:23, NKJV.

Transition Question: But how can a sinful person enter heaven, where God allows no sin?

T is for _______.

Question: If you were driving down the road and someone asked you to turn, what would he or she be asking you to do? *(change direction)*

***Turn* means _____________.**

TURN from something—________ ______ ________

"But unless you repent you will all likewise perish"—Luke 13:3b, NKJV.

TURN to Someone; _________ _________ ________

(The Bible tells us that) ***"Christ died for our sins according to the Scriptures, and that He was buried, and that He rose again the third day according to the Scriptures"—1 Corinthians 15:3b-4, NKJV.***

"If you confess with your mouth the Lord Jesus and believe in your heart that God has raised Him from the dead, you will be saved"—Romans 10:9, NKJV.

H is for ____________.

Heaven is ______________ ______.

____

"I have come that they may have life, and that they may have it more abundantly"—John 10:10b, NKJV.

____

"And if I go and prepare a place for you, I will come again and receive you to Myself; that where I am, there you may be also"—John 14:3, NKJV.

____

How can a person have God's forgiveness, heaven and eternal life, and Jesus as personal Savior and Lord?

Explain based on leaflet picture, F.A.I.T.H. (Forsaking All I Trust Him), Romans 10:9.

Introducing . . . a Sunday School Moment

You are approaching the midpoint of your FAITH training. Is there anything you could do each week that is more important than FAITH? Is anything more focused on the purposes Jesus gave the church in the Great Commission?

As you give priority to learning the FAITH Visit Outline over the next six weeks, keep in your thoughts and prayers the many ways our Sunday School ministry undergirds FAITH. Because each week you are meeting people face-to-face, at their point of need, you are becoming aware of what Sunday School as strategy truly means. In what ways is our Sunday School undergoing transformation, to become more focused in purpose?

According to *Sunday School for a New Century,* five principles support Sunday School as strategy, including Foundational Evangelism. Does the following statement characterize the experience you and others have had in FAITH? *Sunday School creates a great center for missionary power as people tell and live the wondrous story of Christ's redeeming love.* It can.

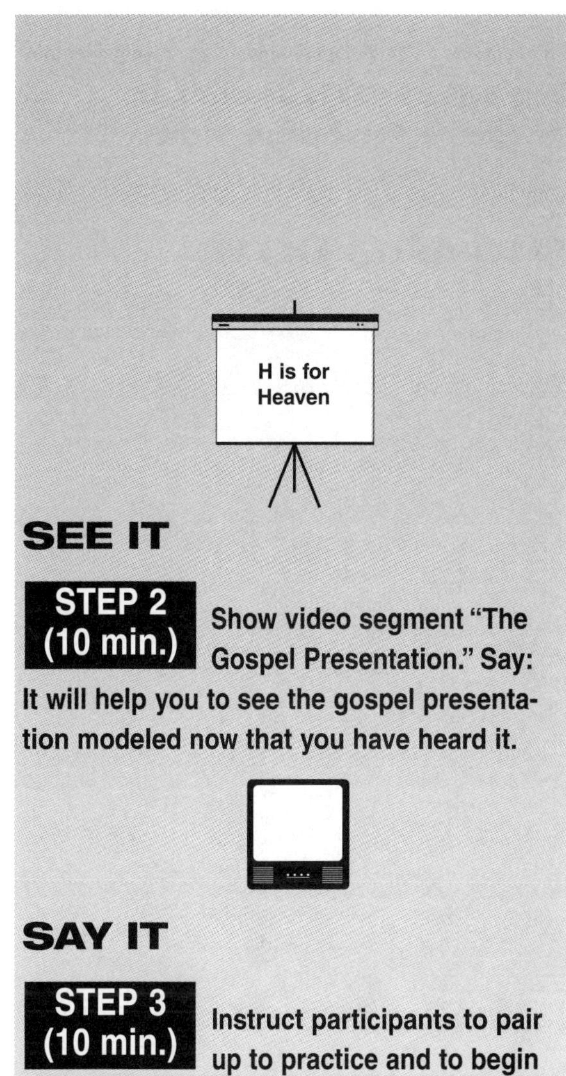

SEE IT

STEP 2 (10 min.) **Show video segment "The Gospel Presentation." Say: It will help you to see the gospel presentation modeled now that you have heard it.**

SAY IT

STEP 3 (10 min.) **Instruct participants to pair up to practice and to begin with the Key Question. They may use notes.**

STUDY IT

STEP 4 (5 min.) **Overview Home Study Assignments for Session 5.**

- **Memorize—FAITH Visit Outline, adding the letter *F* (FORGIVENESS)**
- **Read—*Evangelism Through the Sunday School* assignments, FAITH Tip: "Nurturing a New Christian"**
- **Journal—Your Journey in Faith**

Close with "Introducing . . . a Sunday School Moment" content.

(5 min.) Transition to assemble with FAITH Teams to prepare for home visits.

Visitation Time

(110 min.) DO IT

DO IT

What a joy is yours to share the gospel with someone who does not know Christ! By sharing the gospel presentation with an unsaved person, you may experience the wonderful privilege of seeing God work in that person's life. Watch as your Team Leader moves with sensitivity from the gospel presentation into the ***Invitation.*** And remember, you are not responsible for results, but for sharing the good news.

By sharing the gospel presentation in a FAITH visit, you can be a part of helping someone:

- see his or her need for God's forgiveness;
- recognize God's great love, desire to forgive, and provision of forgiveness, at great cost;
- understand he cannot save himself;
- realize that salvation is possible only through Jesus;
- repent and change direction in life;
- know assurance of eternal life and heaven personally.

You can experience the joy of seeing someone come to saving faith in Christ. You will never be the same!

Celebration Time

(30 min.) SHARE IT

SHARE IT

What an encouragement when these types of visits are made! Share highlights of results so everyone can pray and follow up appropriately. All Teams will have exciting reports to share so, just as you learned to present your Sunday School and evangelistic testimonies concisely, share reports briefly. Take turns sharing results.

In some visitation reports, for the privacy of the individuals involved, your reports may need to include the person's first name only.

- Testimonies and reports
- Session 5 Evaluation Card
- Participation Card
- Visitation assignments updated with results

Home Study Assignments

You may want to read your session notes again once blanks have been filled in from Teaching Time. A good time to review your notes is before doing Home Study Assignments each week.

Memorize the following points of the FAITH Visit Outline, adding the letter *F* (FORGIVENESS). Be prepared to recite them to your Team Leader during Session 6 Team Time.

FAITH VISIT OUTLINE

Preparation

INTRODUCTION
INTERESTS
INVOLVEMENT
  Church Experience/Background
    Ask about the person's church background.
    Listen for clues about the person's spiritual involvement.
  Sunday School Testimony
    Tell general benefits of Sunday School.
    Tell a current personal experience.
  Evangelistic Testimony
    Tell a little of your pre-conversion experience.
    Say: "I had a life-changing experience."
    Tell recent benefits of your conversion.
INQUIRY
Key Question: In your personal opinion, what do you understand it takes for a person to go to heaven?
  Possible answers: Faith, works, unclear, no opinion
Transition Statement: I'd like to share with you how the Bible answers this question, if it is all right. There is a word that can be used to answer this question: FAITH *(spell out on fingers).*

Presentation

F is for FORGIVENESS.

We cannot have eternal life and heaven without God's forgiveness.

"In Him [meaning Jesus] we have redemption through His blood, the forgiveness of sins"—Ephesians 1:7a, NKJV.

A (AVAILABLE)
I (IMPOSSIBLE)
T (TURN)
H (HEAVEN)

Invitation

INQUIRE
INVITE
INSURE

Share your evangelistic testimony with two different persons you know to be believers. Record how long it took you to share your testimony.

Write their names in the space provided.

In *Evangelism Through the Sunday School: A Journey of FAITH* by Bobby Welch, read: "The Person God Uses" (pp. 119-126). Are you a person God can use? Pray that He will strengthen your growth in needed areas.

Also read the testimonies on pages 112 and 149.

Read the following FAITH Tip: "Nurturing a New Christian."

Nurturing a New Christian

"A new believer may wonder: *What would God have me do with my life now that I've repented of my sins and placed my faith in Jesus?* Because of the ultimate sacrifice of Jesus, God has accepted your repentant heart, and He wants to begin His work of transforming you into the likeness of His son" (*Jesus by Heart,* p. 16).

Because a decision to accept Christ is only the beginning, follow-up of new Christians is an intentional and integral part of FAITH. If your FAITH team makes a visit in which there is a decision to (1) accept Christ as Savior and (2) make commitments to share that decision publicly and/or enroll in Sunday School, your Team also will follow up on that person.

Follow-up may include providing resources to help a new Christian begin to grow in the Lord.

What resources do we take to a new Christian?

____

____

Much of the nurture and support needed by people who accept Christ in FAITH visits will continue every week in the Sunday School class.

As a class member, what are some specific ways I might help a new Christian to grow?

____

____

As you reach out to the unchurched and the unsaved, you may be faced with needs that exceed your ability to handle. A referral may be needed. Or some nurturing visits may lead to the development of (or sharing information about) short-term, special-interest, or ongoing classes or studies.

What short-term/special-interest classes are provided by our church? What needs have surfaced in FAITH visits that may indicate a unique need?

____

____

Nurturing also may call for members to intentionally spend time with a new convert beyond Sunday—praying together, educating the person about basics of the faith, encouraging him to fully surrender his life; leading her to understand the qualities of a Spirit-filled life.

When you meet a new friend, you must take time to get acquainted, share initial experiences, and find out something about each other. But if the new friendship is to become a meaningful relationship, you do not stop there.The level of sharing deepens as you continue to do things together. The investment of time and trust endures. The same is true after a person becomes a Christian; the process of discipling and nurturing continues.

Adapted from "Making a Visit to Nurture a New Christian," Roy T. Edgemon in *Going … One on One: A Comprehensive Guide for Making Personal Visits* (Nashville: Convention Press, 1994), 216–19. Out of print.

Your Journey in Faith

Read Isaiah 53 and 2 Corinthians 4:13-18. Summarize what you understand to be a key truth of the gospel, as it relates to the fact that:

We cannot have eternal life without God's forgiveness:

Forgiveness is available but not automatic:

It is impossible for God to allow sin into heaven:

Repentance means turning from sin/self to Christ only:

Heaven is eternal life here and hereafter:

What are you learning or being reminded of concerning the gospel as you overview the words and phrases in the FAITH gospel presentation?

What are the most important things you have learned thus far in observing and participating in FAITH visits?

Prayer Concerns

Answers to Prayer

SESSION 6

F is for Forgiveness

In this session you will

CHECK IT: engage in Team Time activities;

HEAR IT: learn and be able to recite the FORGIVENESS portion of the gospel presentation—meaning of the letter *F,* descriptive statement, and accompanying Bible verse;

SEE IT: view the video segment on FORGIVENESS;

SAY IT: practice FORGIVENESS with a partner;

STUDY IT: overview Home Study Assignments for Session 6;

DO IT: make visits—be able to share your evangelistic testimony;

SHARE IT: celebrate.

In Advance

- Pray for Teams as they learn the gospel presentation and have reaffirmed for themselves the significance of God's forgiveness.
- Search the Internet or newspapers for recent local/national events that illustrate people's need for forgiveness (instances of crime, miscommunication, violation of ethics/dishonesty, and so forth).
- Preview teaching suggestions and all session content. Use the Session 6 computer presentation slides or the overhead cels (#33, 46-47) for teaching support. ***Note:*** Cel #33 was first used in Session 5.
- Cue the video to Session 6, "F-FORGIVENESS."

(15 MIN.) CHECK IT

If the computer presentation is used, display the agenda frame for Team Time, as desired. Add other points as needed.

Team Time

CHECK IT

Your Team Leader directs this important time, checking off memory work, reviewing previous sessions and completed assignments, answering questions, and providing guidance to strengthen home visits.

Agenda:
✓ FAITH Visit Outline
✓ Other Home Study Assignments
✓ Session 5 debriefing
✓ Help for strengthening a visit

❑ ***Outline memorized?—check it!***

Team Leader: In the adjacent box, check off each word as the Learner recites it correctly. In the space provided for sign-off, indicate your approval by signing your name.

FAITH VISIT OUTLINE

❑ *Preparation*

- ❑ **INTRODUCTION**
- ❑ **INTERESTS**
- ❑ **INVOLVEMENT**
  - ❑ **Church Experience/Background**
    - ❑ **Ask about the person's church background.**
    - ❑ **Listen for clues about the person's spiritual involvement.**
  - ❑ **Sunday School Testimony**
    - ❑ **Tell general benefits of Sunday School.**
    - ❑ **Tell a current personal experience.**
  - ❑ **Evangelistic Testimony**
    - ❑ **Tell a little of your pre-conversion experience.**
    - ❑ **Say: "I had a life-changing experience."**
    - ❑ **Tell recent benefits of your conversion.**
- ❑ **INQUIRY**
- ❑ **Key Question: In your personal opinion, what do you understand it takes for a person to go to heaven?**
  - ❑ **Possible answers: Faith, works, unclear, no opinion**
- ❑ **Transition Statement: I'd like to share with you how the Bible answers this question, if it is all right. There is a word that can be used to answer this question: *FAITH (spell out on fingers).***

❑ *Presentation*

❑ **F is for FORGIVENESS.**

❑ **We cannot have eternal life and heaven without God's forgiveness.**

- ❑ ***"In Him [meaning Jesus] we have redemption through His blood, the forgiveness of sins"—Ephesians 1:7a, NKJV.***

❑ **A** (AVAILABLE)

❑ **I** (IMPOSSIBLE)

❑ **T** (TURN)

❑ **H** (HEAVEN)

❑ *Invitation*

❑ **INQUIRE**

❑ **INVITE**

❑ **INSURE**

____________________ *Team Leader Sign-off*

❑ ***Other Home Study Assignments completed?—check it!***

Are you on track with your Home Study Assignments, including assignments from *Evangelism Through the Sunday School: A Journey of FAITH?* Are you a person God is using?

❑ ***Any questions from Session 5?—check it!***

What questions do you have about Session 5? Since the gospel presentation was overviewed then for the first time, you may have some questions. Does any part seem awkward to you? What parts will be easy to remember? If time allows, practice the gospel presentation with your Team Leader or a fellow Learner.

Team Leader: As needed, review any information from Session 5 that will appear on the written review in Session 16. (Allow time for similar help in Sessions 6-10 as the gospel presentation is being fully developed.) Learners also will be required to present the entire FAITH Visit Outline in Sessions 12-16.

❑ ***Need help in strengthening a visit?—here's how!***

Dialogue about ways you have discovered to strengthen a visit.

(5 min.) Transition to classrooms for instruction on the content of the session.

The Need Is Obvious

The need we have to forgive and to be forgiven permeates all of life. How we get along with our families and friends—plus the major incidents that capture headline attention—illustrate our need for forgiveness. We hurt one another because of how we think and act—because of our sinful nature.

Businesses conduct seminars on forgiveness for their employees; talk shows highlight unforgiving people or the results or their unforgiving actions as well as occasionally showing the healing impact of forgiveness; crime victims reveal our capacity to hurt one another in many cruel ways. We need both to forgive and to be forgiven, whether or not we realize that need.

The Bible makes apparent our need for forgiveness and the message of God's forgiveness. New Testament usages of the Greek word for forgiveness include these meanings, among others: "to let go," "to leave," "to leave behind," "to remit." Several New Testament Scriptures that highlight forgiveness include Matthew 6:14, 26:28; Mark 1:4, 2:5; Acts 5:31, 8:22, Romans 3:25, 4:7.

As described in the New Testament, forgiveness is almost always of God (as compared to people forgiving others); is constantly needed; is granted when requested as long as there is a readiness to forgive others; and is based in the saving act of Christ. It also indicates future blessing. Related concepts make it plain that forgiveness:

- is God's responsibility as Judge;
- has its basis in His saving act in Christ;
- brings total renewal in the future;
- is received when God's judgment is affirmed in the confession of sin.[1]

Appropriately, the FAITH gospel presentation begins with forgiveness—which we desperately need and which only God can provide.

You will recall there are several possible responses to the Key Question. For example, many people believe their good works earn them God's favor, and thus entry into heaven. They may think they are good because they have not done any serious crimes. We know that this is not the case.

Introducing God's forgiveness at this point helps the person being visited begin to see his or her need, sinfulness, and inadequacy. It also helps establish God's great love, His ability and desire to forgive, and His provision of salvation at great cost: through the death of His only Son.

At a later time in a visit, you will help a person see that a specific choice—a decision to repent and turn—must be made.

Teaching Time

HEAR IT

STEP 1 (10 min.) **Highlight the need for forgiveness using "The Need Is Obvious" content.**

After commenting on the first two paragraphs, ask the group to brainstorm events from recent headlines that illustrate humanity's need for forgiveness. (Be prepared to offer suggestions.)

Ask: In all instances, would you be able to totally forgive the wrongdoer? Make the point that only God can provide the kind of forgiveness needed for our sin.

STEP 2 (5 min.) Direct Learners to fill in the blanks for the meaning of *F,* descriptive sentence, and verse. Use "F is for Forgiveness: God's Forgiveness" content and media support.

Note: The same cel used in Session 5, Step 1 (FORGIVENESS), is used here.

STEP 3 (5 min.) Instruct Learners to fill in the blanks while you share "Truths About God's Forgiveness" using computer slide or cel. As needed, use key verses (Titus 3:5; Ps.130:4; Neh. 9:17; Acts 10:43; Luke 23:34; and Heb. 9:22).

SEE IT

STEP 4 (5 min.) Show "F-FORGIVENESS" segment of video.

F Is for God's Forgiveness

Last session overviewed the entire gospel presentation that is such a significant part of the FAITH Visit Outline. Each letter in the word *FAITH* relates to a word that helps explain how to know Jesus as Savior. Each word is easy to remember. By using the word for the letter *F,* you have the opportunity at this point in a visit to remind people of their need for forgiveness and to establish the fact that only God can provide it.

The letter F stands for ________________________.
We cannot have eternal life and heaven without God's forgiveness.

Each letter in the gospel presentation has one or more verses of Scripture to explain the significance of that word. The verse(s) are used in the presentation to help you confirm what God says in the Bible. There are many wonderful verses in God's Word that highlight forgiveness. Ephesians 1:7*a* is the verse we use to highlight the importance of forgiveness.

____
____
____

—Ephesians 1:7a, NKJV

Truths About God's Forgiveness

As you share with someone about God's forgiveness, these are the important biblical truths you are helping that person understand or think about, perhaps for the first time:

- Forgiveness is ________ based on what we have done, how good we are, or how sincere we are.
- Forgiveness is based on the _______________ that Jesus Christ made for our sins when He died on the cross.
- It is by ______ _________, and His blood alone, that we may be forgiven.
- It is through Him that a person can experience the _______ of being forgiven.

Jesus Focused on the Lost, and We Should, Too

To share God's forgiveness with sensitivity and respect involves having some understanding of what it means to be lost. Throughout His earthly ministry, Jesus focused on lost people, on the "sick"—on prostitutes, tax collectors, lepers, crowds of common people. While the focus of His life angered His critics, . . "Jesus continued to live with the people. Rather than wait for them to come to Him, He moved in their circles. He lived a lost-centered life."[2]

An Exercise: You Can Be Lost and Not Know It[3]

Can you think of a time when you were lost physically but did not know it? Focusing on that experience, how it happened and how you felt, can help you empathize with non-Christians who are spiritually lost and are unaware. See if these questions help you reflect on your experience:

- What factors caused you to realize you were going the right direction when in reality you were lost?
- How long did you drive before you knew you were lost?
- While you were lost, did you remain confident that you were going in the right direction?

Now think about non-Christians you have known who were lost spiritually but did not know it. Consider the following questions:

Where would your friends rank *themselves* on the following scale? Write the person's name above the number. Where would *you* rank your friends? Write the person's name under the number.

Sure they are not lost 1 _____ 2 _____ 3 _____ 4 _____ 5 _____ *Sure they are lost*

- What did your non-Christian friends say and do that expressed their confidence that they had nothing to worry about spiritually?
- What do you think causes non-Christians to move from being sure they are not lost spiritually to being less sure about their spiritual condition and to say "I may be spiritually lost"?

SAY IT

STEP 5 (5 min.) **Practice FORGIVENESS with a partner. Begin with the Key Question. Allow each person a turn.**

HEAR IT

STEP 6 (10 min.) **Encourage Learners to develop an understanding of lostness, using "Jesus Focused on the Lost, and We Should, Too" content. Allow them to experience what it feels like to be lost by doing the exercise "You Can Be Lost and Not Know It."**

Encourage Learners to reflect on the questions in their home study, especially as they read the "24 Laws of Lostology" FAITH Tip.

STUDY IT

STEP 7 (5 min.) **Overview Home Study Assignments for Session 6.**

- **Memorize—FAITH Visit Outline adding the letter *A* (AVAILABLE)**
- **Write—Class assignment**
- **Read—*Evangelism Through the Sunday School* assignments, FAITH Tips: "God's Wonderful Work of Salvation," "24 Laws of Lostology"**
- **Journal—Your Journey in Faith**

Close by commenting that FAITH Teams have an opportunity to help others begin their journey of faith.

(5 min.) Transition to assemble with FAITH Teams to prepare for home visits.

Help Others Begin Their Journey

By accepting God's forgiveness at a specific point in time, you embarked on your personal journey of faith. As a person who shares your faith with others, you are helping someone else learn about God's forgiveness and possibly begin his or her own journey in faith. You may never know the complete results of a visit or other contact in someone's life.

Just as you have rethought what it may feel like to be lost, this is a good time to think again about the implications of God's forgiveness in your life. As you consider both the urgency of lostness and the grace of forgiveness, you will find yourself even more motivated to share God's love and forgiveness.

---

[1] Geoffrey W. Bromley, *Theological Dictionary of the New Testament,* Gerhard Kittell and Gerhard Friedrich, eds., Geoffrey W. Bromley, trans. (Grand Rapids, MI: William B. Eerdmans Publishing Co., 1985), 88.

[2] Adapted from John Kramp, *Out of Their Faces and Into Their Shoes* (Nashville: Broadman & Holman Publishers, 1995), 125.

[3] Ibid., 35-36.

Visitation Time

(110 min.) DO IT

DO IT

Be prepared, at your Team Leader's cue, to share your evangelistic testimony in a visit.

As you go, and your visits include nonbelievers, ask yourself: *What truths about forgiveness does a nonbeliever need to know?* Watch what happens in a visit, or evaluate the visit as you return to the church. As you make ministry visits, ask yourself: *What truths about forgiveness are helpful for sharing with another believer?* Watch what happens in visits to believers, and evaluate appropriately as you return to the church.

Celebration Time

(30 min.) SHARE IT

SHARE IT

- Testimonies and reports
- Session 6 Evaluation Card
- Participation Card
- Visitation assignments updated with results

Home Study Assignments

You may want to read your session notes again once blanks have been filled in from Teaching Time. A good time to review your notes is before doing Home Study Assignments each week.

Memorize the following points of the FAITH Visit Outline, adding the letter *A* (AVAILABLE). Be prepared to recite them to your Team Leader during Session 7 Team Time.

FAITH VISIT OUTLINE

Preparation

INTRODUCTION
INTERESTS
INVOLVEMENT
  Church Experience/Background
    Ask about the person's church background.
    Listen for clues about the person's spiritual involvement.
  Sunday School Testimony
    Tell general benefits of Sunday School.
    Tell a current personal experience.
  Evangelistic Testimony
    Tell a little of your pre-conversion experience.
    Say: "I had a life-changing experience."
    Tell recent benefits of your conversion.
INQUIRY
Key Question: In your personal opinion, what do you understand it takes for a person to go to heaven?
  Possible answers: Faith, works, unclear, no opinion
Transition Statement: I'd like to share with you how the Bible answers this question, if it is all right. There is a word that can be used to answer this question: FAITH *(spell out on fingers).*

Presentation

F is for FORGIVENESS.

We cannot have eternal life and heaven without God's forgiveness.

"In Him [meaning Jesus] we have redemption through His blood, the forgiveness of sins"—Ephesians 1:7a, NKJV.

A is for AVAILABLE.

Forgiveness is available. It is—

AVAILABLE FOR ALL

"For God so loved the world that He gave His only begotten Son, that whoever believes in Him should not perish but have everlasting life"—John 3:16, NKJV.

BUT NOT AUTOMATIC

"Not everyone who says to Me, 'Lord, Lord,' shall enter the kingdom of heaven"—Matthew 7:21a, NKJV.

I (IMPOSSIBLE)
T (TURN)
H (HEAVEN)

Invitation

INQUIRE
INVITE
INSURE

Think of two or three persons who might have a particular interest in knowing that God's forgiveness is available for them. List ways you feel you and/or your Sunday School class could initiate contact with these individuals.

From *Evangelism Through the Sunday School: A Journey of FAITH* by Bobby Welch, read: "Today's Satanic Strategy" (pp. 88-90). How is FAITH training helping you confront Satan's strategy?

Also read the testimonies on pages 46 and 78.

Read the FAITH Tip "God's Wonderful Work of Salvation." Thank God for His initiative in providing salvation for you and for the people you will be visiting during FAITH. Thank Him for forgiving you, and ask Him to give you greater capacity to forgive others.

Read the FAITH Tip "24 Laws of Lostology." Consider how many statements differ from your thinking about what it means to be lost. How will these new thoughts affect how you visit?

God's Wonderful Work of Salvation

Salvation involves the redemption of the whole man and is offered freely to all who accept Jesus Christ as Lord and Savior, who by His own blood obtained eternal redemption for the believer. In its broadest sense, salvation includes regeneration, sanctification, and glorification.

A. Regeneration, or the new birth, is a work of God's grace whereby believers become new creatures in Christ Jesus. It is a change of heart wrought by the Holy Spirit through conviction of sin, to which the sinner responds in repentance toward God and faith in the Lord Jesus Christ.

Repentance and faith are inseparable experiences of grace. Repentance is a genuine turning from sin toward God. Faith is the acceptance of Jesus Christ and commitment of the entire personality to Him as Lord and Savior. Justification is God's gracious and full acquittal upon principles of His righteousness of all sinners who repent and believe in Christ. Justification brings the believer into a relationship of peace and favor with God.

B. Sanctification is the experience, beginning in regeneration, by which the believer is set apart to God's purposes, and is enabled to progress toward moral and spiritual perfection through the presence and power of the Holy Spirit dwelling in him. Growth in grace should continue throughout the regenerate person's life.

C. Glorification is the culmination of salvation and is the final blessed and abiding state of the redeemed. . . .

Way of Salvation

Sin separated man from God. The fellowship depicted in Eden was broken. But God proposed to restore it. At Sinai He gave His law to Israel (Ex. 20). In essence, Paul says that God wrote this same law into the hearts of pagans (Rom. 2:14-16). In a sense God called from the heights of His holiness for man to come up to Him. Failure to do so brought judgment in keeping with either code of law given to man (Rom. 2:1-13). Jesus Himself told the rich young ruler that to inherit eternal life he must keep the commandments (Matt. 19:16-17). But they must be kept perfectly. Failure in one law made one as guilty as though he had failed in all. No man does as good as he knows. So no man keeps God's law perfectly, whether it be the written law or that in pagan hearts. Someone may object that God is unjust in making such a demand. The perfect life of Jesus speaks to the contrary. He proved God "just" in His demand for perfect righteousness. Having done so, God in Christ became the "justifier of him which believeth in Jesus" (Rom. 3:26). This He did by paying the price for man's sin in His atoning death, that through faith in Him man might receive the righteousness of God which is in His Son. . . . Jesus came to seek and to save that which was lost. And this salvation is offered freely to all who receive Jesus Christ as Lord and Savior.[1]

[1]Herschel H. Hobbs, "Salvation," in *The Baptist Faith and Message* (Convention Press: Nashville, Tennessee, 1971), 48–50.

The 24 Laws of Lostology

1. Being lost can be fun.
2. No one gets lost on purpose.
3. It is easy to get lost.
4. You can be lost and not know it.
5. You cannot force people to admit they are lost.
6. Admitting you are lost is the first step in the right direction.
7. When you are lost, you are out of control.
8. Just because you are lost does not mean you are stupid.
9. It is tough to trust a stranger.
10. People ask for directions without revealing their true emotions.
11. Directions are always confusing.
12. Unnecessary details make directions more confusing.
13. A search reveals your values.
14. Searches are always costly.
15. Love pays whatever a search costs.
16. A search becomes your consuming priority.
17. A search is also lost-centered, not searcher-centered.
18. A search is urgent because the lost are in danger.
19. Coordinate resources to maximize the search.
20. Discouragement threatens a successful search.
21. Waiting is part of the search.
22. Successful searches do not always have happy endings.
23. If you are searching, the lost may find you.
24. Always celebrate when the lost are found.

John Kramp, "The 24 Laws of Lostology," *Out of Their Faces and Into Their Shoes* (Nashville: Broadman & Holman, Publishers, 1995), 185.

Your Journey in Faith

From what you have experienced in FAITH visits, what are some evidences people show of being interested in spiritual things?

Read Hebrews 9:22. Write what you think Jesus would say to you about why He shed His blood in order to forgive you of your sins.

Read Luke 23:34. Write what you think Jesus would say to you about things for which you need forgiveness.

Prayer Concerns

Answers to Prayer

SESSION 7

A is for Available

In this session you will

CHECK IT: engage in Team Time activities;

HEAR IT: learn and be able to recite the AVAILABLE portion of the gospel presentation—meaning of the letter *A,* descriptive statements, and accompanying Bible verses;

SEE IT: view the FORGIVENESS and AVAILABLE video segments;

SAY IT: practice AVAILABLE with a partner;

STUDY IT: overview Home Study Assignments for Session 7;

DO IT: make visits—at Team Leader's cue, be able to share your evangelistic testimony, the Key Question, and FORGIVENESS;

SHARE IT: celebrate.

In Advance

- Pray for a renewed ability to look at all people as the focus of God's love and forgiveness. Pray for Teams as they approach the midpoint of their FAITH training journey.
- Preview teaching suggestions and all session content. Use Session 7 overhead cels (#34-35) or the computer presentation slides. ***Note:*** Both cels were first used in Session 5; there are no new cels.
- Cue the Training Video to segment "F-FORGIVENESS" to view *F* and *A*. Or use the role-play segments communicating FORGIVENESS and AVAILABLE (pp. 75-76, Administrative Guide) as another way to demonstrate a visit.

(15 min.) CHECK IT

If the computer presentation is used, display the agenda frame for Team Time, as desired. Add other points as needed.

Team Time

CHECK IT

Your Team Leader directs this important time, checking off memory work, reviewing previous sessions and completed assignments, answering questions, and providing guidance to strengthen home visits.

Agenda:

✓ FAITH Visit Outline

✓ Practice

✓ Other Home Study Assignments

✓ Session 6 debriefing

✓ Help for strengthening a visit

❑ ***Outline memorized?—check it!***

Team Leader: In the adjacent box, check off each word as the Learner recites it correctly. In the space provided for sign-off, indicate your approval by signing your name.

FAITH VISIT OUTLINE

❑ *Preparation*

❑ **INTRODUCTION**
❑ **INTERESTS**
❑ **INVOLVEMENT**
- ❑ **Church Experience/Background**
  - ❑ **Ask about the person's church background.**
  - ❑ **Listen for clues about the person's spiritual involvement.**
- ❑ **Sunday School Testimony**
  - ❑ **Tell general benefits of Sunday School.**
  - ❑ **Tell a current personal experience.**
- ❑ **Evangelistic Testimony**
  - ❑ **Tell a little of your pre-conversion experience.**
  - ❑ **Say: "I had a life-changing experience."**
  - ❑ **Tell recent benefits of your conversion.**

❑ **INQUIRY**
❑ **Key Question: In your personal opinion, what do you understand it takes for a person to go to heaven?**
- ❑ **Possible answers: Faith, works, unclear, no opinion**

❑ **Transition Statement: I'd like to share with you how the Bible answers this question, if it is all right. There is a word that can be used to answer this question: *FAITH (spell out on fingers).***

❑ *Presentation*

❑ **F is for FORGIVENESS.**

❑ **We cannot have eternal life and heaven without God's forgiveness.**

- ❑ ***"In Him [meaning Jesus] we have redemption through His blood, the forgiveness of sins"—Ephesians 1:7a, NKJV.***

❑ **A is for AVAILABLE.**

❑ **Forgiveness is available. It is—**

❑ **AVAILABLE FOR ALL**

- ❑ ***"For God so loved the world that He gave His only begotten Son, that whoever believes in Him should not perish but have everlasting life"—John 3:16, NKJV.***

❑ **BUT NOT AUTOMATIC**

- ❑ ***"Not everyone who says to Me, 'Lord, Lord,' shall enter the kingdom of heaven"—Matthew 7:21a, NKJV.***

❑ **I** (IMPOSSIBLE)

❑ **T** (TURN)

❑ **H** (HEAVEN)

❑ *Invitation*

❑ **INQUIRE**

❑ **INVITE**

❑ **INSURE**

____________________ *Team Leader Sign-off*

❑ ***Other Home Study Assignments completed?—check it!***

Are you aware that, even though directed to your Team Leader, the Team Leader Supplement pages also can give you some additional details? They can be particularly helpful as you then see the situations in actual visits. Hopefully, some day you will be a Team Leader, too!

❑ ***Any questions from Session 6?—check it!***

What questions do you have about Session 6? Ask your Team Leader now.

❑ ***Need help in strengthening a visit?—here's help!***

If an opportunity was available last session to give your evangelistic testimony, how comfortable were you in sharing it? How was it received?

You will not be asked to share anything in a visit before you have been trained. For example, in this session's Visitation Time, you would only be expected to share through FORGIVENESS in the outline. Your Team Leader will not interrupt the flow of a visit for you to "do your part"; as he or she can involve you very naturally and appropriately, he or she will ask you to share. You should know in advance how you might be involved.

Until you have learned the gospel presentation and the ***Invitation,*** your Team Leader may take the lead with a non-Christian. As you learn more of the gospel presentation, your Team Leader will allow you to share more during a visit; he or she will assume the lead again in issuing the all-important ***Invitation.***

Each week as you learn new information pray, watch, and talk about what happens in actual visits. You will learn a lot as you watch your Team Leader; however, you will learn more as you actually use the opportunities available to you to share with nonbelievers.

A good setting in which to build confidence and to learn how to share parts of the gospel presentation is with another Christian. For example, your Team visits the Joe Smith family. Joe is a Christian, as are the other family members.

It is very appropriate for your Team Leader to ask: "Joe, we're learning how to visit and share the gospel with people who need to know the Lord. It's been good celebrating with you what the Lord is doing in your life. Would you mind if __________ *(a Team member's name)* shared his evangelistic testimony and some important truths he has learned for sharing with a non-Christian? It would be a real encouragement, if you have a few more moments."

(5 min.) Transition to classrooms for instruction on the content of the session.

Part of the wise use of travel time is deciding how to handle situations before they arise. Practice with another Christian, here and in a home visit, also can help.

The All's of the Great Commission

Although there are several places in the New Testament where the Great Commission is given, Matthew 28:18-20 probably is the most familiar expression of Jesus' command to us. Read it again now:

> *"All authority has been given to Me in heaven and on earth. Go therefore and make disciples of* all *the nations, baptizing them in the name of the Father and of the Son and of the Holy Spirit, teaching them to observe* all *things whatever I have commanded you; and lo, I am with you always, even to the end of the age" (Matt. 28:18-20, NKJV).*

God's forgiveness is available for all. Fill in a key word in the blanks.

- _____ authority or power is given to Jesus (Jesus has the authority to tell us what to do!)
- Christ has told us to go and make disciples of _____ nations.
- We are to teach people to do _____ things Christ has commanded us to do.
- Remember that He is with us in _____ ways, times, and places.

If you remember the *all's* in the Great Commission, you will have an easy time remembering the *all's* for whom God's forgiveness is available.

Good News: God's Forgiveness Is Available for All!

In response to someone's answer to the Key Question and willingness to know what the Bible has to say, you already have shared that we cannot have eternal life and heaven without God's forgiveness. You now have the opportunity to share that there is good news.

The letter A in FAITH is for ________________.
God's forgiveness is ________________ . It is
_______________ _____ ______.

John 3:16 is the verse we use to highlight God's forgiveness—for ourselves and for all people. Write your name in each blank of the following paraphrase, recalling again the personal nature of God's love.

Teaching Time

HEAR IT

STEP 1 (5 min.) **Briefly review the letter *F* (FORGIVENESS) if a review is still needed after Team Time.**

Then direct Learners to focus on the "all's" of the Great Commission.

STEP 2 (5 min.) **Using "Good News: God's Forgiveness Is Available for All!" content and media support, instruct Learners to take notes on:**

- **The meaning of letter *A***
- **Descriptive sentence**
- **One subpoint/verse**

***Note:* The same cel used in Session 5, (A is for AVAILABLE), is used here.**

STEP 3 (5 min.) **Lead Learners to personalize John 3:16.**

STEP 4 (5 min.) **Using "His Forgiveness Is Not Automatic" content and media support, instruct Learners to take notes on the second subpoint/verse:**

- **BUT NOT AUTOMATIC**
- **Matthew 7:21*a***

Note: **The same cel used in Session 5, (BUT NOT AUTOMATIC), is used here.**

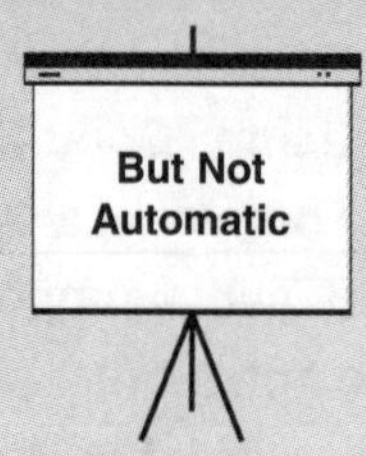

SEE IT

STEP 5 (10 min.) **View "F-FORGIVENESS" and "A-AVAILABLE" segments.**

Watch as Andrew, George, and Myra communicate essential truths about salvation. Ask: In what ways does Tony show initial conviction of sin and recognition of some need for God's forgiveness?

SAY IT

STEP 6 (5 min.) **Practice AVAILABLE with a partner, making sure each person has a turn.**

For God so loved ________________________ that He gave His only "one-of-a-kind" Son that if ________________________ believes in Him, ________________________ will not perish but will have eternal life.

What does it mean to you that forgiveness is available for all? Unless you understand and believe that God's love is available for each person—including each person you potentially will contact in FAITH visits—you have missed the full impact of God's forgiveness.

His Forgiveness Is Not Automatic

What does it mean to you that God's forgiveness is not automatic? It is much easier to understand that God's forgiveness is available for all than to recognize His forgiveness is not automatic.

God wants all people to accept His forgiveness. It is our responsibility to share, even though not everyone will accept the good news.

God's forgiveness is available. It is AVAILABLE FOR ALL,

_____ ______ _______________.

Many verses in Scripture remind us that God wants all people to accept His forgiveness. Many also indicate that not everyone will choose to accept it. Matthew 7:13*b*-14 (NIV) underscores this reality: "For wide is the gate and broad is the road that leads to destruction, and many enter through it. But small is the gate and narrow the road that leads to life, and only a few find it."

Also from Matthew, chapter 7, is our verse for the next point, BUT NOT AUTOMATIC. Write it here:

____

____

____

—Matthew 7:21*a*, NKJV.

It is important to remember that God's forgiveness is not automatic. He has made it available at great cost: through the death of His Son, Jesus. And not everyone will choose to accept His great gift.

Do you truly believe that the only way to God is through Jesus? If so, you will find yourself focusing on the lost with greater urgency.

Ways to Focus on the Lost

Evaluate yourself, our church, and your Sunday School class in focusing on the lost. Commit to these and other ways to be more inclusive of *all* who are lost without Christ:

- Go the lost rather than expecting the lost to come to you.
- Meet the physical and emotional needs, as well as spiritual needs, of lost people.
- Value non-Christians as people and seek to develop relationships. This can be done naturally through our Sunday School ministry.
- Encourage church and Sunday School leaders to devote time and resources to reach the lost, rather than to focus on Christians who already are part of the church.
- Join with other Christians to learn more about lost people.
- Make it easy for non-Christians to explore their beliefs in your church. Make sure new people feel welcome.
- Lovingly challenge your non-Christian friends to commit their lives to Christ.[1]

---

[1] Adapted from John Kramp, *Out of Their Faces and Into Their Shoes* (Nashville: Broadman & Holman Publishers, 1995), 128.

Visitation Time

DO IT

If visits allow, your Team Leader will call on you to present your evangelistic testimony, the Key Question, and the FORGIVENESS portion of the gospel presentation. He or she will continue the presentation.

If a prospect is uncertain about accepting God's forgiveness at this time, ask whether you may leave a copy of *Exploring Faith.* God's Holy Spirit may convict and convince long after you have left the home.

Celebration Time

SHARE IT

- Testimonies and reports
- Session 7 Evaluation Card
- Participation Card
- Visitation assignments updated with results

Hear IT

Point out ways to focus more intentionally on the lost, especially through Sunday School classes and the FAITH strategy.

STUDY IT

STEP 8 (5 min.) **Call attention to Home Study Assignments for Session 7.**

- **Memorize—FAITH Visit Outline, adding the letter *I* (IMPOSSIBLE)**
- **Read—*Evangelism Through the Sunday School* assignments, FAITH Tip: "Sunday School Intentionally Reaching People"**
- **Journal—Your Journey in Faith**

(5 min.) Transition to assemble with FAITH Teams to prepare for home visits.

(110 min.) DO IT

(30 min.) SHARE IT

Memorize the following points of the FAITH Visit Outline, adding the letter *I* (IMPOSSIBLE). Be prepared to recite them to your Team Leader during Session 8 Team Time.

FAITH VISIT OUTLINE

Preparation

INTRODUCTION
INTERESTS
INVOLVEMENT
Church Experience/Background
Ask about the person's church background.
Listen for clues about the person's spiritual involvement.
Sunday School Testimony
Tell general benefits of Sunday School.
Tell a current personal experience.
Evangelistic Testimony
Tell a little of your pre-conversion experience.
Say: "I had a life-changing experience."
Tell recent benefits of your conversion.
INQUIRY
Key Question: In your personal opinion, what do you understand it takes for a person to go to heaven?
Possible answers: Faith, works, unclear, no opinion
Transition Statement: I'd like to share with you how the Bible answers this question, if it is all right. There is a word that can be used to answer this question: FAITH *(spell out on fingers).*

Presentation

F is for FORGIVENESS.

We cannot have eternal life and heaven without God's forgiveness.

"In Him [meaning Jesus] we have redemption through His blood, the forgiveness of sins"—Ephesians 1:7a, NKJV.

A is for AVAILABLE.

Forgiveness is available. It is—

AVAILABLE FOR ALL

"For God so loved the world that He gave His only begotten Son, that whoever believes in Him should not perish but have everlasting life"—John 3:16, NKJV.

BUT NOT AUTOMATIC

"Not everyone who says to Me, 'Lord, Lord,' shall enter the kingdom of heaven"—Matthew 7:21a, NKJV.

I is for IMPOSSIBLE.

It is impossible for God to allow sin into heaven.

GOD IS—

- **LOVE**

  John 3:16, NKJV

- **JUST**

  "For judgment is without mercy"—James 2:13a, NKJV.

MAN IS SINFUL

"For all have sinned and fall short of the glory of God"—Romans 3:23, NKJV.

Question: But how can a sinful person enter heaven, where God allows no sin?

T (TURN)

H (HEAVEN)

Invitation

INQUIRE

INVITE

INSURE

From *Evangelism Through the Sunday School: A Journey of FAITH* by Bobby Welch, read "Five Frank Facts" (pp. 91-96) and the testimony on page 97. Which of the five facts most gripped your heart and soul, encouraging you to "keep on keeping on" in FAITH?

How does sharing your faith have worldwide implications?

Read the FAITH Tip: "Sunday School Intentionally Reaching People." Think about how our Sunday School does some things well; how might we reach more people?

FAITH *Tip*

Sunday School Intentionally Reaching People

Sunday School is not an educational entity. It is not a program or an organization. Sunday School is a strategy, a plan for doing the work of the church. It becomes foundational to everything we do: *Sunday School is the foundational strategy in a local church for leading people to faith in the Lord Jesus Christ and for building Great Commission Christians through Bible study groups that engage people in evangelism, discipleship, fellowship, ministry, and worship.*

Sunday School is designed to reach people. Sunday School has responsibility for and opportunity to reach people, witness to the unsaved, teach the Bible, care for members and nonmembers, provide opportunity for Christian fellowship, and to pray. As such, it becomes a plan and a strategy for doing the church's work of evangelism, discipleship, fellowship, ministry, and worship. Sunday School is a seven-day-a-week plan for involving people in the kingdom of God.

Sunday School is designed for believers and nonbelievers. A non-Christian cannot join our church (or any other church). A nonbeliever can indeed be a member of our Sunday School.

Any person who agrees to be enrolled can be a member of the Sunday School ministry. Sunday School is for people in every age, background, life situation, need, and experience. A person can be enrolled any time, even without attending, as long as he or she agrees. We do people a favor by asking to enroll them in our small-group Bible study experience.

We are more successful in reaching people when we identify and seek to reach specific target groups who have such things in common as age or generational situations, life circumstances, or transitions. When Sunday School is strategy, we are constantly looking for opportunities and audiences for whom a new unit is needed.

Frequently we find success in targeting people who are in a special life transition or affinity group such as single adults, newlyweds, homebound persons, individuals who work on Sunday, and so forth. We are more successful in reaching unreached people when we start new Bible study groups designed to target people in affinity groups. People we are seeking to reach are less likely to join a group that has been in existence for more than a year.

We are more successful in reaching and assimilating new people as we activate class members to take responsibilities, helping to accomplish the purpose of the Sunday School class.

Your Journey in Faith

Read 1 John 2:1-2. Imagine that you are standing at the foot of the cross and looking into the eyes of Jesus. Jesus looks at your and says, "Even if no one else were on this earth, I would have done this for you." What would you say to Jesus?

What are you learning about the role of Sunday School in making forgiveness available for all? What can you do through your Sunday School class to help people who do not know of Christ's forgiveness?

What have you been learning about forgiveness through FAITH training?

Prayer Concerns

Answers to Prayer

Dear Learner:

You're Making It!

"I can do all things through Christ which strengtheneth me!" (Phil. 4:13).

In all the years I have taught this first level of training I am always amazed at how quickly we arrive at the halfway point. Sadly, some drop out of training now. Please, don't you do that! Stop and think:

- *What would you do with this time that is more productive for the Lord than FAITH? ("Nothing," is always the answer I receive.)*
- *Think not of the things you have struggled with, but of the things you already have learned.*

FAITH is about faithfulness, commitment, obedience, discipline, and focus—not just an emotional decision. FAITH is bigger than just you. Family and friends will be changed because you continue. The grown son of Karen, one of our Learners, was saved when she was at this point in FAITH training. What if she had dropped out?

Remember, this is a 16-week commitment you have made. With Christ's help, you can overcome just about any excuse and make it. The vast majority will continue "full speed ahead" to the last week. You can do that, too; hang in there!

Team Time and Celebration Time attendance are critical at this point. If you feel a need for encouragement or help, go to your Team Leader, fellow Team member, or pastor. We're all in this together, as a team! (By the way, pray for these three people now and go to them this week and encourage them. They need support, too.)

Again, I have gotten down on my knees and prayed for you and the other people who might read this note of encouragement:

Dear Lord Jesus, we claim the promise that we really* can *do all all things through You. Right now we are setting our hearts and minds to be determined to "stick by the stuff" in the second half of FAITH. Thank You for the joy of blessings and growth that are ahead for us!

Would you like to write a prayer for yourself and your FAITH Team in the space provided?

____

____

With You in His Certain FAITH Victory!

Bobby

Bobby

SESSION 8

I is for Impossible

In this session you will

CHECK IT: engage in Team Time activities;

HEAR IT: learn the IMPOSSIBLE portion of the gospel presentation—meaning of the letter *I,* descriptive statements, and accompanying Bible verses;

SEE IT: view the FORGIVENESS, AVAILABLE, and IMPOSSIBLE video segments;

SAY IT: practice IMPOSSIBLE with a partner;

STUDY IT: overview Home Study Assignments for Session 8;

DO IT: make visits—at Team Leader's cue, be able to share FORGIVENESS and AVAILABLE;

SHARE IT: celebrate.

In Advance

- Pray for Team Leaders by name as they guide their FAITH Teams.
- Preview teaching suggestions and session content. Also review Session 6 FAITH Tip, "God's Wonderful Work of Salvation" and this session's FAITH Tip, "God Cannot Allow Sin into Heaven." Use either Session 8 computer slides or the overhead transparencies (#36-38, 48-49) to support teaching. ***Note:*** Cels #36-38 were first used in Session 5.
- Prepare the room for teaching.
- Cue video to segment "F-FORGIVENESS" to view *F-A-I*-(if time is limited, show only "I-IMPOSSIBLE"). Or use the role-play (pp. 75-76, Administrative Guide) as another way to model a visit.
- Are Teams making complete reports? Update Teams on how information is used for follow-up.

(15 min.) CHECK IT

If the computer presentation is used, display the agenda frame for Team Time, as desired. Add other points as needed.

Team Time

CHECK IT

Your Team Leader directs this important time, checking off memory work, reviewing previous sessions and completed assignments, answering questions, and providing guidance to strengthen home visits.

Agenda:
✓ FAITH Visit Outline
✓ Practice
✓ Other Home Study Assignments
✓ Session 7 debriefing
✓ Help for strengthening a visit

❑ ***Outline memorized?—check it!***

Team Leader: In the adjacent box, check off each word as the Learner recites it correctly. In the space provided for sign-off, indicate your approval by signing your name.

FAITH VISIT OUTLINE

❑ *Preparation*

- ❑ **INTRODUCTION**
- ❑ **INTERESTS**
- ❑ **INVOLVEMENT**
  - ❑ **Church Experience/Background**
    - ❑ **Ask about the person's church background.**
    - ❑ **Listen for clues about the person's spiritual involvement.**
  - ❑ **Sunday School Testimony**
    - ❑ **Tell general benefits of Sunday School.**
    - ❑ **Tell a current personal experience.**
  - ❑ **Evangelistic Testimony**
    - ❑ **Tell a little of your pre-conversion experience.**
    - ❑ **Say: "I had a life-changing experience."**
    - ❑ **Tell recent benefits of your conversion.**
- ❑ **INQUIRY**
- ❑ **Key Question: In your personal opinion, what do you understand it takes for a person to go to heaven?**
  - ❑ **Possible answers: Faith, works, unclear, no opinion**
- ❑ **Transition Statement: I'd like to share with you how the Bible answers this question, if it is all right. There is a word that can be used to answer this question: *FAITH (spell out on fingers).***

❑ *Presentation*

❑ **F is for FORGIVENESS.**

❑ **We cannot have eternal life and heaven without God's forgiveness.**

❑ ***"In Him [meaning Jesus] we have redemption through His blood, the forgiveness of sins"—Ephesians 1:7a, NKJV.***

❑ **A is for AVAILABLE.**

❑ **Forgiveness is available. It is—**

❑ **AVAILABLE FOR ALL**

❑ ***"For God so loved the world that He gave His only begotten Son, that whoever believes in Him should not perish but have everlasting life"—John 3:16, NKJV.***

❑ **BUT NOT AUTOMATIC**

❑ ***"Not everyone who says to Me, 'Lord, Lord,' shall enter the kingdom of heaven"—Matthew 7:21a, NKJV.***

❑ **I is for IMPOSSIBLE.**

❑ **It is impossible for God to allow sin into heaven.**

❑ **GOD IS—**

❑ **• LOVE**

❑ ***John 3:16, NKJV***

❑ **• JUST**

❑ ***"For judgment is without mercy"—James 2:13a, NKJV.***

❑ **MAN IS SINFUL**

❑ ***"For all have sinned and fall short of the glory of God"—Romans 3:23, NKJV.***

❑ **Question: But how can a sinful person enter heaven, where God allows no sin?**

❑ **T** (TURN)

❑ **H** (HEAVEN)

❑ *Invitation*

❑ **INQUIRE**

❑ **INVITE**

❑ **INSURE**

_________________ *Team Leader Sign-off*

❑ ***Other Home Study Assignments completed?—check it!***

How are FAITH Tips enhancing your study? Have you been able to keep up with these and other Home Study Assignments? Journaling can be a particularly significant exercise at this point in FAITH training. Acknowledge that, since memorization is at its most intense level now, it may be more difficult to keep up.

❑ ***Any questions from Session 7?—check it!***

What questions do you have about Session 7? Ask your Team Leader now.

❑ ***Need help in strengthening a visit?—here's how!***

Be prepared to share your evangelistic testimony and other parts of the FAITH Visit Outline you have learned, if such an opportunity presents itself in this session.

(5 min.) Transition to classrooms for instruction on the content of the session.

On Our Own, Heaven Is Impossible

Just a reminder: the letter *F* stands for FORGIVENESS and the letter *A* represents AVAILABLE. Forgiveness is available for all, but it is not automatic.

Every attribute that is ________ ______ ________ can be used to describe God *(Almighty, Righteous,* and so forth; the following are only a few Scriptures that highlight attributes of God: Pss. 86:8-15; 94:9-23; 99:1-5; 130; 139:1-14; 145:3-20; Isa. 6:1-5; Rev. 1:17-18.) God created man as His most prized possession to bless us and enjoy fellowship with us. Man rebelled against God and thus rejected a perfect relationship with a perfect and caring God.

When we recognize the perfection and holiness of God and compare it with our imperfection and sinfulness, we begin to recognize we cannot have a right relationship with God _____ ________ ________.

There are two primary reasons it is impossible for someone to go to heaven or be in the presence of God on our own—*(1) because of who He is and (2) because of who we are.* Because God is perfect, He cannot allow sin (or unredeemed sinners) in His presence.

Sin is part of our rebellious ___________. All of us are blemished to the point that we cannot be allowed, on our own, into the presence of God. Sin is that serious. Sin not only is doing something bad or wrong, it also is direct rebellion against God. James 4:17 reminds us that failure to do the things we should do is sin as well. Sin _______________ us from God. (These are a few Scriptures that highlight characteristics of sinful humanity: Pss. 73:3-19,27; 94:1-7; Isa. 1:2-9; Rom. 3:10-18; Gal. 5:19-21; Col. 3:5-10; Titus 3:3.)

Likely you already have encountered, and will continue to meet, people who see themselves as "good, moral" individuals. Some think they have not sinned because they do not commit serious or harmful acts. In their understanding of what sin is, they are sinless. This view is contrary to what the Bible teaches.

The consequences of sin must be ________. John 3:16 is used a second time in a FAITH visit, as a reminder of God's love as previously discussed but now to communicate the righteousness and justice of God. The word ____________ in John 3:16 points out the seriousness of sin to God and the impossibility of our situation.

Teaching Time

HEAR IT

STEP 1 (5 min.) **Review the letters learned earlier *(F* and *A)* if still needed after Team Time.**

STEP 2 (10 min.) **Using either the cel or computer slide and "On Our Own, Heaven Is Impossible" content, direct Learners to fill in the blanks.**

On Our Own,
Heaven Is
Impossible

Explain the impossibility of having a right relationship with God on our own. Using selected Scriptures (in advance ask someone to read them aloud), highlight:

- **God's holiness (attributes of God)**
- **Our sinfulness (our nature, sinful acts, sin of omission)**
- **Consequences of sin (Use John 3:16 to highlight *perish;* choose from selected Scriptures—including Rom. 1:26-27; 1:28-32; 2:12; 6:23; 8:13—to further emphasize consequences of sin.)**

STEP 3 (5 min.) Using the "I is for Impossible" content and the presentation slide or cel, instruct Learners to write the:

- Meaning of letter *I*
- Verse for GOD IS LOVE—John 3:16
- Verse for GOD IS JUST—James 2:13*a*
- Verse for MAN IS SINFUL—Romans 3:23

Note: The same cel used in Session 5, Step 1 (IMPOSSIBLE), is used here.

SEE IT

Show "F-FORGIVENESS," "A-AVAILABLE," and "I-IMPOSSIBLE" video segments.

If time is limited, show only the "I-IMPOSSIBLE" segment.

I is for Impossible

The letter *I* in the gospel presentation is for ________________. It is impossible for God to allow sin into heaven.

Why? Because of Who He is and who we are.

The Scriptures you share for IMPOSSIBLE show how:

- God is both loving and just; and
- Man is sinful.

By this time in a visit, you already have talked with someone about God's love. John 3:16 is used again to remind a person that God is loving.

If you have not already used your small New Testament, this would be a good time to show the person a verse in your Bible. John 3:16 is easy to locate. It is appropriate for the person to read the verse aloud with you. Someone who is not familiar with the Bible can see that everything you are sharing indeed is from God's Word.

GOD IS LOVE

____

____

____

____

—John 3:16, NKJV.

Many passages of Scripture indicate that God is love. These are a few: 1 Kings 8:23; Psalm 25:4-7; Jeremiah 31:3; John 15:9-13; Romans 5:8; Ephesians 2:4-5; 1 John 4:16.

Not only is God loving, He also is just and righteous. Because He is just, God cannot accept sinfulness—and us as sinful creatures. While it is acknowledged that the book of James was written to Christians, James 2:13*a* affirms the fact that the judgment of God upon lost man's sin is without mercy.

GOD IS JUST

____

—James 2:13*a*, NKJV.

God's judgment is against sin. Many verses in Scripture call attention to the just nature of God and His judgment against sin. These are a few verses that refer to the fact that God is just and proclaims judgment against sin: Deuteronomy 32:4; Psalm 9:16; Jeremiah 30:11; Matthew 12:36; Hebrews 9:27; Revelation 16:7.

Romans 3:23 reveals our sinfulness before God.

MAN IS SINFUL

____

____

—Romans 3:23, NKJV.

There are many words in Hebrew and Greek that are translated "sin" or "sinner." Some words mean "missing the mark," "ethical wrong," "rebellion or transgression against God," "to refuse to obey a command," "some wrong done to someone else," "a departure from that which is right," "a lack of belief," "unfaithfulness or the betrayal of a trust," "to satisfy desire," "covetousness," "a desire for something forbidden as in lust," "a hatred or enmity against God."[1]

These are but a few of the many verses that call attention to the fact that we are sinners in need of a Savior: Deuteronomy 24:16; Psalm 51:1-4; John 8:34; Romans 7:5; 1 John 1: 5-7.

By this time in a visit, a nonbeliever may have recognized for the first time the impossible situation he or she is in. Asking the question **But how can a sinful person enter heaven, where God allows no sin?** can reinforce this truth and open up the opportunity to share God's solution.

I is for IMPOSSIBLE.
It is impossible for God to allow sin into heaven.
GOD IS—

- **LOVE**
  "For God so loved the world that He gave His only begotten Son, that whoever believes in Him should not perish but have everlasting life"—John 3:16, NKJV.
- **JUST**
  "For judgment is without mercy"—James 2:13a, NKJV.

MAN IS SINFUL
"For all have sinned and fall short of the glory of God"—Romans 3:23, NKJV.

Question: But how can a sinful person enter heaven, where God allows no sin?

Be Sensitive to Seeker Signals

When seekers (those who show some openness to the gospel) take a step of action in their spiritual searches, they are not carrying a sign that says: "Don't miss me. I'm ready to talk about God." Usually, their signals are subtle. Assume that if any of the following things happen (as they can on a FAITH visit), a seeker is signaling spiritual interest:

STEP 5 (5 min.) **Ask:**
From what you have experienced in FAITH visits, what are some evidences people show of being interested in spiritual things?

Allow for a few responses; then share the "Be Sensitive to Seeker Signals" content.

SAY IT

STEP 6 (5 min.) **Practice IMPOSSIBLE with a partner, making sure each person has a turn. Include the transition question. Use the notes in your Journal showing all of *I* is for IMPOSSIBLE.**

STUDY IT

STEP 7 (5 min.) **Overview Home Study Assignments for Session 8.**

- **Memorize—FAITH Visit Outline, adding the letter *T* (TURN)**
- **Practice—First four letters of FAITH**
- **Write—Sunday School class actions**
- ***Read—Evangelism Through the Sunday School* assignments, FAITH Tips: "God Cannot Allow Sin into Heaven," "An Urgency Transfusion"**
- **Journal—Your Journey in Faith**

• *The Question Signal:* Pay attention to any question that has to do with spiritual matters. Seekers do not ask questions about the Bible or about attending church because they are suddenly curious. The questions show some sort of spiritual activity in their lives.

• *The Church Attendance Signal:* It is always significant when seekers come to church. . . . Christians should assume God is at work in their lives.

• *The Christian Literature Signal:* Pay attention when seekers tell you they have started reading the Bible or a religious book. What they read indicates a need in their lives.

• *The Christian Broadcasting Signal:* When non-Christians mention they listened to a Christian radio program or watched a Christian program on television, ask some follow-up questions. Find out what they thought about the program. Ask them to tell you about the speaker's message.

• *The Christian Fellowship Signal:* If seekers join with Christians in some sort of fellowship activity, the event has spiritual significance. . . The seekers will evaluate the Christians in the fellowship setting to see if there is anything distinctive in their lives.[2]

(5 min.) Transition to assemble with FAITH Teams to prepare for home visits.

---

[1]C. B. Hogue, *The Doctrine of Salvation* (Nashville: Convention Press, 1978), 22–43. Out of print.
[2]John Kramp, *Out of Their Faces and into Their Shoes* (Nashville: Broadman & Holman Publishers, 1995), 74–75.

Visitation Time

(110 min.) DO IT

DO IT

We are all sinners by nature, and we are visiting people who are sinners by nature. The difference for us (and for the Christians we visit) is that we have realized we are sinners and cannot do anything apart from acknowledging that Jesus paid the penalty for our sins.

Be very careful when you are visiting that you do not come across as judgmental. Remember, you can identify with the most hardened of sinners. Until you chose God's way over your own, you were just as guilty.

Celebration Time

(30 min.) SHARE IT

SHARE IT

- Testimonies and reports
- Session 8 Evaluation Card
- Participation Card
- Visitation assignments updated with results

Home Study Assignments

You may want to read your session notes again once blanks have been filled in from Teaching Time. A good time to review your notes is before doing Home Study Assignments each week.

Memorize the following points of the FAITH Visit Outline, adding the letter *T* (TURN). Be prepared to recite them to your Team Leader during Session 9 Team Time.

FAITH VISIT OUTLINE

Preparation

INTRODUCTION
INTERESTS
INVOLVEMENT
  Church Experience/Background
    Ask about the person's church background.
    Listen for clues about the person's spiritual involvement.
  Sunday School Testimony
    Tell general benefits of Sunday School.
    Tell a current personal experience.
  Evangelistic Testimony
    Tell a little of your pre-conversion experience.
    Say: "I had a life-changing experience."
    Tell recent benefits of your conversion.
INQUIRY
Key Question: In your personal opinion, what do you understand it takes for a person to go to heaven?
  Possible answers: Faith, works, unclear, no opinion
Transition Statement: I'd like to share with you how the Bible answers this question, if it is all right. There is a word that can be used to answer this question: FAITH *(spell out on fingers).*

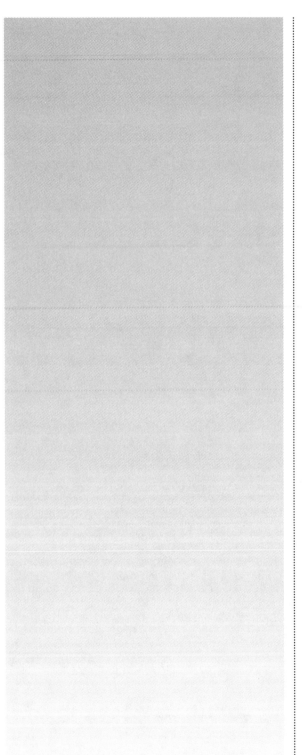

Presentation

F is for FORGIVENESS.

We cannot have eternal life and heaven without God's forgiveness.

"In Him [meaning Jesus] we have redemption through His blood, the forgiveness of sins"—Ephesians 1:7a, NKJV.

A is for AVAILABLE.

Forgiveness is available. It is—

AVAILABLE FOR ALL

"For God so loved the world that He gave His only begotten Son, that whoever believes in Him should not perish but have everlasting life"—John 3:16, NKJV.

BUT NOT AUTOMATIC

"Not everyone who says to Me, 'Lord, Lord,' shall enter the kingdom of heaven"—Matthew 7:21a, NKJV.

I is for IMPOSSIBLE.

It is impossible for God to allow sin into heaven.

GOD IS—

- LOVE

  John 3:16, NKJV

- JUST

  "For judgment is without mercy"—James 2:13a, NKJV.

MAN IS SINFUL

"For all have sinned and fall short of the glory of God"—Romans 3:23, NKJV.

Question: But how can a sinful person enter heaven, where God allows no sin?

T is for TURN.

Question: If you were driving down the road and someone asked you to turn, what would he or she be asking you to do? *(change direction)*

***Turn* means repent.**

TURN from something—sin and self

"But unless you repent you will all likewise perish"—Luke 13:3b, NKJV.

TURN to Someone; trust Christ only

(The Bible tells us that) ***"Christ died for our sins according to the Scriptures, and that He was buried, and that He rose again the third day according to the Scriptures"—1 Corinthians 15:3b-4, NKJV.***

"If you confess with your mouth the Lord Jesus and believe in your heart that God has raised Him from the dead, you will be saved"—Romans 10:9, NKJV.

H (HEAVEN)

Invitation

INQUIRE
INVITE
INSURE

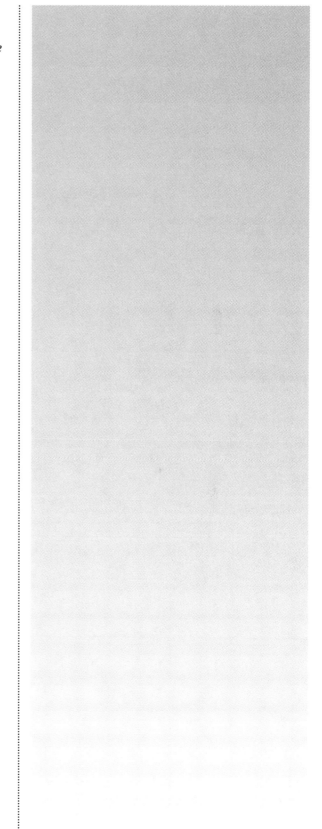

List actions your Sunday School class could take to follow up by ministering to or encouraging a person who is a believer. List actions your Sunday School class could take to follow up by ministering to or encouraging a person if he or she is not a believer.

BELIEVER	NONBELIEVER
______________________	______________________
______________________	______________________
______________________	______________________

From *Evangelism Through the Sunday School: A Journey of FAITH* by Bobby Welch, read:

- "Avoid the No-Win Collision Course" (p. 107)
- "Hurry, Hurry, Hurry!" (p. 163)
- "When the Light Comes On" (pp. 44-48).

Read the testimony on page 131.

Read the FAITH Tips: "God Cannot Allow Sin into Heaven" and "An Urgency Transfusion."

FAITH *Tip*

God Cannot Allow Sin into Heaven

God cannot allow sin into heaven because of who He is: holy, righteous, just, sinless. The words *justice* and *righteous* are based in the same root word in Greek. God's nature is completely opposite anything unholy or unrighteous. Everything that is perfect can be used to describe God.

God cannot allow sin into heaven because of who we are: sinful and rebellious creatures. Sin is foreign and detestable to God. Not only do we have wrong thoughts and do things that displease God, we also neglect to do those things we should do. Sin is a part of our nature, and it separates us from God, both now and for eternity. Without Christ, we are out of fellowship with God because of sin.

Sin deserves punishment, or God's judgment on it. God's judgment on sin is severe; the punishment of sin is death, or eternal separation from God. This is why it is impossible for anyone to have heaven on his or her own. Investigate Romans 3:23-26 and Romans 6:23 to get a glimpse of the contrast between God's justice and love and the inevitable consequence of sin: death.

Even understanding that God is the perfect picture of love ("God so loved the world that He gave His only begotten Son . . ., John 3:16), we cannot begin to get away from the consequences of His judgment on us because of our sin ("perish," John 3:16).

The contrast between God's judgment of us and His justice toward us is easier to understand when we consider our own difficulty in rightly judging persons we love. Think about how you feel when a child or another family member wrongs you; does not the wrong act usually deserve punishment? If we desire and would be allowed to punish someone who wrongs us, how much more should a sinless God punish sin and the sinner? Do you always punish the person who offends you, or is your justice tempered with mercy toward this one you love more than life?

The contrasts are vivid. In God there is life (both abundant in the present and eternal in the future); in sin there is death. God's judgment against sin is without mercy. On the other hand, God is full of mercy: In Jesus He provided the payment for our sins and the sins of the world.

What saves us, if we choose to accept it, is that Jesus has paid the penalty for us so that we might be judged righteous in God's sight. A person who continues to choose sin is choosing death over life.

With the Holy Spirit's prompting, a nonbeliever can both catch a glimpse of the severity of sin in his or her life and the inescapable consequence God requires for sin—and, at the same time, the great love and mercy God shows us in Christ.

FAITH *Tip*

An Urgency Transfusion

Why do many Christians lack urgency in their search for lost people? Here are three possible reasons:

(1) Some question whether non-Christians are really lost.
(2) Others wonder if the lost are in ultimate danger.
(3) Some Christians toy with the idea that those who die without Christ will simply die without any future life whatsoever.

No matter how plausible or appealing these views may be, they deny biblical reality. These views offer false hope. This is why few evangelical Christians admit they hold these beliefs. Put on the spot, they affirm that Jesus is the only way to God and that those without Christ will spend eternity in hell. Still the undercurrent of doubt remains.

Christians sing the words—we affirm the biblical truths about evangelism. But our lives do not play the music—we do not share our faith with lost people. Somewhere, somehow, something has dulled our sense of urgency. So we search infrequently and without urgency. We must ask why. . .

A friend of mine has an intriguing habit. On a regular basis he takes a sheet of paper and writes affirmations he holds central in his life. For example, one day he wrote, "I believe Jesus really is the Christ." Then throughout the day, he thought about that affirmation and drew it into focus in his life. . . . Another day he wrote, "I believe the Bible is God's Word." That day he centered his thinking on the Bible and made that affirmation burn bright in his life once again.

A simply practice like my friend's affirmation sheet can help us discipline our thinking with central truths. As "lostologists," we can use this practice to transfuse our spiritual system with urgency for evangelism. Why not start with these affirmations?

- Jesus is the only way to God.
- Every person deserves to hear about Jesus.
- I can tell others what Jesus has done for me.
- All who die without Christ will spend eternity in hell.
- I must tell others about God's gift of eternal life.
- Deep down, people long for a relationship with God.
- It is wrong to keep the good news of Jesus to myself.

Use one of these affirmations (or write one of your own) and focus on it for one full day. Pray about it. Think about it. Evaluate your life by it. The next day, move on to another affirmation and repeat the process. Continue this pattern for a full week. Ask God to rejuvenate your sense of urgency about sharing Christ with those around you. He will!

Adapted from John Kramp, *Out of Their Faces and Into Their Shoes* (Nashville: Broadman & Holman, Publishers, 1995), 134-135.

Your Journey in Faith

Read 1 John 1:8 and Romans 6:23. Describe when you realized your sinfulness was punishable by eternal separation from God.

What are you learning about nonbelievers through FAITH training?

What are you learning about God through FAITH training?

What are you learning about yourself through FAITH training?

Prayer Concerns

Answers to Prayer

SESSION 9

T is for Turn

In this session you will

CHECK IT: engage in Team Time activities;

HEAR IT: learn the TURN portion of the gospel presentation—meaning of the letter *T,* descriptive statements, and accompanying Bible verses;

SEE IT: view the FORGIVENESS, AVAILABLE, IMPOSSIBLE, and TURN video segments;

SAY IT: practice TURN with a partner;

STUDY IT: overview Home Study Assignments for Session 9;

DO IT: make visits—at your Team Leader's cue, be able to share the FORGIVENESS, AVAILABLE, and IMPOSSIBLE segments in a visit;

SHARE IT: celebrate.

In Advance

- Pray for unsaved people Team members will visit.
- Preview teaching suggestions and all session content. Use Session 9 computer presentation slides or overhead cels (#39-42, 50-51). ***Note:*** Cels #39-42 were first used in Session 5.
- Cue the video to segment "F-FORGIVENESS" to view *F-A-I-T;* if time is limited, only show "T-TURN." Or use the role-play segment (Administrative Guide, pp. 76-77) as another way to demonstrate or practice.
- Is Team Time beginning and ending on time each week? Remind Teams of the importance of using this period well so there is sufficient time for teaching and visits.
- Prepare the room for teaching.

(15 min.) CHECK IT

If the computer presentation is used, display the agenda frame for Team Time, as desired. Add other points as needed.

Team Time

CHECK IT

Your Team Leader directs this important time, checking off memory work, reviewing previous sessions and completed assignments, answering questions, and providing guidance to strengthen home visits.

Agenda:
✓ FAITH Visit Outline
✓ Practice
✓ Other Home Study Assignments
✓ Session 8 debriefing
✓ Help for strengthening a visit

❑ ***Outline memorized?—check it!***

Team Leader: In the adjacent box, check off each word as the Learner recites it correctly. In the space provided for sign-off, indicate your approval by signing your name.

FAITH VISIT OUTLINE

❑ *Preparation*

- ❑ **INTRODUCTION**
- ❑ **INTERESTS**
- ❑ **INVOLVEMENT**
  - ❑ **Church Experience/Background**
    - ❑ **Ask about the person's church background.**
    - ❑ **Listen for clues about the person's spiritual involvement.**
  - ❑ **Sunday School Testimony**
    - ❑ **Tell general benefits of Sunday School.**
    - ❑ **Tell a current personal experience.**
  - ❑ **Evangelistic Testimony**
    - ❑ **Tell a little of your pre-conversion experience.**
    - ❑ **Say: "I had a life-changing experience."**
    - ❑ **Tell recent benefits of your conversion.**
- ❑ **INQUIRY**
- ❑ **Key Question: In your personal opinion, what do you understand it takes for a person to go to heaven?**
  - ❑ **Possible answers: Faith, works, unclear, no opinion**

❑ **Transition Statement: I'd like to share with you how the Bible answers this question, if it is all right. There is a word that can be used to answer this question:** ***FAITH (spell out on fingers).***

❑ *Presentation*

❑ **F is for FORGIVENESS.**

❑ **We cannot have eternal life and heaven without God's forgiveness.**

 ❑ ***"In Him [meaning Jesus] we have redemption through His blood, the forgiveness of sins"—Ephesians 1:7a, NKJV.***

❑ **A is for AVAILABLE.**

❑ **Forgiveness is available. It is—**

❑ **AVAILABLE FOR ALL**

 ❑ ***"For God so loved the world that He gave His only begotten Son, that whoever believes in Him should not perish but have everlasting life"—John 3:16, NKJV.***

❑ **BUT NOT AUTOMATIC**

 ❑ ***"Not everyone who says to Me, 'Lord, Lord,' shall enter the kingdom of heaven"—Matthew 7:21a, NKJV.***

❑ **I is for IMPOSSIBLE.**

❑ **It is impossible for God to allow sin into heaven.**

❑ **GOD IS—**

 ❑ **• LOVE**

  ❑ ***John 3:16, NKJV***

 ❑ **• JUST**

  ❑ ***"For judgment is without mercy"—James 2:13a, NKJV.***

❑ **MAN IS SINFUL**

  ❑ ***"For all have sinned and fall short of the glory of God"—Romans 3:23, NKJV.***

❑ **Question: But how can a sinful person enter heaven, where God allows no sin?**

❑ **T is for TURN.**

❑ **Question: If you were driving down the road and someone asked you to turn, what would he or she be asking you to do?** ***(change direction)***

❑ ***Turn*** **means repent.**

❑ **TURN from something—sin and self**

- ❑ ***"But unless you repent you will all likewise perish"—Luke 13:3b, NKJV.***

❑ **TURN to Someone; trust Christ only**

- ❑ **(The Bible tells us that)** ***"Christ died for our sins according to the Scriptures, and that He was buried, and that He rose again the third day according to the Scriptures"—1 Corinthians 15:3b-4, NKJV.***
- ❑ ***"If you confess with your mouth the Lord Jesus and believe in your heart that God has raised Him from the dead, you will be saved"—Romans 10:9, NKJV.***

❑ **H** (HEAVEN)

❑ *Invitation*

❑ **INQUIRE**

❑ **INVITE**

❑ **INSURE**

____________________ *Team Leader Sign-off*

❑ ***Other Home Study Assignments completed?—check it!***

Do you see ways your Sunday School class can encourage believers and can follow up on nonbelievers? Are you recognizing how your class helps nurture a new believer through Bible study, fellowship, and other experiences?

Do class/department members who are not participating in FAITH still see themselves as a part of this ministry? In what ways? Are you sharing prayer needs and results of visits with fellow class members? Are they praying for you and for people you and your Team will visit? Is your class, department, and church growing spiritually and numerically?

❑ ***Any questions from Session 8?—check it!***

What questions do you have about Session 8? Ask your Team Leader now.

❑ ***Need help in strengthening a visit?—here's how!***

How does it encourage and help you to share what you have learned with another Christian who is not a part of FAITH? How might it encourage him or her?

If time allows, practice with a partner as much of the FAITH Visit Outline as you have learned. Share first as if with a nonbeliever; share the second time as if with a believer. Notice and discuss any difference.

(5 min.) Transition to classrooms for instruction on the content of the session.

Teaching Time

HEAR IT

STEP 1 (5 min.) Review *F-A-I* (if still needed after Team Time.)

STEP 2 (5 min.) Using "The Image—and Importance—of Turning" content and computer presentation slides or cels, instruct Learners to fill in the blanks for meanings of *T.*

Note: The same cels used in Session 5, Step 1 (TURN), are used here.

The Image—and Importance—of Turning

The Bible was written in picturesque languages. Most of the Old Testament was written in Hebrew; the New Testament, in Greek. Both languages take abstract concepts and use simple and beautiful images to depict them. *Turning* is a significant image in Scripture—and a significant action in the salvation experience.

God desires us to have a full and a fulfilled life. He offers forgiveness available to and for all people, but His forgiveness is not automatic. Our sinfulness makes it impossible on our own to have a right relationship with God and to spend eternity in His presence. God chose to intervene.

The T in FAITH is for ________.

Imagine you are driving down the road and someone tells you to turn. What would he or she be asking you to do? You are to *change direction.*

Significantly, you are to ask a similar question and affirm a similar response at this point in the gospel presentation. Such a question intentionally involves the person in this important part of the visit.

Question: If you were driving down the road and someone asked you to turn, what would he or she be asking you to do? ***(change direction)***

***Turn* means __________.**

Turn also can mean to ________ __________ ________.

TURN from ____________—_____ _____ ______.

TURN to ____________; _______ _________ ______.

To *turn* is a very straightforward image. We are to turn, to change the direction of our lives. Turn means repent.

Turning from, Turning to

We are to turn *from* something—sin and self. We are to turn *to* Someone—to Jesus Christ only, in whom we put our trust. A number of Scripture passages show the vivid imagery of *turning from* sin and self and *turning to* Christ only for forgiveness and eternal life (repentance).

• Isaiah 45:20-22*a* draws a _________ ____________ between idol gods and the true God. We are to turn *from* idols *to* Him to be saved.

• Isaiah 55:7 paints a vivid picture of *turning from* ____________________ and *turning to* _____ ________ for mercy and pardon.

• Ezekiel 33:10-11 indicates God takes _____ _____________ in the death of the wicked; rather, He desires that "they turn from their ways and live" (NIV).

• Acts 3:19 makes clear what we are to do: "___________, then, and turn to God, so that your sins may be wiped out" (NIV).

• Peter (in 1 Pet. 3:10-11) quotes from Psalm 34 (vv. 12-16) to encourage people to *turn away* from _______.

• In a familiar and much-loved passage—Luke 15—Jesus taught about lostness using three parables: a lost sheep, a lost coin, and a lost son. In each case Jesus gave a beautiful picture of God's _________________—and the seriousness He places on one person out of relationship with Him.

We must turn from sin and self (repent) and turn to Christ only to be forgiven and to receive heaven and life everlasting.

T is for TURN. If you were driving down the road and someone asked you to turn, what would he or she be asking you to do? *(change direction)*

***Turn* means repent.**

TURN from something—sin and self

____

____

—Luke 13:3*b*, NKJV.

TURN to Someone; trust Christ only

(The Bible tells us that) ______________________________

____

____

____

____,

—1 Corinthians 15:3*b*-4, NKJV.

"____

____

____

____

____

—Romans 10:9, NKJV.

STEP 3 (5 min.) **Using "Turning from, Turning to" content, overview some Scriptures emphasizing repentance:**

- **Isaiah 45:20-22*a***
- **Isaiah 55:7**
- **Ezekiel 33:10-11**
- **Luke 15**
- **Acts 3:19**
- **1 Peter 3:10-11**

STEP 4 (5 min.) **Using the computer presentation slides or cels, lead Learners to write the verses for the letter *T*:**

- **Luke 13:3*b*, NKJV**
- **1 Corinthians 15:3*b*-4, NKJV**
- **Romans 10:9, NKJV**

SEE IT

STEP 5 (10 min.) **View the video segments "F-FORGIVENESS," "A-AVAILABLE," "I-IMPOSSIBLE," and "T-TURN."**

If time is limited, show only "T-TURN" (less than 3 minutes).

SAY IT

STEP 6 (10 min.) **Practice TURN with a partner, making sure each person has a turn.**

STUDY IT

STEP 7 (5 min.) **Overview Home Study Assignments for Session 9.**

- **Memorize—FAITH Visit Outline, adding the letter *H* (HEAVEN)**
- **Read—*Evangelism Through the Sunday School* assignments**
- **Journal—Your Journey in Faith**

Conclude by saying: When the lost are found, celebration occurs in heaven. What happens on earth must mirror the heavenly party in spirit and joy.

(5 min.) Transition to assemble with FAITH Teams to prepare for home visits.

(110 min.) DO IT

(30 min.) SHARE IT

If your Celebration Time does not mirror the same joy that occurs in heaven when the lost have been found, make special effort to celebrate all victories by FAITH Teams.

After you have shared verses on turning from sin and turning to Christ only, consider further involving the person. Ask: What will happen if you are willing to turn to Christ and Christ only? *(You will have eternal life and heaven)*

Interestingly, Jesus' classic parables on lostness (Luke 15) have celebration as a central theme. When the shepherd found the missing sheep, he celebrated with friends and neighbors (vv. 5-6). The woman, on finding her coin, called her friends and neighbors together, saying: 'Rejoice with me; I have found my lost coin' (v. 9). On his son's return, the father instructed his servants: 'Quick! Bring the best robe and put it on him. Put a ring on his finger and sandals on his feet. Bring the fattened calf and kill it. Let's have a feast and celebrate. For this son of mine was dead and is alive again; he was lost and is found.' So they began to celebrate' (vv. 22-24). . . . Jesus left no doubt. When the lost are found, celebration occurs in heaven. What happens on earth must mirror the heavenly party in spirit and joy."[1]

[1] Adapted from John Kramp, *Out of Their Faces and Into Their Shoes* (Nashville: Broadman & Holman Publishers, 1995), 176-177.

Visitation Time

DO IT

Be prepared to present *F-A-I* in a visit, under the guidance of your Team Leader. As you prepare to visit and to observe your Team Leader in visits, and try to anticipate these situations: If you were a nonbeliever, what aspects of turning and trusting would appeal to you? What questions would come to mind? As a believer, what aspects of turning and trusting would encourage or help you celebrate your faith journey?

This part of the FAITH Visit Outline describes the pivotal choice a person must make to receive God's forgiveness. Pray that the persons you visit will recognize their need to turn to Christ and to Christ only.

Celebration Time

SHARE IT

- Reports and testimonies
- Session 9 Evaluation Card
- Participation Card
- Visitation forms updated with results of visits

Home Study Assignments

You may want to read your session notes again once blanks have been filled in from Teaching Time. A good time to review your notes is before doing Home Study Assignments each week.

Learn and present the entire gospel presentation to your Team Leader. Session 12 will give you opportunity to practice the entire FAITH Visit Outline.

FAITH VISIT OUTLINE

Preparation

INTRODUCTION
INTERESTS
INVOLVEMENT
 Church Experience/Background
  Ask about the person's church background.
  Listen for clues about the person's spiritual involvement.
 Sunday School Testimony
  Tell general benefits of Sunday School.
  Tell a current personal experience.
 Evangelistic Testimony
  Tell a little of your pre-conversion experience.
  Say: "I had a life-changing experience."
  Tell recent benefits of your conversion.
INQUIRY
Key Question: In your personal opinion, what do you understand it takes for a person to go to heaven?
 Possible answers: Faith, works, unclear, no opinion
Transition Statement: I'd like to share with you how the Bible answers this question, if it is all right. There is a word that can be used to answer this question: *FAITH (spell out on fingers).*

Presentation

F is for FORGIVENESS.
We cannot have eternal life and heaven without God's forgiveness.

"In Him [meaning Jesus] we have redemption through His blood, the forgiveness of sins"—Ephesians 1:7a, NKJV.

A is for AVAILABLE.
Forgiveness is available. It is—
AVAILABLE FOR ALL

"For God so loved the world that He gave His only begotten Son, that whoever believes in Him should not perish but have everlasting life"—John 3:16, NKJV.

BUT NOT AUTOMATIC

"Not everyone who says to Me, 'Lord, Lord,' shall enter the kingdom of heaven"—Matthew 7:21a, NKJV.

I is for IMPOSSIBLE.
It is impossible for God to allow sin into heaven.
GOD IS—

- LOVE
  John 3:16, NKJV
- JUST
  "For judgment is without mercy"—James 2:13a, NKJV.

MAN IS SINFUL

"For all have sinned and fall short of the glory of God" —Romans 3:23, NKJV.

Question: But how can a sinful person enter heaven, where God allows no sin?

T is for TURN.
Question: If you were driving down the road and someone asked you to turn, what would he or she be asking you to do? *(change direction)*
Turn **means repent.**
TURN from something—sin and self

"But unless you repent you will all likewise perish" —Luke 13:3b, NKJV.

TURN to Someone; trust Christ only

(The Bible tells us that) *"Christ died for our sins according to the Scriptures, and that He was buried, and that He rose again the third day according to the Scriptures"—1 Corinthians 15:3b-4, NKJV.*

"If you confess with your mouth the Lord Jesus and believe in your heart that God has raised Him from the dead, you will be saved"—Romans 10:9, NKJV.

H is for HEAVEN.

Heaven is eternal life.

HERE

"I have come that they may have life, and that they may have it more abundantly"—John 10:10b, NKJV.

HEREAFTER

"And if I go and prepare a place for you, I will come again and receive you to Myself; that where I am, there you may be also"—John 14:3, NKJV.

HOW

How can a person have God's forgiveness, heaven and eternal life, and Jesus as personal Savior and Lord?

Explain based on leaflet picture, F.A.I.T.H. (Forsaking All I Trust Him), Romans 10:9.

Invitation

INQUIRE

INVITE

INSURE

From *Evangelism Through the Sunday School: A Journey of FAITH* by Bobby Welch read "The Risk of Evangelism" (p. 157) and the testimony on page 155.

What risks do you find yourself more willing to take as a result of your FAITH training?

____
____
____
____
____
____

Your Journey in Faith

Write those things you experienced that helped you know you were deciding to turn from a sinful lifestyle and intentionally choosing to follow (turn to) God's leadership in your life.

Read Proverbs 3:5. What lessons have you learned regarding putting your trust in Christ alone?

Read James 1:2-3. What experiences have you faced recently that have tested your trust in Christ?

What advice about trusting Christ would you give to a person considering a new or growing relationship with Jesus?

Prayer Concerns

Answers to Prayer

SESSION 10

H is for Heaven

In this session you will

CHECK IT: engage in Team Time activities;

HEAR IT: learn and be able to recite the HEAVEN portion of the gospel presentation—meaning of the letter *H,* descriptive statements, and accompanying Bible verses; understand the way HOW makes transition into the ***Invitation;***

SEE IT: view the video segment of letter *H* (or entire gospel presentation, if time allows);

SAY IT: practice HEAVEN with a partner;

STUDY IT: overview Home Study Assignments for Session 10;

DO IT: make visits—at Team Leader's cue, be able to share FORGIVENESS, AVAILABLE, IMPOSSIBLE, and TURN;

SHARE IT: celebrate.

In Advance

- Pray that Team members will have opportunities to share the gospel during Visitation Time.
- Study teaching suggestions and all session content. (Also review Session 6 FAITH Tip, "God's Wonderful Work of Salvation.") Many important points need to be covered in this session. Use Session 10 computer presentation slides or overhead cels (#43-45, 52-54) for teaching support. ***Note:*** Cels #43-45 were first used in Session 5.
- Give each person a copy of *A Step of Faith* to use in Home Study Assignments.
- Cue the video to "H-HEAVEN"; if time allows, show the video segment of the entire gospel presentation (Session 5, "The Gospel Presentation"). Or use the role play (p. 77, Administrative Guide) to model.

(15 min.) CHECK IT

If the computer presentation is used, display the agenda frame for Team Time, as desired. Add other points as needed.

Team Time

CHECK IT

Your Team Leader directs this important time, checking off memory work, reviewing previous sessions and completed assignments, answering questions, and providing guidance to strengthen home visits.

Agenda:
✓ FAITH Visit Outline
✓ Practice
✓ Other Home Study Assignments
✓ Session 9 debriefing
✓ Help for strengthening a visit

❑ ***Outline memorized?—check it!***

Team Leader: In the adjacent box, check off each word as the Learner recites it correctly. In the space provided for sign-off, indicate your approval by signing your name.

FAITH VISIT OUTLINE

❑ *Preparation*

- ❑ **INTRODUCTION**
- ❑ **INTERESTS**
- ❑ **INVOLVEMENT**
  - ❑ **Church Experience/Background**
    - ❑ **Ask about the person's church background.**
    - ❑ **Listen for clues about the person's spiritual involvement.**
  - ❑ **Sunday School Testimony**
    - ❑ **Tell general benefits of Sunday School.**
    - ❑ **Tell a current personal experience.**
  - ❑ **Evangelistic Testimony**
    - ❑ **Tell a little of your pre-conversion experience.**
    - ❑ **Say: "I had a life-changing experience."**
    - ❑ **Tell recent benefits of your conversion.**
- ❑ **INQUIRY**
- ❑ **Key Question: In your personal opinion, what do you understand it takes for a person to go to heaven?**
  - ❑ **Possible answers: Faith, works, unclear, no opinion**
- ❑ **Transition Statement: I'd like to share with you how the Bible answers this question, if it is all right. There is a word that can be used to answer this question: *FAITH (spell out on fingers).***

❑ *Presentation*

❑ F is for FORGIVENESS.

❑ We cannot have eternal life and heaven without God's forgiveness.

- ❑ *"In Him [meaning Jesus] we have redemption through His blood, the forgiveness of sins"—Ephesians 1:7a, NKJV.*

❑ A is for AVAILABLE.

❑ Forgiveness is available. It is—

❑ AVAILABLE FOR ALL

- ❑ *"For God so loved the world that He gave His only begotten Son, that whoever believes in Him should not perish but have everlasting life"—John 3:16, NKJV.*

❑ BUT NOT AUTOMATIC

- ❑ *"Not everyone who says to Me, 'Lord, Lord,' shall enter the kingdom of heaven"—Matthew 7:21a, NKJV.*

❑ I is for IMPOSSIBLE.

❑ It is impossible for God to allow sin into heaven.

❑ GOD IS

- ❑ • LOVE
    - ❑ *John 3:16, NKJV*
- ❑ • JUST
    - ❑ *"For judgment is without mercy"—James 2:13a, NKJV.*

❑ MAN IS SINFUL

- ❑ *"For all have sinned and fall short of the glory of God"—Romans 3:23, NKJV.*

❑ Question: But how can a sinful person enter heaven, where God allows no sin?

❑ T is for TURN.

❑ Question: If you were driving down the road and someone asked you to turn, what would he or she be asking you to do? *(change direction)*

❑ *Turn* means repent.

❑ TURN from something—sin and self

- ❑ *"But unless you repent you will all likewise perish"—Luke 13:3b, NKJV.*

- ❑ TURN to Someone; trust Christ only
  - ❑ (The Bible tells us that) ***"Christ died for our sins according to the Scriptures, and that He was buried, and that He rose again the third day according to the Scriptures"—1 Corinthians 15:3b-4, NKJV.***
  - ❑ ***"If you confess with your mouth the Lord Jesus and believe in your heart that God has raised Him from the dead, you will be saved"—Romans 10:9, NKJV.***

- ❑ **H is for HEAVEN.**
- ❑ **Heaven is eternal life.**
- ❑ **HERE**
  - ❑ ***"I have come that they may have life, and that they may have it more abundantly"—John 10:10b, NKJV.***
- ❑ **HEREAFTER**
  - ❑ ***"And if I go and prepare a place for you, I will come again and receive you to Myself; that where I am, there you may be also"—John 14:3, NKJV.***
- ❑ **HOW**
  - ❑ **How can a person have God's forgiveness, heaven and eternal life, and Jesus as personal Savior and Lord?**
  - ❑ **Explain based on leaflet picture, F.A.I.T.H. (Forsaking All I Trust Him), Romans 10:9.**

❑ *Invitation*

- ❑ **INQUIRE**
- ❑ **INVITE**
- ❑ **INSURE**

___________________ *Team Leader Sign-off*

❑ ***Other Home Study Assignments completed?—check it!***

How has the Lord given you everything you need to carry out the Great Commission? How has FAITH training impacted your life, as well as the lives of your family members? (*Evangelism Through the Sunday School* reading)

❑ ***Any questions from Session 9?—check it!***

What questions do you have about Session 9? Ask your Team Leader now.

❑ ***Need help in strengthening a visit?—here's how!***

Be prepared to share as much of the gospel presentation as you feel comfortable doing in this week's visits. By now, you may be ready to present to someone the significant points of FORGIVENESS, AVAILABLE, IMPOSSIBLE, and TURN. Your Team Leader will resume the presentation to help the prospect know about HEAVEN—as well as about HOW God's forgiveness and heaven might be his/hers.

You will not be asked to do anything you do not feel ready to handle in a home visit.

(5 min.) Transition to classrooms for instruction on content of the session

Teaching Time

HEAR IT

STEP 1 (5 min.) **Using "Our Hope Now and for Eternity" content and computer slide or cel, overview meanings of the letter *H*.**

***Note:* If using cels, use the same cels used in Session 5, Step 1 (HEAVEN).**

STEP 2 (5 min.) **Using "Our Hope Now" content, overview the nature of abundant life.**

Keep the HEAVEN cel up or use the computer presentation slide to help Learners write John 10:10*b*, the verse expressing heaven in the present.

Our Hope Now and for Eternity

One of the most meaningful doctrines of our faith is that God, who resides in heaven, invites the righteous to live forever in His presence. Heaven is the epitome of beauty, glory, and joy. It is best understood as the place where God's holy presence dwells.

To be in the presence of God is the most joyful, fulfilling experience one can have. Christians have accepted God's initiative in Christ and have had their sins paid for by the sacrificial death of Jesus; they will be in God's presence for eternity. *Eternal life* is described not only as living in heaven later, but also as enjoying abundant life in fellowship with God now.

H is for ____________.

Heaven is ______________ ________.

The letter *H* in the gospel presentation stands for HEAVEN. If a person trusts in Christ and receives Him as Savior, he or she will receive eternal life and heaven. Heaven is both here and hereafter.

Our Hope Now

Did you realize that, when you asked Jesus to be your Savior, He gave you the capacity to have life that is complete, full, and at its greatest potential? You were created to live in complete fellowship with God and to enjoy the potential of being His most prized creation. The verse we use at this point in the gospel presentation clearly expresses the truth of HEAVEN HERE—full, complete, even superabundant life.

HERE

____

____

____

—John 10:10b, NKJV.

What does *abundant* mean? In this verse the Greek word "denotes the *superabundance* (italics added by author) of the life Christ brings."[1] The dictionary indicates that the word means "present in great quantity; more than adequate; well supplied; abounding; richly supplied."[2] These definitions would indicate that abundant life is complete, full, and being lived to its highest potential and beyond our expectations.

Abundant life does not mean that you will never have sorrows, crises, disappointments, or defeats. Abundant life does mean that you will have the God who created you to personally nurture and direct your life.

While *abundant life* also refers to heaven (the future), the quality of abundant life begins now. These are but a few Scriptures highlighting the quality of life that becomes available to us as Christians (Rom. 8:12-17; Rom. 8:26-30; Gal. 2:20; Gal. 3:26-27; Gal. 5:22-25; Eph. 1:9-14).

Second Corinthians 5:17 reminds us that life in the spiritual dimension begins when a person accepts Jesus as Savior and is freed from the eternal consequences of rebellion against God. These are some benefits from living in right relationship to God:

- __________________ with God;
- ___________, ________, and _______;
- God's ________________, which are yours, now and forever;
- Change of perspective—seeing situations and people from ________ __________________, realizing that you are loved and can/should show compassion for others, as God does;
- Awareness that ______ ____ ____ __________, no matter the circumstances, and that His plan is perfect;
- Recognition that _____________ can separate us from God's love;
- Life filled with _________;
- A new way of living—_____ _________, learning to trust God for everything.

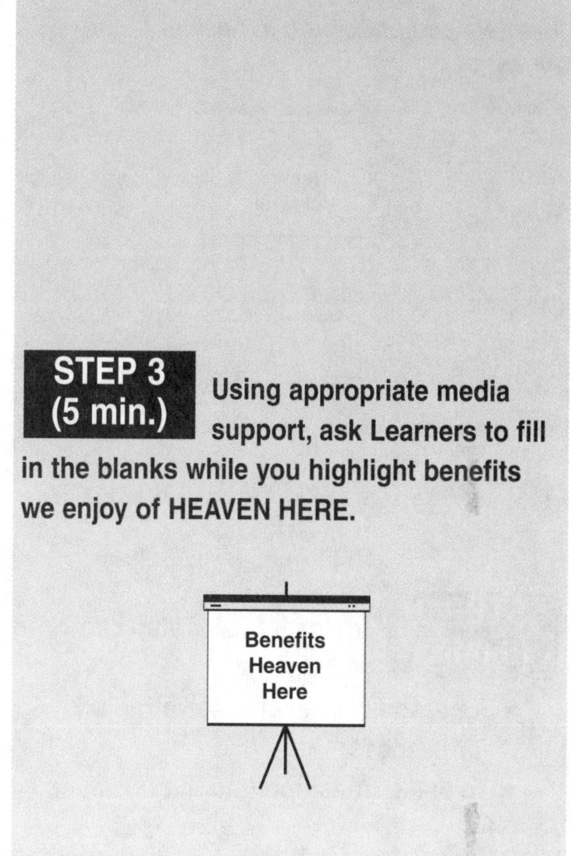

STEP 3 (5 min.) **Using appropriate media support, ask Learners to fill in the blanks while you highlight benefits we enjoy of HEAVEN HERE.**

Our Hope for Eternity

Just as verses can help us relate to heaven now, so do key passages help us relate to heaven in the hereafter: John 3:16; Ephesians 2:1-10; 1 Peter 1:3-9; Revelation 21:1-6. At this point in the gospel presentation, we use John 14:3 to highlight the hope Christ gives us for all of eternity:

HEREAFTER

____

____

____

____

—John 14:3, NKJV.

STEP 4 (5 min.) **Using "Our Hope for Eternity," discuss *H* as also meaning HEAVEN HEREAFTER. Use the computer presentation slide or the HEREAFTER cel from Session 5.**

Keeping the HEREAFTER cel up or using the computer slide, ask Learners to write John 14:3, the verse to be learned for HEAVEN HEREAFTER.

STEP 5 (5 min.) **Using benefits content and media support, describe what we can anticipate in heaven in the hereafter.**

Thank God again for the benefits we anticipate with heaven in the hereafter:

- ______________ fellowship with God;
- Capacity to more ___________ see God's perfect plan and more completely experience His love;
- ___________ ______ _____ and death, freeing us from all temptation and consequences of sin (will not experience spiritual death);
- Being beneficiaries of God's ____________ ______ _________;
- Knowledge that, because of Christ; we will live in the glory of _______ _______________ _____________. Those who do not accept Jesus as Savior will live ___________ _______________ from God's favor—that judgment will be eternal hell.
- Ability to _____ ____________; there no longer will be a need for faith.
- __________________ of our hope; there no longer will be a need for hope.

STEP 6 (5 min.) **Indicate how H also can mean HOW:**

- **A person can receive salvation and forgiveness;**
- **To make transition into the *Invitation.***

By this point in the gospel presentation, a person may be thinking, *How can I have this forgiveness and heaven?*

HOW

At this point give an _____________________ _____ _________ a person can have forgiveness and eternal life/heaven and Jesus as Savior and Lord.

Notice that the letter *H* also can stand for HOW—how God took the initiative to save us through the death of His Son, Jesus, and how a person can have God's forgiveness and eternal life/heaven. It may be helpful to ask, acknowledging the question a person may have: How can a person have God's forgiveness, heaven and eternal life, and Jesus as personal Savior and Lord? You will answer this question by using the leaflet *A Step of Faith.*

SEE IT

STEP 7 (5 min.) **Show the video segment "H-HEAVEN."**

If time allows, show "The Gospel Presentation" video segment, first used in Session 5.

Explaining how a person can receive God's forgiveness and heaven sets the stage for the most important question of the visit:

Understanding what we have shared, would you like to receive this forgiveness by trusting in Christ as your personal Savior and Lord?

With this question the visit moves into the ***Invitation***—when someone has the opportunity to receive personally what you know to be true and have shared. Allow God to direct you and your Team with sensitivity as you share how someone can have heaven here and in the hereafter.

---

[1]Geoffrey W. Bromley, *Theological Dictionary of the New Testament,* Gerhard Kittell and Gerhard Friedrich, eds., Geoffrey W. Bromley, trans. (Grand Rapids, MI: William B. Eerdmans Publishing Co., 1985), 829.

[2]*The Random House Unabridged Dictionary, Second Edition* (New York: Random House, Inc., 1993), 9.

SAY IT

STEP 8 (5 min.) Practice the letter *H* with a partner. Each person should share. If time allows, practice the entire gospel presentation beginning with the Key Question.

STUDY IT

STEP 9 (5 min.) Overview Home Study Assignments for Session 10.

- Memorize—FAITH Visit Outline, adding the *Invitation*
- Read—*Evangelism Through the Sunday School* assignments and FAITH Tips about *A Step of Faith*
- Journal—Your Journey in Faith

(5 min.) Transition to assemble with FAITH Teams to prepare for home visits.

Visitation Time

DO IT

Be able to share the *F-A-I-T* portions of the presentation in a visit. Your Team Leader will resume the presentation at *H* and will handle the ***Invitation.*** As in previous weeks, he or she will appropriately re-enter the presentation by thanking you for sharing.

(110 min.) DO IT

Celebration Time

SHARE IT

- Reports and testimonies
- Session 10 Evaluation Card
- Participation Card
- Visitation forms updated with results of visits

(30 min.) SHARE IT

You may want to read your session notes again once blanks have been filled in from Teaching Time. A good time to review your notes is before doing Home Study Assignments each week.

Memorize the following points of the FAITH Visit Outline; add the ***Invitation.*** Be prepared to recite the ***Invitation*** to your Team Leader during Session 11 Team Time.

FAITH VISIT OUTLINE

Preparation

INTRODUCTION
INTERESTS
INVOLVEMENT
Church Experience/Background
Ask about the person's church background.
Listen for clues about the person's spiritual involvement.
Sunday School Testimony
Tell general benefits of Sunday School.
Tell a current personal experience.
Evangelistic Testimony
Tell a little of your pre-conversion experience.
Say: "I had a life-changing experience."
Tell recent benefits of your conversion.
INQUIRY
Key Question: In your personal opinion, what do you understand it takes for a person to go to heaven?
Possible answers: Faith, works, unclear, no opinion
Transition Statement: I'd like to share with you how the Bible answers this question, if it is all right. There is a word that can be used to answer this question: FAITH *(spell out on fingers).*

Presentation

F is for FORGIVENESS.

We cannot have eternal life and heaven without God's forgiveness.

"In Him [meaning Jesus] we have redemption through His blood, the forgiveness of sins"—Ephesians 1:7a, NKJV.

A is for AVAILABLE.

Forgiveness is available. It is—

AVAILABLE FOR ALL

"For God so loved the world that He gave His only begotten Son, that whoever believes in Him should not perish but have everlasting life"—John 3:16, NKJV.

BUT NOT AUTOMATIC

"Not everyone who says to Me, 'Lord, Lord,' shall enter the kingdom of heaven"—Matthew 7:21a, NKJV.

I is for IMPOSSIBLE.

It is impossible for God to allow sin into heaven.

GOD IS—

- LOVE

  John 3:16, NKJV.

- JUST

  "For judgment is without mercy"—James 2:13a, NKJV.

MAN IS SINFUL

"For all have sinned and fall short of the glory of God"
—Romans 3:23, NKJV.

Question: But how can a sinful person enter heaven, where God allows no sin?

T is for TURN.

Question: If you were driving down the road and someone asked you to turn, what would he or she be asking you to do? *(change direction)*

Turn means repent.

TURN from something—sin and self

"But unless you repent you will all likewise perish"—
Luke 13:3b, NKJV.

TURN to Someone; trust Christ only

(The Bible tells us that) *"Christ died for our sins according to the Scriptures, and that He was buried, and that He rose again the third day according to the Scriptures"—1 Corinthians 15:3b-4, NKJV.*

"If you confess with your mouth the Lord Jesus and believe in your heart that God has raised Him from the dead, you will be saved" —Romans 10:9, NKJV.

H is for HEAVEN.

Heaven is eternal life.

HERE

"I have come that they may have life, and that they may have it more abundantly"—John 10:10b, NKJV.

HEREAFTER

"And if I go and prepare a place for you, I will come again and receive you to Myself; that where I am, there you may be also" —John 14:3, NKJV.

HOW

How can a person have God's forgiveness, heaven and eternal life, and Jesus as personal Savior and Lord?

Explain based on leaflet picture, F.A.I.T.H. (Forsaking All I Trust Him), Romans 10:9.

Invitation

INQUIRE

Understanding what we have shared, would you like to receive this forgiveness by trusting in Christ as your personal Savior and Lord?

INVITE

Pray to accept Christ.

Pray for commitment/recommitment.

Invite to join Sunday School.

INSURE

Use *A Step of Faith* to insure decision.

Personal Acceptance

Sunday School Enrollment

Public Confession

From *Evangelism Through the Sunday School: A Journey of FAITH* by Bobby Welch, read "Heart Failure Killing Churches" (pp. 21-24), and "Can We Sleep When People Die?" (pp. 53-54); and the testimony on page 112.

Also read "Making Much of Jesus" (pp. 143-145). Write your thoughts about this sentence: "Jesus is the Christian's unique distinctive and the sole basis for the Great Commission and the salvation of this world" (p. 144).

How are you learning to make much of Jesus?

Read the two important FAITH Tips "Meanings of *A Step of Faith* Picture" and "Using *A Step of Faith* During a Visit." Reflect on the picture, noting the reactions people experience when they realize that their sin nailed Jesus on the cross and that He willingly took their place.

Overview the Commitment panel *(panel 5).* Become comfortable with options for leading a person to express his or her commitment to accept Jesus, enroll in Bible study, or plan to stand with other believers at the church. Become familiar with ways to encourage a person to begin growing in his or her (new) faith.

Study the Response Card panel for information to be completed and returned to the church.

FAITH *Tip*

Meaning of A Step of Faith *Picture*

Nearly every picture has different meanings or can be interpreted in different ways. Some meanings are obvious while others are more subtle.

The central focus of this picture is on the foot of the cross. Notice the nail-pierced feet of Jesus. Salvation comes when we realize and accept that Jesus died for you and me.

The people at the foot of the cross are intentionally contemporary. They represent you and me. They also represent the different cultures that intersect our lives. Although not every distinct ethnic group is represented, the people might be said to represent the world.

Notice the mallets (hammers) and spikes lying at the foot of the cross—dropped by some of the people who are looking into the face of Jesus. Some are still clutching the tools that were used to nail Jesus to the cross.

What does this imagery say to you? ___________

____

____

____

Perhaps it represents the fact that because of our sin we, intentionally or unintentionally, placed Jesus on the cross. *We* are the ones who should have been sentenced to die for our rebellion against God. Instead, Jesus was willingly nailed on the cross because of the sins of the world, your sins and mine. Our journey of faith begins when we realize that Jesus died for each one of us, individually and personally.

Evident in the picture are heartfelt emotions of persons who realize that Jesus died for them personally. *We* too experience remorse, shock, grief, and overwhelming unworthiness when we realize what we have done and how Jesus still shows His grace and unconditional love for us.

Joy, peace, and hope are not as evident in the picture, but are definite continuing results of the salvation experience. The reality of wonder and conviction still embraces those of us who are invited to take our mallets and spikes and look into Jesus' face.

The picture, painted by a believer (Stephen S. Sawyer of Versailles, KY), has already been used by God to convict and to convince. The persons selected as models for the people at the foot of the cross have their own stories of reflection, reaction, and revival. Realizing they were depicting someone who was looking into the face of Jesus, upon driving spikes into His hands and feet, several wept openly.

Where do you find yourself in this picture?

How do you see yourself using this picture to help someone else take a step of faith?

Using A Step of FAITH *During a Visit*

This FAITH Tip is designed to familiarize you with *A Step of Faith* so you will be comfortable using it in any visit. Leaving this leaflet with someone after the visit reinforces all that has been shared. It gives the person a tangible memento of what Christ did for him or her, as well as a reminder about key actions to take in the journey of faith. *A Step of Faith* provides a way to record important information needed by the class/department, Sunday School, and church staff in following up with someone who makes a decision.

As you conclude the gospel presentation, use *A Step of Faith* to explain how the person can have God's forgiveness and Jesus as Savior and Lord.

First, show the cover of *A Step of Faith.* Help the person identify with individuals in this illustration and to personally realize the sacrifice Jesus unashamedly made for him or her. Identify yourself with those who put Jesus on the cross, and conclude that Christ's sacrifice is how we are able to have God's forgiveness and salvation.

Forsaking

All "... God so loved the world ..." (John 3:16, NKJV)

I "... Christ died for our sins ..." (1 Cor. 15:3*b*, NKJV)

Trust "... if you confess with your mouth the Lord Jesus and believe in your heart that God has raised Him from the dead, you will be saved." (Rom. 10:9, NKJV)

Him

2

JESUS was not ashamed to die on the cross for you.

"Whosoever believeth on him (Jesus) shall not be ashamed" (Rom. 10:11).

YOU can commit your life to Christ and so begin a wonderful journey of faith.

3

Open the leaflet so the shadow of the cross appears across two panels of copy *(panels 2 and 3).* After reviewing another meaning of F.A.I.T.H. (Forsaking All I Trust Him) and Romans 10:9, put the leaflet aside.

• Decision to Accept Christ

If the person acknowledges a willingness to ask Jesus for salvation, review and clarify what it means to turn from sin and turn to Christ. Without reading the Salvation Prayer *(panel 4)* in *A Step of Faith,* lead the person to pray a salvation prayer. Continue by saying something like "You seem to be sincere about your salvation. I would like to lead you in a prayer of commitment." Lead the person to pray a prayer based on the Commitment Prayer (*panel 5)* in *A Step of Faith.*

If the person expresses disinterest or chooses not to accept Jesus, express thanks for openness and an opportunity to share. Remind the person about Bible study opportunities, inviting him or her to enroll in Sunday School.

• Expressions of Commitment

After the prayers you may want to refer briefly back to the front picture, saying something like "I am so thankful Jesus was not ashamed to die for us, aren't you?" With *panels 2 and 3* open, highlight the words *Jesus was not ashamed to die on the cross for you* and Romans 10:11. Continue unfolding *A Step of Faith* so *panels 2, 4, and 5* are open. Say: Jesus expected those who followed Him to publicly profess Him—and to do so quickly. Overview both Mark 8:38 and Matthew 10:32-33 as Scriptures reinforcing this important concept.

For the person who has just accepted Christ, this introduces the idea that Jesus was not ashamed and he, too, can commit his life unashamedly to Christ. This concept is central to the rest of the leaflet.

Now refer to the Commitment panel *(5)*. As you draw attention to it, you have opportunity to explain the importance of these expressions of commitment. Move through the three opportunities the person has to indicate growth in Christ. As you call attention to the Commitment panel *(5),* you have opportunity to briefly explain the importance of these expressions of commitment.

If the person prayed to receive Christ, help him/her check the first box on the commitment card and to fill in the date/place of the decision. You will be leaving the leaflet as a reminder of this step of faith.

Remind the person of opportunities to grow through the Sunday School. Offer an invitation to enroll in the class.

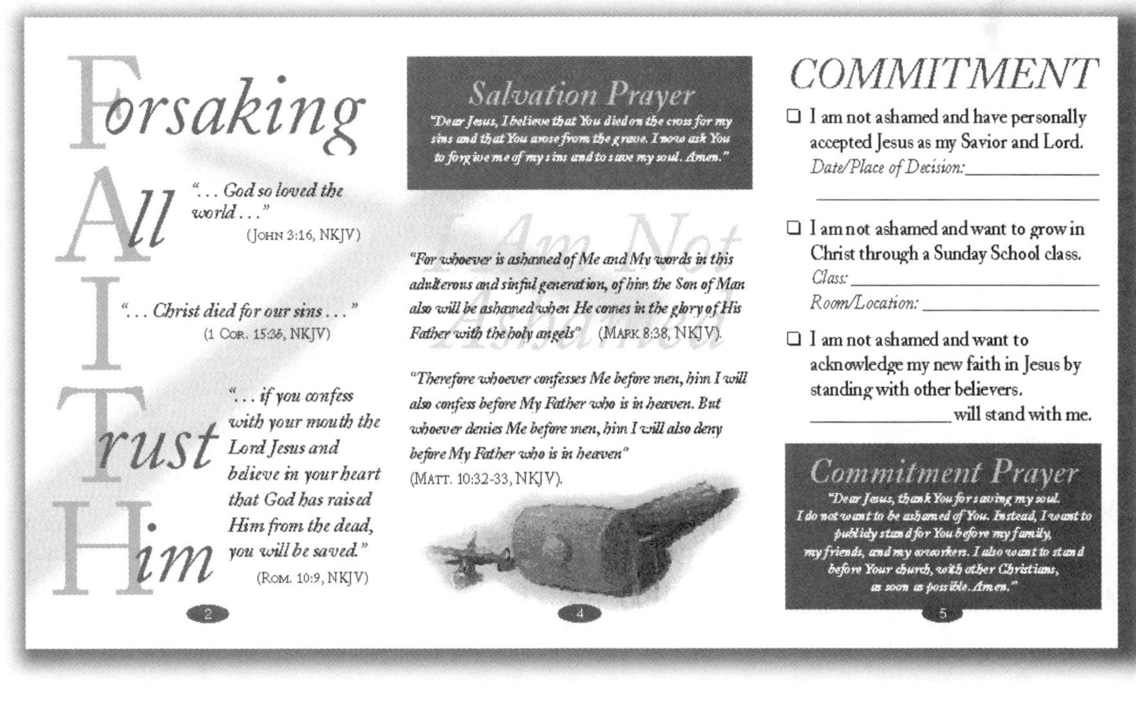

Forsaking
All
"... God so loved the world..."
(John 3:16, NKJV)
I
"... Christ died for our sins..."
(1 Cor. 15:3, NKJV)
Trust
"... if you confess with your mouth the Lord Jesus and believe in your heart that God has raised Him from the dead, you will be saved."
Him
(Rom. 10:9, NKJV)
2

Salvation Prayer
"Dear Jesus, I believe that You died on the cross for my sins and that You arose from the grave. I now ask You to forgive me of my sins and to save my soul. Amen."

I Am Not Ashamed
"For whoever is ashamed of Me and My words in this adulterous and sinful generation, of him the Son of Man also will be ashamed when He comes in the glory of His Father with the holy angels" (Mark 8:38, NKJV).
"Therefore whoever confesses Me before men, him I will also confess before My Father who is in heaven. But whoever denies Me before men, him I will also deny before My Father who is in heaven"
(Matt. 10:32-33, NKJV).
4

COMMITMENT
❑ I am not ashamed and have personally accepted Jesus as my Savior and Lord.
Date/Place of Decision:______________
____
❑ I am not ashamed and want to grow in Christ through a Sunday School class.
Class:______________
Room/Location:______________
❑ I am not ashamed and want to acknowledge my new faith in Jesus by standing with other believers.
______________will stand with me.

Commitment Prayer
"Dear Jesus, thank You for saving my soul. I do not want to be ashamed of You. Instead, I want to publicly stand for You before my family, my friends, and my coworkers. I also want to stand before Your church, with other Christians, as soon as possible. Amen."
5

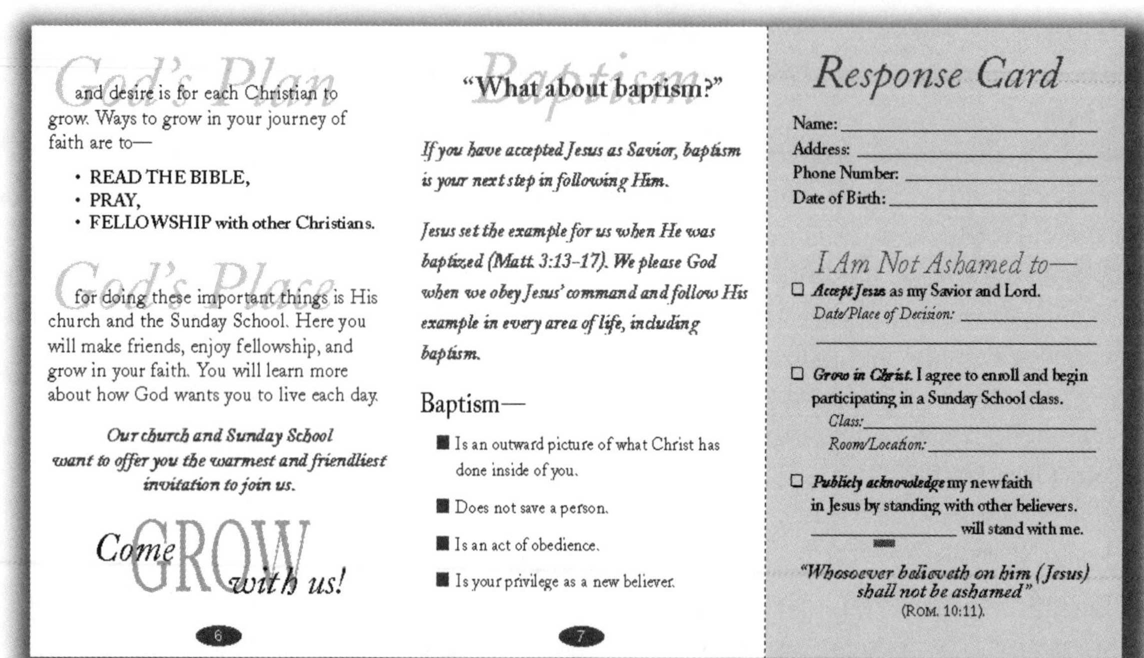

God's Plan and desire is for each Christian to grow. Ways to grow in your journey of faith are to—

- READ THE BIBLE,
- PRAY,
- FELLOWSHIP with other Christians.

God's Place for doing these important things is His church and the Sunday School. Here you will make friends, enjoy fellowship, and grow in your faith. You will learn more about how God wants you to live each day.

Our church and Sunday School want to offer you the warmest and friendliest invitation to join us.

Come GROW with us!

6

Baptism

"What about baptism?"

If you have accepted Jesus as Savior, baptism is your next step in following Him.

Jesus set the example for us when He was baptized (Matt. 3:13-17). We please God when we obey Jesus' command and follow His example in every area of life, including baptism.

Baptism—

- Is an outward picture of what Christ has done inside of you.
- Does not save a person.
- Is an act of obedience.
- Is your privilege as a new believer.

7

Response Card

Name: ____________________
Address: ____________________
Phone Number: ____________________
Date of Birth: ____________________

I Am Not Ashamed to—

☐ ***Accept Jesus*** as my Savior and Lord.
Date/Place of Decision: ____________________

☐ ***Grow in Christ.*** I agree to enroll and begin participating in a Sunday School class.
Class: ____________________
Room/Location: ____________________

☐ ***Publicly acknowledge*** my new faith in Jesus by standing with other believers.
____________________ will stand with me.

"Whosoever believeth on him (Jesus) shall not be ashamed"
(ROM. 10:11).

Allow the individual to check the second action. A Team member should write the specific location of the class and, if possible, the name/phone number of someone in the class.

If the person prayed to receive Christ, explain how your church wants to celebrate with him in his new faith by having him come and stand with other new believers at the end of next Sunday's worship service. Lead the new believer to check the third box; a Team member should write the name of someone (perhaps a FAITH Team member) who will stand alongside the new Christian as all new believers are introduced.

If not already done, it is appropriate now to unfold the leaflet so *panels 6 and 7* and the Response Card are visible This card is to be completed and returned to the church. Any member of the FAITH Team could complete the card on behalf of the person making the decision. Clarify information on the Response Card after completing the visit. Record on the front of the Response Card all information on everyone who makes a commitment.

For many people it may be overwhelming to consider commitment to Christ, enrollment in Sunday School, public profession, and baptism all at one time. Unless questions about baptism come up, point out the "Baptism" panel *(7)* and indicate that the person may want to read this information at his or her convenience. Your Team will make an initial follow-up visit within the next two weeks to persons who make a decision to accept Christ. Additional follow-up will be done through your Sunday School class/department. More people who "walk the aisle" or otherwise publicly acknowledge their new decision ultimately are baptized, as compared to those who pray to receive Christ during one-on-one opportunities in which there is no intentional follow-up. Do not overlook the importance of follow-up.

The back of the leaflet is blank so you, your class/department, or church can customize or personalize it. Information such as address, telephone number, and times of worship and Bible study can be helpful.

As you use *A Step of Faith* prayerfully, be aware of ways the Holy Spirit works in persons' lives as seeds of faith are planted, cultivated, or bear fruit.

Your Journey in Faith

Read John 19:1-24. Imagine that you are standing before Jesus on the cross. What do you think Jesus would say to you?

Read John 19:25-37. What would you say to Jesus?

Study Romans 10:11, Mark 8:38, and Matthew 10:32-33 as they relate to not being ashamed to follow Jesus.

What are ways you have seen the Holy Spirit work in the lives of persons visited by your Team?

What are ways you have seen the Holy Spirit work in the lives of your FAITH Team members?

Write a prayer describing your personal (re)commitment to the Lord.

Prayer Concerns

Answers to Prayer

SESSION 11

Inviting Persons to Saving Faith

In this session you will

CHECK IT: practice the ***Invitation*** and use *A Step of Faith* with a partner;

HEAR IT: learn and be able to recite different points of the ***Invitation*** portion of the FAITH Visit Outline, and understand different uses of *A Step of Faith*;

SEE IT: view the video showing the ***Invitation*** portion of the outline;

STUDY IT: overview Home Study Assignments for Session 11;

DO IT: make visits—observe your Team Leader's use of *A Step of Faith*;

SHARE IT: celebrate.

In Advance

- Pray for church and Sunday School leaders—that their vital work will intersect the lives of people with life-changing Bible study and worship experiences, fellowship, and ministry.
- Preview all teaching suggestions and session content. Use Session 11 computer presentation slides or overhead transparencies (#55-59). ***Note:*** Additional computer presentation slides are available for this session. Many important points will be covered; look closely at this week's schedule.
- Place a copy of *A Step of Faith* at every person's place.
- Cue the video segment "The Invitation" for use early in the session. If the role play is preferred, enlist several people well in advance and practice this important segment (pp. 77-81).

(15 min.) CHECK IT

If the computer presentation is used, display the agenda frame for Team Time, as desired. Add other points as needed.

Team Time

CHECK IT

Your Team Leader directs this important time, checking off memory work, reviewing previous sessions and completed assignments, answering questions, and providing guidance to strengthen home visits.

Agenda:
✓ FAITH Visit Outline: Invitation
***✓ Practice Invitation using* A Step of Faith**
✓ Other Home Study Assignments
✓ Session 10 debriefing
✓ Help for strengthening a visit

❑ ***Outline memorized?—check it!***

Team Leader: Because time is at a premium in this session, Learners are to recite the ***Invitation*** only in Team Time, beginning with HOW. In the space provided for sign-off, indicate your approval by signing your name.

FAITH VISIT OUTLINE

HOW

- ❑ **How can a person have God's forgiveness, heaven and eternal life, and Jesus as personal Savior and Lord?**
- ❑ **Explain based on leaflet picture, F.A.I.T.H. (Forsaking All I Trust Him), Romans 10:9.**

❑ *Invitation*

- ❑ **INQUIRE**
- ❑ **Understanding what we have shared, would you like to receive this forgiveness by trusting in Christ as your personal Savior and Lord?**
- ❑ **INVITE**
  - ❑ **Pray to accept Christ.**
  - ❑ **Pray for commitment/recommitment.**
  - ❑ **Invite to join Sunday School.**
- ❑ **INSURE**
- ❑ **Use *A Step of Faith* to insure decision.**
  - ❑ **Personal Acceptance**
  - ❑ **Sunday School Enrollment**
  - ❑ **Public Confession**

_______________________ *Team Leader Sign-off*

❑ **Invitation** ***practiced with*** **A Step of Faith*?—check it!***

Keep this important practice segment brief.

❑ ***Other Home Study Assignments completed?—check it!***

How are you learning to make much of Jesus? *(Evangelism Through the Sunday School: A Journey of FAITH* assignment)

Two FAITH Tips helped you overview the use of *A Step of Faith.* That help will continue in Teaching Time. Not every visit in which the gospel is shared will result in a profession of faith. You may not have seen your Team Leader use *A Step of Faith* for a decision to accept Christ. Because of this fact, your Team Leader will continue to guide a person to pray to receive Christ, using *A Step of Faith* as a tool, at least through Session 12.

What you may have seen modeled by this point in FAITH training is the leaflet's use to enroll someone in Sunday School. Don't forget you can use the Response Card in *A Step of Faith* to invite someone to be part of your Sunday School class.

❑ ***Any questions from Session 10?—check it!***

What questions do you have about Session 10? Ask your Team Leader now. You have learned the gospel presentation and now are seeing how to make transition into the ***Invitation.***

❑ ***Need help in strengthening a visit?—here's how!***

(1) Practice using *A Step of Faith* with a friend outside the class session.

(2) Pay careful attention to your Team Leader as he or she guides a person through the leaflet in an actual visit.

Are people who have accepted Christ as Savior in FAITH visits also standing with other believers at the church? Are you finding this expression of commitment to be encouragement to continue in your FAITH visits? Such public follow-up of decisions also encourages the church, as members see God at work in their midst and celebrate together. Church members also are reminded of their responsibility to nurture and cultivate new Christians.

You may be at the point of FAITH training in which you are tired or are wondering how you will get all the memory work done. Recall these new Christians and your part in reaching them, and keep on keeping on.

(5 min.) Transition to classrooms for instruction on the content of the session.

Teaching Time

HEAR IT

STEP 1 (5 min.) **Based on "A Life-Changing Decision" content, overview three main parts of the *Invitation.* Use cel or computer slide to help Learners fill in the blanks easily.**

A Life-Changing Decision

By this point in a visit, you have helped someone understand how salvation is possible and how he or she may have God's forgiveness, too. You have come to a crucial moment in the visit as you invite a person to make the most important life-changing decision he or she will ever be asked to consider. Note the overview of the ***Invitation*** and how certain key elements are a part.

Invitation

INQUIRE
INVITE
INSURE

As this point in the visit, a Team member will INQUIRE about the person's:

- ________________ regarding *A Step of Faith* picture;
- ________________________ of the gospel presentation;
- __________________ to accept God's forgiveness and salvation in Jesus Christ, using this question: **Understanding what we have shared, would you like to receive this forgiveness by trusting in Christ as your personal Savior and Lord?**

Another crucial part is to INVITE the person to pray to make the appropriate decision:

- Pray to ______________ Christ;
- Pray for ____________________ or ______________________ (as appropriate); and
- Invite to _______ Sunday School class.

The person may indicate he or she does not understand some part of what you have shared. If so, or if there is any sense that the person is unclear about some part of the presentation, there may be a need to confirm or INSURE the decision. Do so in one or more of these ways:

- _________ with the person;
- Share and ________________ *A Step of Faith;* and
- ____________ ___________________ ______ ____________ used earlier in FAITH.

While optional, insuring a decision should be done if there is any doubt about the person's understanding.

KEY ACTIONS TO TAKE DURING THE INVITATION

____

____

____

____

A Tool to Help Someone Take a Step of Faith

A Step of Faith will be used in a significant way as you issue an invitation and begin bringing the visit to a close. Use of the cover picture can be very meaningful.

Pictures have different messages to different people. The wonderful thing about pictures is that the person's response or opinion is correct to him or her.

To anticipate how others may respond, think about these questions:

What do you think this picture represents? Why?

____

____

What do you think Jesus is saying to you personally in this picture?

____

____

What would you say to an unsaved person about this picture?

____

____

As you begin using the picture during visits, briefly call attention to Jesus on the cross paying the price for our sins; to the different people, who represent you and me; to the wide range of emotions that are evident—deep remorse, grief, and shock—when these individuals realized their sins put Jesus on the cross.

Call attention to the mallets (hammers) and spikes. These people have been or still are holding mallets; it is as though they have been driving the

SEE IT

STEP 2 (10 min.) **Say: Watch the video to see how our visit has been leading up to the *Invitation.* As you view it, note key actions taken during this part of a visit.**

Show the videotape segment entitled "The Invitation."

HEAR IT

STEP 3 (5 min.) **Describe meanings/uses of *A Step of Faith* based on "A Tool to Help Someone Take a Step of Faith" content. Since Learners are not taking notes, but are examining *A Step of Faith,* demonstrate or emphasize any points needed.**

Say:

While you are using *A Step of Faith* to help a person accept God's forgiveness and make important commitments for growth, do not give the leaflet to the person(s) until the end of the visit. Then it becomes a significant memento of his or her decision.

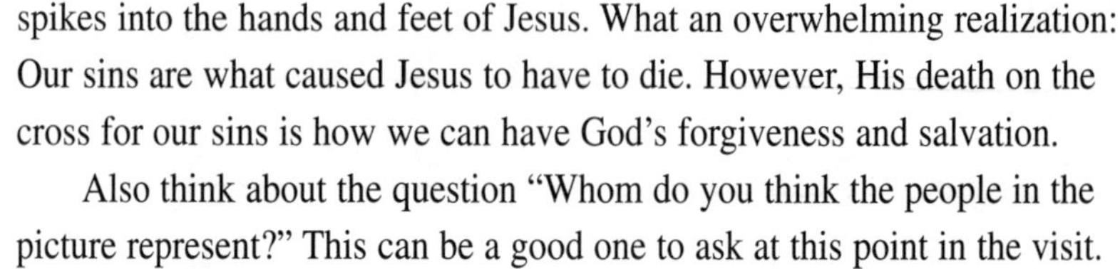

spikes into the hands and feet of Jesus. What an overwhelming realization: Our sins are what caused Jesus to have to die. However, His death on the cross for our sins is how we can have God's forgiveness and salvation.

Also think about the question "Whom do you think the people in the picture represent?" This can be a good one to ask at this point in the visit. One obvious answer is they represent people from different cultural/ethnic groups. A person could look at the picture and identify a friend, neighbor, or associate. This gives you a chance to say, "They represent you and me. Jesus died for everyone."

By calling attention to the mallets and spikes, you clarify that your sins and the sins of the person you are visiting are what put Jesus on the cross. Yet despite this, He still offers forgiveness to all who turn from sin to Him.

After using the picture, clarify if needed by using Romans 10:9, a verse associated with *turn.* You also can summarize by indicating that another meaning of F.A.I.T.H. is Forsaking All I Trust Him. After briefly examining the picture and discussing responses, put the leaflet aside.

You have used your hand at several points in the visits. As it is natural and comfortable for you, reemphasize what you have said by leaning forward and extending your hand. Say: "I've been talking about my hand and my faith. You have your own hand and can have your own faith. With your hand of faith, you can reach out and receive God's gift of grace . . ." Do what is most comfortable for you and for the person hearing the ***Invitation.***

The important thing is to support, not detract from, the message. Your main goal is to move to the second inquiry question in the FAITH Visit Outline.

INQUIRE

Understanding what we have shared, would you like to receive this forgiveness by trusting in Christ as your personal Savior and Lord?

The invitation is very simple—and very important. The invitation has three parts: (1) to accept Christ; (2) to commit or recommit one's life to Christ; and (3) to join a Sunday School class.

Invite to Pray

During visits in which someone is invited to accept Christ, you will have the opportunity both to share the good news and to lead a person to pray to receive Christ. If a person prays this important prayer, you may be able to help him or her express newfound faith in personal commitments.

Leading someone to pray a ___________ ____ ________________ becomes a meaningful expression of that person's decision to accept God's offer of forgiveness and salvation and to begin to follow Christ. God does not want or expect eloquent words or particular phrases in a prayer.

He wants someone to come to Him and to ask, confess, and believe. Some people you visit have never prayed. It becomes meaningful to help by having them ____________ after you a short prayer, one phrase at a time. Become familiar and comfortable enough with this prayer that you do not have to read it. While the words chosen are not as important as the attitudes and changes they reflect, you may be able to help someone begin to learn how to pray.

A short, very basic prayer of faith is printed in *A Step of Faith.*

SALVATION PRAYER

"Dear Lord Jesus, *(repeat)*
I believe that You died on the cross for my sins *(repeat)*
and that You arose from the grave. *(repeat)*
I now ask You to forgive me of my sins *(repeat)*
and to save my soul. Amen." *(repeat)*

What is more natural after accepting God's forgiveness and salvation than to want to express one's commitment to Christ? After you lead a person to pray to receive Christ, it also will be significant to lead the person to pray aloud a prayer of commitment. It may seem very natural to move from the Salvation Prayer into the ________________________ ____________ printed in *A Step of Faith,* almost as if they were one prayer. Lead the person to make these important commitments, just as you helped him pray for salvation, without reading the printed prayer.

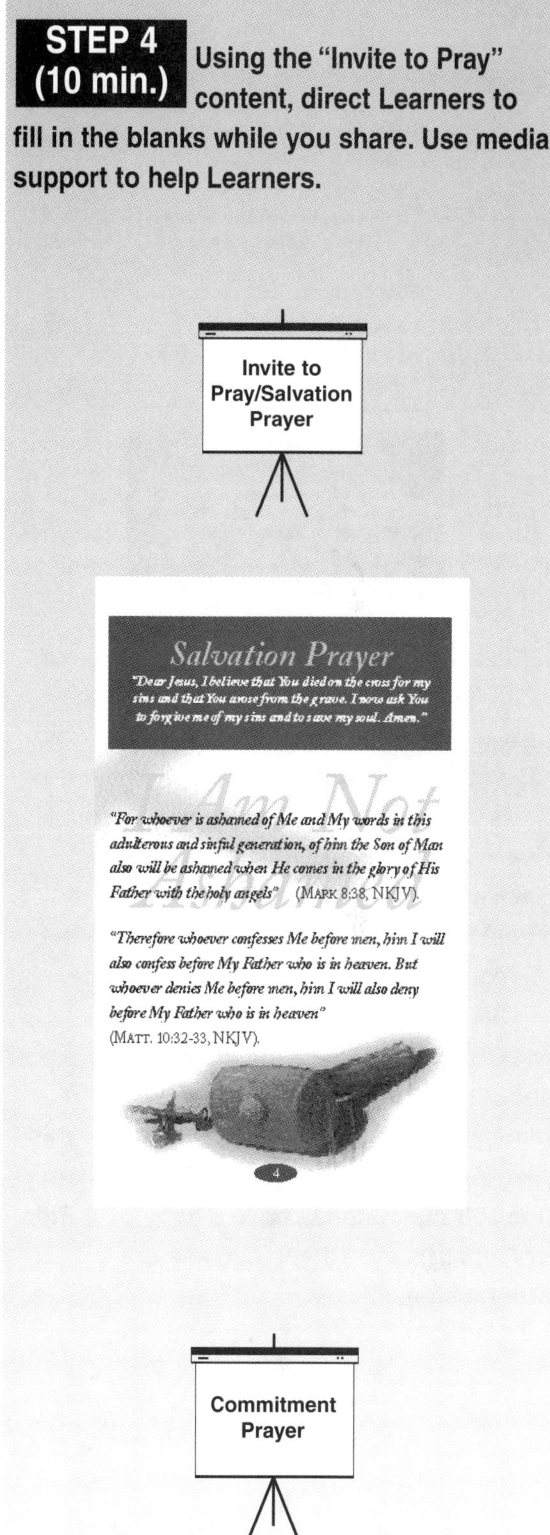

STEP 4 (10 min.)
Using the "Invite to Pray" content, direct Learners to fill in the blanks while you share. Use media support to help Learners.
Invite to Pray/Salvation Prayer
Salvation Prayer
"Dear Jesus, I believe that You died on the cross for my sins and that You arose from the grave. I now ask You to forgive me of my sins and to save my soul. Amen."
"For whoever is ashamed of Me and My words in this adulterous and sinful generation, of him the Son of Man also will be ashamed when He comes in the glory of His Father with the holy angels" (MARK 8:38, NKJV).
"Therefore whoever confesses Me before men, him I will also confess before My Father who is in heaven. But whoever denies Me before men, him I will also deny before My Father who is in heaven" (MATT. 10:32-33, NKJV).
4
Commitment Prayer

COMMITMENT

☐ I am not ashamed and have personally accepted Jesus as my Savior and Lord.
Date/Place of Decision: ______________
____

☐ I am not ashamed and want to grow in Christ through a Sunday School class.
Class: ______________
Room/Location: ______________

☐ I am not ashamed and want to acknowledge my new faith in Jesus by standing with other believers.
______________ will stand with me.

Commitment Prayer

"Dear Jesus, thank You for saving my soul. I do not want to be ashamed of You. Instead, I want to publicly stand for You before my family, my friends, and my coworkers. I also want to stand before Your church, with other Christians, as soon as possible. Amen."

5

STEP 5 (10 min.) **Overview "Commitments of a New Believer" content. Use *A Step of Faith,* FAITH Tips from Session 10, and cels/computer slides to assist Learners. Ask Learners to fill in the blanks with the information you provide.**

Say:

On the next few pages write notes about using *A Step of Faith,* to help you remember significant ideas to share in this part of the visit. As you listen and glance through the material, have a copy of *A Step of Faith* in hand so you can see the progression.

COMMITMENT PRAYER

"Dear Jesus, thank You for saving my soul. *(repeat)*
I do not want to be ashamed of You. *(repeat)*
Instead, I want to publicly stand for You before my family, *(repeat)*
my friends, and my coworkers.*(repeat)*
I also want to stand before Your church, *(repeat)*
with other Christians, as soon as possible. Amen. *(repeat)*

While it is most desirable to pray these prayers one after the other, recognize that persons will have comments or questions about what they have experienced. The video shows you an effective way to respond to someone's comments and move without interruption back into the ***Invitation.***

Commitments of a New Believer

Once you have prayed for the person making a commitment to Christ, use *A Step of Faith* again. This leaflet may help the person begin identifying specific actions to take as a new believer. *A Step of Faith* will be left with the person whatever the response. You will find three basic parts to the leaflet.

- **Briefly ______________ the Message of the Gospel Presentation**

First, there is a brief review of the gospel presentation. The letters in the word FAITH have been used throughout. You can summarize by saying, "F.A.I.T.H. also stands for Forsaking All I Trust Him." Notice the verses. You can use the leaflet or your own New Testament to read Romans 10:9.

- **Offer Opportunity to __________ ______________________**

As you open the panel so "I Am Not Ashamed" is on the middle panel *(panel 4),* you have opportunity to reinforce verses and the concept of not being ashamed to follow Christ. Remind the person that Jesus has no private followers; He expects everyone who follows Him to publicly profess Him. You may want to read Mark 8:38 and Matthew 10:32-33 from the leaflet.

The Commitment panel *(panel 5)* on the right of the trifold gives you an opportunity to walk the person through three types of commitment. When you use the Commitment section, likely you are following up with a person who has just accepted Christ. This gives you an opportunity, without pressuring the person, to point him to the church as the Holy Spirit leads.

Someone who has made a decision for Christ sincerely wants to grow in her new faith, and you are providing opportunities for her to express her newfound faith.

There are several options on how this might be done. The videotape showed us one effective approach. Write others in your Notes column.

In general, lead the person to check the box adjacent to the first statement and to write the date/place of his or her ________________ _____ ____________. Since this leaflet will be left with the person, *A Step of Faith* can be a meaningful memento of the decision.

Move to the second statement on the Commitment panel *(panel 5).* Remind the person of the benefits of Sunday School and that your Team represents the same Sunday School class (or department). Invite the person to allow you to ____________ him or her in the class. Ask whether he will check the second box.

Explain how excited everyone is about the person's decision to follow Christ. Explain how new believers are encouraged to take a stand with the pastor at the end of the worship service so he can ____________________ them to the church.

Explain what will happen in your church. For example, "Mrs. Jones, our pastor, Jim Smith, will call you by name. He likes to know who you are, and he wants others in our church to know you and begin to support you. He'll pray a sweet prayer for you and others who are standing. Some, if not all, of us will be by your side, since we're all in the same Sunday School class. It's a special time in our church and will help you feel welcome." Ask whether you can check the third box and write the name of someone who will stand with her.

The Response Card reveals another use of *A Step of Faith:* to record information about a person's decision(s) so people at the church have the correct information. There are several ways to gather this information; indicate the options in your notes.

- **Provide Information About ______________ as a New Christian**

Another use of the leaflet is to provide basic information about growing as a Christian and about baptism. Suggest that the person read through *A Step of Faith* as a reminder of the decisions and of the visit. The leaflet will introduce him to important concepts such as baptism, which can be dealt with as part of follow-up.

❑ **Accept Christ**

❑ **Enroll in Sunday School**

❑ **Stand with other believers**

STUDY It

STEP 6 (5 min.) **Overview Home Study Assignments for Session 12.**

- **Memorize—Entire FAITH Visit Outline; be prepared to practice**
- **Read—*Evangelism Through the Sunday School* assignments, FAITH Tip: "Importance of the Follow-up Visit"**
- **Journal—Your Journey in Faith**

(5 min.) Transition to assemble with FAITH Teams to prepare for home visits.

Visitation Time

(110 min.) DO IT

DO IT

There is no more important time in a visit than when you offer someone the opportunity to receive what you have been describing. Watch how your Team Leader handles the ***Invitation*** in FAITH visits. Pray both for your Team Leader and the person(s) being visited—that your Team Leader will communicate clearly and in love and that the person will understand and accept the life-changing nature of God's forgiveness. Also, think about how *you* will present the ***Invitation*** when an opportunity becomes available in a visit for which you are responsible.

There are opportunities during the ***Invitation*** to help review the gospel presentation or to insure a decision, if the person seems uncertain about what he or she is doing. Remember, your Team also will make a follow-up decision to a person who makes a decision, to help that person get off to a good start on his or her journey of faith.

Allow God to do His saving work through you and your Team, and thank Him for the ways He is using you. Recognize again the nature of the divine appointments you have been given in FAITH visits,.

Celebration Time

(30 min.) SHARE IT

SHARE IT

- Reports and testimonies
- Session 11 Evaluation Card
- Participation Card
- Visitation forms updated with results of visits

Home Study Assignments

You may want to read your session notes again once blanks have been filled in from Teaching Time. A good time to review your notes is before doing Home Study Assignments each week.

Learn and present the entire FAITH Visit Outline to your Team Leader. Session 12 will give you opportunity to practice the entire FAITH Visit Outline.

FAITH VISIT OUTLINE

Preparation

INTRODUCTION
INTERESTS
INVOLVEMENT
Church Experience/Background
Ask about the person's church background.
Listen for clues about the person's spiritual involvement.
Sunday School Testimony
Tell general benefits of Sunday School.
Tell a current personal experience.
Evangelistic Testimony
Tell a little of your pre-conversion experience.
Say: "I had a life-changing experience."
Tell recent benefits of your conversion.
INQUIRY
Key Question: In your personal opinion, what do you understand it takes for a person to go to heaven?
Possible answers: Faith, works, unclear, no opinion
Transition Statement: I'd like to share with you how the Bible answers this question, if it is all right. There is a word that can be used to answer this question: ***FAITH (spell out on fingers).***

Presentation

F is for FORGIVENESS.

We cannot have eternal life and heaven without God's forgiveness.

"In Him [meaning Jesus] we have redemption through His blood, the forgiveness of sins"—Ephesians 1:7a, NKJV.

A is for AVAILABLE.

Forgiveness is available. It is—

AVAILABLE FOR ALL

"For God so loved the world that He gave His only begotten Son, that whoever believes in Him should not perish but have everlasting life"—John 3:16, NKJV.

BUT NOT AUTOMATIC

"Not everyone who says to Me, 'Lord, Lord,' shall enter the kingdom of heaven"—Matthew 7:21a, NKJV.

I is for IMPOSSIBLE.

It is impossible for God to allow sin into heaven.

GOD IS—

- **LOVE**

  John 3:16, NKJV
- **JUST**

  "For judgment is without mercy"—James 2:13a, NKJV.

MAN IS SINFUL

"For all have sinned and fall short of the glory of God" —Romans 3:23, NKJV.

Question: But how can a sinful person enter heaven, where God allows no sin?

T is for TURN.

Question: If you were driving down the road and someone asked you to turn, what would he or she be asking you to do? ***(change direction)***

Turn **means repent.**

TURN from something—sin and self

"But unless you repent you will all likewise perish" —Luke 13:3b, NKJV.

TURN to Someone; trust Christ only

(The Bible tells us that) *"Christ died for our sins according to the Scriptures, and that He was buried, and that He rose again the third day according to the Scriptures"—1 Corinthians 15:3b-4, NKJV.*

> ***"If you confess with your mouth the Lord Jesus and believe in your heart that God has raised Him from the dead, you will be saved"—Romans 10:9, NKJV.***

H is for HEAVEN.
Heaven is eternal life.
HERE

> ***"I have come that they may have life, and that they may have it more abundantly"—John 10:10b, NKJV.***

HEREAFTER

> ***"And if I go and prepare a place for you, I will come again and receive you to Myself; that where I am, there you may be also"—John 14:3, NKJV.***

HOW

How can a person have God's forgiveness, heaven and eternal life, and Jesus as personal Savior and Lord?
Explain based on leaflet picture, F.A.I.T.H. (Forsaking All I Trust Him), Romans 10:9.

Invitation

INQUIRE
Understanding what we have shared, would you like to receive this forgiveness by trusting in Christ as your personal Savior and Lord?
INVITE

Pray to accept Christ.
Pray for commitment/recommitment.
Invite to join Sunday School.

INSURE
Use *A Step of Faith* to insure decision.

Personal Acceptance
Sunday School Enrollment
Public Confession
Public Confession

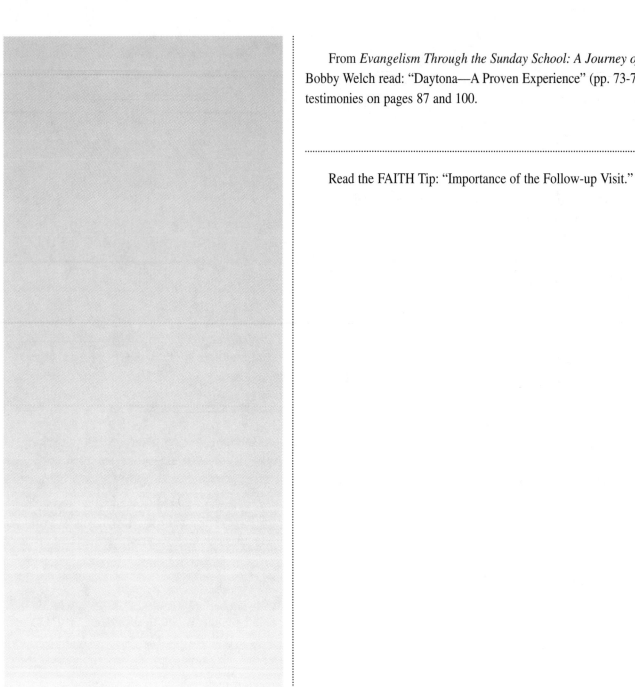

From *Evangelism Through the Sunday School: A Journey of FAITH* by Bobby Welch read: "Daytona—A Proven Experience" (pp. 73-79); and the testimonies on pages 87 and 100.

Read the FAITH Tip: "Importance of the Follow-up Visit."

Importance of the Follow-up Visit

If you visit someone who makes a decision to accept Christ, know that your Team will be following up with this person the next week during Visitation Time. Your Team Leader has been helping you with the important follow-up visit and how to handle different situations. Use this FAITH Tip as a reminder of several types of follow-up visits and the kinds of things that might be discussed.

- *The follow-up visit is a good time to review what happened in the previous visit.*

Your Team Leader probably will begin by asking how the person feels about the decision he or she made. If there are any questions about the decision, this is a time to give positive, reassuring answers.

- *The follow-up visit can be a time to further explain baptism.*

Together look at *A Step of Faith.* Refer to the panel on baptism *(panel 7)* and discuss baptism further. Again, your Team Leader will assume this part of the conversation. Explain the baptism procedure for your church.

- *If the person attended Sunday School and worship, the follow-up visit can be a time to further explain what happens and to get their impressions.*

Questions can be answered about additional ways to become involved. You might share what the previous week's Bible study meant to you.

- *If a desire to stand publicly has been expressed but not yet done, affirm in the follow-up visit that you/other Team members still want to stand with the new believer.*

- *A follow-up visit may need to be a time to find out why someone has not followed up on expressed commitments.* Your Team Leader will provide this kind of sensitive help and leadership.

Follow-up is extremely important. Your FAITH Team will initiate follow-up; additional follow-up will continue through the Sunday School.

Your Journey in Faith

Read Matthew 16:13-20. Who do the people you have visited say Jesus is? Reflect on some of the people your Team has visited and write about their spiritual background and response(s) to Jesus.

What have you learned about Jesus during the past several months that you would be willing to share with someone else?

Read Matthew 16:21-26. What does this passage say to you? How would you seek to encourage someone with these words of Christ?

Prayer Concerns

Answers to Prayer

Dear Learner:

You're in the "Homestretch" Now!

Beloved, you are in the "homestretch" of this semester of training, and there are not but a few lessons to the finish. I can almost hear all of heaven and our Father crying out, "Go on home! Go on home!"

If you have not shared FAITH in a home or are not caught up with all your lessons, you might feel a bit discouraged now. Don't be; "hang in there" for the next few weeks. You are heading into some of the most important and useful lessons: "FAITH in Daily Life" and "Dealing with Difficulties." This is the precise point in FAITH training in which many receive the exact encouragement and help they need to win their own family members and nearest and dearest friends.

My Team and I went seven weeks one semester before we found anyone at home. That was rare indeed, but after that the floodgates opened! The Lord used that experience to teach us endurance and patience in following Him. God is at work; stick with it, you are almost to the finish line.

At the Daytona 500 Speedway the entire crowd stands as the cars come out of the fourth and final turn and as the announcer cries out in exhilaration, "And they are in the homestretch headed for the finish line!" The crowd goes wild! Little wonder everyone is cheering because those they are watching are sparing nothing at this point in their all-out dash for the finish line.

Many people here on earth are praying for us to finish these last few weeks of FAITH. I cannot help but believe that all of heaven watches and cheers you now as you go for the finish line, "You are in the homestretch now. Go on, finish! Go on, finish!"

On my knees over this letter I have prayed:

Dear Lord, help us all to keep looking unto Jesus, the Author and Finisher of our faith and let us run with endurance the race that is set before us—all the way to the finish line!

Would you like to jot down a prayer for yourself and your Team?

____

____

____

With You in His Certain FAITH Victory!

Bobby

Bobby

SESSION 12

Practicing FAITH

In this session you will

CHECK IT: engage in Team Time activities—practice the FAITH Visit Outline with your Team Leader;

DO IT: make visits—be able to share the FAITH Visit Outline up to the ***Invitation*** (which your Team Leader will handle), as the situation merits;

SHARE IT: celebrate.

In Advance

- Pray for Team members as they take the lead in visits.
- There is no Teaching Time content for this session. Instead, plan to stay in Teams for practice, each person sharing with his or her Team Leader.
- Use cels or computer slides from previous sessions to reinforce any part of the practice session.
- Preview Home Study Assignments for Session 12: read assignments from *Evangelism Through the Sunday School: A Journey of FAITH* and the FAITH Tips "Understanding the Role of Cultivation" and "Keep the Strategy Balanced" and continue journal assignments.

(15 min.) CHECK IT

This session is important in reinforcing the sequence of the entire FAITH Visit Outline. It provides Learners time to practice.

Team members have learned the entire FAITH Visit Outline. Although they have been practicing aspects of the outline as they have learned them, this session will be a time to practice all aspects of the visit.

Keep Teams together. While one person shares with the Team Leader, the other might evaluate. Rotate responsibilities.

In any time available with the entire group, answer questions about Session 11, focusing on the important *Invitation.* Members need to be comfortable with the content, process, resources, and possibilities for moving into the *Invitation.* Also highlight any information that will appear on the written review in Session 16.

Team Time

CHECK IT

Your Team Leader directs this important time, checking off memory work, reviewing previous sessions and completed assignments, answering questions, and providing guidance to strengthen home visits.

Agenda:

✓ *Practice with Team Leader/other Learners*

❑ *Entire presentation, including* Invitation, *practiced and evaluated?—check it!*

Team Leader: In the adjacent box, check off each word as the Learner recites it correctly. In the space provided for sign-off, indicate your approval by signing your name.

FAITH VISIT OUTLINE

❑ *Preparation*

- ❑ INTRODUCTION
- ❑ INTERESTS
- ❑ INVOLVEMENT
  - ❑ **Church Experience/Background**
    - ❑ **Ask about the person's church background.**
    - ❑ **Listen for clues about the person's spiritual involvement.**
  - ❑ **Sunday School Testimony**
    - ❑ **Tell general benefits of Sunday School.**
    - ❑ **Tell a current personal experience.**
  - ❑ **Evangelistic Testimony**
    - ❑ **Tell a little of your pre-conversion experience.**
    - ❑ **Say: "I had a life-changing experience."**
    - ❑ **Tell recent benefits of your conversion.**
- ❑ INQUIRY
- ❑ **Key Question: In your personal opinion, what do you understand it takes for a person to go to heaven?**
  - ❑ **Possible answers: Faith, works, unclear, no opinion**
- ❑ **Transition Statement: I'd like to share with you how the Bible answers this question, if it is all right. There is a word that can be used to answer this question:** ***FAITH (spell out on fingers).***

❑ *Presentation*

❑ F is for FORGIVENESS.

❑ We cannot have eternal life and heaven without God's forgiveness.

❑ *"In Him [meaning Jesus] we have redemption through His blood, the forgiveness of sins"—Ephesians 1:7a, NKJV.*

❑ A is for AVAILABLE.

❑ Forgiveness is available. It is—

❑ AVAILABLE FOR ALL

❑ *"For God so loved the world that He gave His only begotten Son, that whoever believes in Him should not perish but have everlasting life"—John 3:16, NKJV.*

❑ BUT NOT AUTOMATIC

❑ *"Not everyone who says to Me, 'Lord, Lord,' shall enter the kingdom of heaven"—Matthew 7:21a, NKJV.*

❑ I is for IMPOSSIBLE.

❑ It is impossible for God to allow sin into heaven.

❑ GOD IS—

❑ • LOVE

❑ *John 3:16, NKJV*

❑ • JUST

❑ *"For judgment is without mercy"—James 2:13a, NKJV.*

❑ MAN IS SINFUL

❑ *"For all have sinned and fall short of the glory of God" —Romans 3:23, NKJV.*

❑ Question: But how can a sinful person enter heaven, where God allows no sin?

❑ T is for TURN.

❑ Question: If you were driving down the road and someone asked you to turn, what would he or she be asking you to do? *(change direction)*

❑ *Turn* means repent.

❑ TURN from something—sin and self

❑ *"But unless you repent you will all likewise perish" —Luke 13:3b, NKJV.*

- ❑ TURN to Someone; trust Christ only
  - ❑ (The Bible tells us that) *"Christ died for our sins according to the Scriptures, and that He was buried, and that He rose again the third day according to the Scriptures"—1 Corinthians 15:3b-4, NKJV.*
  - ❑ *"If you confess with your mouth the Lord Jesus and believe in your heart that God has raised Him from the dead, you will be saved" —Romans 10:9, NKJV.*

- ❑ H is for HEAVEN.
- ❑ Heaven is eternal life.
- ❑ HERE
  - ❑ *"I have come that they may have life, and that they may have it more abundantly"—John 10:10b, NKJV.*
- ❑ HEREAFTER
  - ❑ *"And if I go and prepare a place for you, I will come again and receive you to Myself; that where I am, there you may be also" —John 14:3, NKJV.*
- ❑ HOW
  - ❑ How can a person have God's forgiveness, heaven and eternal life, and Jesus as personal Savior and Lord?
  - ❑ Explain based on leaflet picture, F.A.I.T.H. (Forsaking All I Trust Him), Romans 10:9.

❑ *Invitation*

- ❑ INQUIRE
- ❑ Understanding what we have shared, would you like to receive this forgiveness by trusting in Christ as your personal Savior and Lord?
- ❑ INVITE
  - ❑ Pray to accept Christ.
  - ❑ Pray for commitment/recommitment.
  - ❑ Invite to join Sunday School.
- ❑ INSURE
- ❑ Use *A Step of Faith* to insure decision.
  - ❑ Personal Acceptance
  - ❑ Sunday School Enrollment
  - ❑ Public Confession

____________________ *Team Leader Sign-off*

Visitation Time

DO IT

Be prepared to take the lead in a visit. As the situation allows, move into the gospel presentation. Your Team Leader will be ready to handle the ***Invitation,*** if appropriate. One way to transition to the ***Invitation*** (or to any part of the presentation you are unable to handle) is to say "____________ *(your Team Leader's name),* what do you think about this?' He or she will be ready to pick up the conversation from this point. Your Team Leader always will be ready to resume the FAITH Visit Outline at any point you feel you cannot continue.

As always, discuss plans in the car en route to the visit. There should be no surprises; your purpose and goals are too important. Pray for God to lead you personally and to help your Team be sensitive to opportunities for sharing the gospel.

(110 min.) DO IT

Celebration Time

SHARE IT

- Reports and testimonies
- Session 12 Evaluation Card
- Participation Card
- Visitation forms updated with results of visits

(30 min.) SHARE IT

You have learned the entire FAITH Visit Outline. You are learning to take the lead in visits. There is no new memory work.

Practice will be important parts of Team Time and Teaching Time. Continue to work through your Home Study Assignments.

You may want to read your session notes again once blanks have been filled in from Teaching Time. A good time to review your notes is before doing Home Study Assignments each week.

From *Evangelism Through the Sunday School: A Journey of FAITH* by Bobby Welch, read: "The Church Devouring Monster" (pp. 140-143) and the testimonies on pages 91 and 106.

Read the FAITH Tips "Understanding the Role of Cultivation" and "Keep the Strategy Balanced."

Understanding the Role of Cultivation

"The purpose of cultivation is to build bridges of friendship and to establish in the prospect confidence in the visitor and the church. When these conditions exist, the climate is right for sowing gospel seed and nurturing it toward conversion" (p. 54).

Cultivation is a term that applies not only to the work of evangelism but also to outreach to saved persons who need to be enrolled in Sunday School or reached for church membership. Cultivation becomes a natural, ongoing part of our ministry through the Sunday School.

In general, everything we are about through FAITH training and FAITH visits speaks of cultivation. We are cultivating and developing one another to become witnesses. More than an activity, cultivation is an attitude.

We live in a secular world. Many unreached people are not ready for God-talk. They are preoccupied with human affairs, lack conviction that they need God, and question the relevance of the church.

People who fit these descriptions often are slow to reach. One or two visits will not be enough. Persistent effort that includes cultivation visits will be required to build trust, to communicate genuine concern, and to demonstrate that following Christ makes a difference in daily living. Caring cultivators get on the prospect's wavelength, speak her language, and share the good news with convincing love.

Cultivation visits and other cultivation activities have a biblical base (see John 4:36-38; 1 Cor. 3:6; 1 Cor. 9:22). Goals of a cultivation visit are to build trust; communicate genuine concern; demonstrate the effectiveness of Christ; and establish a meaningful relationship in Christ.

Marks of an Effective Cultivator

An effective cultivator is—

- Genuine
- Open
- Credible
- Skilled as a listener
- A risk-taker
- A conversationalist
- Sacrificially kind
- Knowledgeable
- Characterized by integrity
- Responsible
- Committed to Christ.

You may not always see the results of cultivation in your visits. However, you may have the opportunity, as witnessing becomes a part of your lifestyle, to become a cultivator. We will give more attention to lifestyle-witness opportunities in Session 13.

Adapted from "Making a Visit to Cultivate a Prospect," C. Ferris Jordan in *Going ... One on One: A Comprehensive Guide for Making Personal Visits* (Nashville: Convention Press, 1994), 52–56. Out of print.

FAITH *Tip*

Keep the Strategy Balanced

The Sunday School class is more than a teaching unit; it is a tool for outreach, assimilation, and teaching. *You can incorporate the entire Great Commission strategy into a single organization, but you cannot do it in one hour.* You will not be able to accomplish all of these functions in a single hour on Sunday morning. In the Sunday morning hour, you may include a time for sharing results of outreach and ministry needs, but the focus will clearly be on teaching. The work of assimilation, fellowship, and evangelism will occur outside the class and at times other than Sunday morning.

The teacher is the key to the effective functioning of the . . . leadership team. The teacher must maintain the team spirit and keep the class involved in the Great Commission strategy. If the teacher sees his or her role as an invited guest lecturer with no connection to the further work of the class, assimilation and evangelistic activities will languish. The teacher should lead the leadership team through prayer, coordination, and inspiration.

There should be regular evaluation to ensure that the above three elements of the work of the class are balanced:

- Are members bringing unsaved friends?
- Does the outreach or FAITH team visit unsaved prospects regularly?
- Has anyone been led to Christ through the ministry of our class?
- Are members being contacted regularly?
- Are care needs being missed?
- Are members attending regularly?
- Are members frequently lost from the class? Why?
- Does the teaching address the spiritual needs of the class?
- Do members participate in class discussion?

Nothing is more important than what we do through the church and therefore we must continually seek to strive for excellence. Continued evaluation and improvement of the integrated work of Sunday School is essential.

Adapted from Ken Hemphill, *Revitalizing the Sunday Morning Dinosaur* (Nashville: Broadman and Holman Publishers), 148.

Your Journey in Faith

Read John 9:1-39. What differences have you seen in your life from the time you started FAITH training until now?

What are the biggest obstacles or tests you have personally faced thus far in FAITH training?

Look back at some prayer concerns you identified at the beginning of FAITH training. What results have you seen?

Prayer Concerns

Answers to Prayer

SESSION 13

FAITH in Daily Life

In this session you will:

CHECK IT: engage in Team Time activities, especially practice;

HEAR IT: learn ways the outline and other principles learned in FAITH can be used in daily life settings;

STUDY IT: overview Home Study Assignments for Session 13;

DO IT: make visits—at your Team Leader's cue and as the situation merits, lead the entire visit, including the ***Invitation;***

SHARE IT: celebrate.

In Advance

- Pray for daily settings in which to share a witness.
- Familiarize yourself with all teaching suggestions and all session content. Use Session 13 computer presentation slides or the overhead transparencies (#60-62).
- Prepare the room for teaching. Preview all media and request necessary equipment. There is no video for this session.
- Think about specific life-witness situations you have recently experienced. Be prepared to share one during Step 6 if time allows.
- During Celebration Time, consider highlighting decisions made beyond those in FAITH visits. In so doing, you encourage Learners to become aware of lifestyle opportunities.

(15 min.) CHECK IT
If the computer presentation is used, display the agenda frame for Team Time, as desired. Add other points as needed.

Team Time

CHECK IT

Your Team Leader directs this important time, checking off memory work, reviewing previous sessions and completed assignments, answering questions, and providing guidance to strengthen home visits.

Agenda:
✓ FAITH Visit Outline
✓ Other Home Study Assignments
✓ Help for strengthening a visit

❑ ***Outline memorized?—check it!***

Team Leader: In the adjacent box, check off each word as the Learner recites it correctly. In the space provided for sign-off, indicate your approval by signing your name.

FAITH VISIT OUTLINE

❑ *Preparation*

- ❑ **INTRODUCTION**
- ❑ **INTERESTS**
- ❑ **INVOLVEMENT**
  - ❑ **Church Experience/Background**
    - ❑ **Ask about the person's church background.**
    - ❑ **Listen for clues about the person's spiritual involvement.**
  - ❑ **Sunday School Testimony**
    - ❑ **Tell general benefits of Sunday School.**
    - ❑ **Tell a current personal experience.**
  - ❑ **Evangelistic Testimony**
    - ❑ **Tell a little of your pre-conversion experience.**
    - ❑ **Say: "I had a life-changing experience."**
    - ❑ **Tell recent benefits of your conversion.**
- ❑ **INQUIRY**
- ❑ **Key Question: In your personal opinion, what do you understand it takes for a person to go to heaven?**
  - ❑ **Possible answers: Faith, works, unclear, no opinion**
- ❑ **Transition Statement: I'd like to share with you how the Bible answers this question, if it is all right. There is a word that can be used to answer this question: *FAITH (spell out on fingers).***

❑ *Presentation*

❑ **F is for FORGIVENESS.**

❑ **We cannot have eternal life and heaven without God's forgiveness.**

❑ ***"In Him [meaning Jesus] we have redemption through His blood, the forgiveness of sins"—Ephesians 1:7a, NKJV.***

❑ **A is for AVAILABLE.**

❑ **Forgiveness is available. It is—**

❑ **AVAILABLE FOR ALL**

❑ ***"For God so loved the world that He gave His only begotten Son, that whoever believes in Him should not perish but have everlasting life"—John 3:16, NKJV.***

❑ **BUT NOT AUTOMATIC**

❑ ***"Not everyone who says to Me, 'Lord, Lord,' shall enter the kingdom of heaven"—Matthew 7:21a, NKJV.***

❑ **I is for IMPOSSIBLE.**

❑ **It is impossible for God to allow sin into heaven.**

❑ **GOD IS —**

❑ **• LOVE**

❑ ***John 3:16, NKJV.***

❑ **• JUST**

❑ ***"For judgment is without mercy"—James 2:13a, NKJV.***

❑ **MAN IS SINFUL**

❑ ***"For all have sinned and fall short of the glory of God" —Romans 3:23, NKJV.***

❑ **Question: But how can a sinful person enter heaven, where God allows no sin?**

❑ **T is for TURN.**

❑ **Question: If you were driving down the road and someone asked you to turn, what would he or she be asking you to do? *(change direction)***

❑ ***Turn* means repent.**

❑ **TURN from something—sin and self**

❑ ***"But unless you repent you will all likewise perish"—Luke 13:3b, NKJV.***

- ❑ TURN to Someone; trust Christ only
  - ❑ (The Bible tells us that) *"Christ died for our sins according to the Scriptures, and that He was buried, and that He rose again the third day according to the Scriptures"—1 Corinthians 15:3b-4, NKJV.*
  - ❑ *"If you confess with your mouth the Lord Jesus and believe in your heart that God has raised Him from the dead, you will be saved" —Romans 10:9, NKJV.*

- ❑ H is for HEAVEN.
- ❑ Heaven is eternal life.
- ❑ HERE
  - ❑ *"I have come that they may have life, and that they may have it more abundantly"—John 10:10b, NKJV.*
- ❑ HEREAFTER
  - ❑ *"And if I go and prepare a place for you, I will come again and receive you to Myself; that where I am, there you may be also" —John 14:3, NKJV.*
- ❑ HOW
  - ❑ How can a person have God's forgiveness, heaven and eternal life, and Jesus as personal Savior and Lord?
  - ❑ Explain based on leaflet picture, F.A.I.T.H. (Forsaking All I Trust Him), Romans 10:9.

❑ *Invitation*

- ❑ INQUIRE
- ❑ Understanding what we have shared, would you like to receive this forgiveness by trusting in Christ as your personal Savior and Lord?
- ❑ INVITE
  - ❑ Pray to accept Christ.
  - ❑ Pray for commitment/recommitment.
  - ❑ Invite to join Sunday School.
- ❑ INSURE
- ❑ Use *A Step of Faith* to insure decision.
  - ❑ Personal Acceptance
  - ❑ Sunday School Enrollment
  - ❑ Public Confession

_______________ *Team Leader Sign-off*

❑ ***Other Home Study Assignments completed?—check it!***

How has practice helped you feel more comfortable sharing the FAITH Visit Outline?

❑ ***Need help in strengthening a visit?—here's how!***

If time constraints keep both Learners from sharing the FAITH Visit Outline in Team Time, one person can share while in the car en route to a visit.

In general, learn to use travel time wisely. Go over the "game plan" for the visit. Make sure there is an agreement between you and your Team Leader on what portion of the FAITH Visit Outline you are willing to share. Do recognize the need for some flexibility if the nature of a specific visit calls for a change in plans.

Remember, the Holy Spirit will strengthen and direct you.

(5 min.) Transition to classrooms for instruction on the content of the session.

Teaching Time

HEAR IT

STEP 1 (5 min.) **Review the Sunday School's responsibility in witnessing and ministry (also refer to Session 4). Continue to keep in front of participants the foundational role of Sunday School and of foundational evangelism, through your FAITH strategy.**

STEP 2 (5 min.) **Lead Teams to review Acts 2:41-47, a description of the early church at its best—showing love.**

Encourage Learners, based on this understanding, to write characteristics of a caring Sunday School ministry in the space provided. Ask them to consider how their class or department can be the point of contact for many unchurched people.

Remind the group of this way of thinking about and doing Sunday School: *Sunday School is the foundational strategy in a local church for leading people to faith in the Lord Jesus Christ and for building Great Commission Christians through Bible study groups that engage people in evangelism, discipleship, fellowship, ministry, and worship.*

Throughout FAITH training you have had opportunities to visit people who are not members of our Sunday School (but who have shown interest or whom we would like to have as members). Many times we call them *guests, prospects, VIPs,* or some other term that indicates how important they are to our Sunday School.

In many situations, you have asked the Key Question and been given an opportunity to share the gospel presentation. One of the main objectives of FAITH training is to discover persons who are open to the gospel and to share with them about God's forgiveness.

FAITH training also gives us opportunity to make ministry visits. Such contacts are with people already assigned to, and perhaps even consistently attending, our Sunday School ministry. We have many ongoing opportunities to touch base with folks in our classes. We can discover prayer concerns, seek to encourage members, provide information about our classes, or attempt to meet a specific need representing Jesus and our church.

Many powerful passages in Scripture help us focus on ministry through our Sunday School ministry. Acts 2:41-47 describes the church at its best—showing love and being a people of love.

For many people their first point of contact with a church is through a caring Sunday School member. Think about how our Sunday School—your class—can be an important point of "connecting" with unchurched people. In special and in numerous ways, Sunday School can minister and thus point people to Christ and to His church.

ACTS 2:41-47

"Those who accepted his message were baptized, and about three thousand were added to their number that day.

"They devoted themselves to the apostles' teaching and to the fellowship, to the breaking of bread and to prayer. Everyone was filled with awe, and many wonders and miraculous signs were done by the apostles. All the believers were together and had everything in common. Selling their possessions and goods, they gave to anyone as he had need. Every day they continued to meet together in the temple courts. They broke bread in their homes and ate together with glad and sincere hearts, praising God and enjoying the favor of all the people. And the Lord added to their number daily those who were being saved" (NIV).

CHARACTERISTICS OF A CARING SUNDAY SCHOOL

____

____

____

____

____

Did you see the importance of:

praying?

sharing with those in need?

studying the Bible together?

enjoying fellowship?

praising God together?

You should have; your Sunday School class does all of these things!

You represent the work of your Sunday School and church, no matter where you are. The work of evangelism and ministry is to be a lifestyle.

FAITH *in Daily Life*

No matter where you are—if with a Team or by yourself—you can offer ______________________ to members needing Christian fellowship. Many Christian members cannot attend regularly but realize their need for a blessing from another Christian. You can share what God is doing in your life and can encourage the person to share what Christ means personally.

You can identify _________ _____________ ______ __________ and can be prepared to share them with others in the church as appropriate. Often class members need to be reminded that people of faith are praying for them.

You provide for many ______________ __________ by merely visiting a person during a crisis. Extended illnesses, bereavements, job loss, accidents, and divorce are among the many personal crises individuals experience. At times like these, visits from fellow Sunday School members are most appreciated.

These contacts give you appropriate opportunities to visit and to offer assistance and encouragement. You can take care packages prepared by class members, be present to listen during a particularly challenging life transition or crisis, or identify special needs calling for more assistance from the church.

On many occasions you will have the opportunity to ______________ with a member at a special time in life. It is important that class members make contact after such events as the birth of a child, a promotion, a wedding, and a retirement. Birthdays and anniversaries also are good times to make contact.

Sometimes you encounter a member who ____________ _____ ____ ____________. This person may not have a (______________) ______________________ with Christ. Your ministry to this person can be a source of scriptural accountability and encouragement.

STEP 3 (10 min.) **Using "FAITH in Daily Life" content, direct Learners to fill in the blanks.**

Use cels or computer presentation slides to help Learners easily see answers.

STEP 4 (10 min.) **Instruct Learners to fill in the blanks while you share the "Importance of a Witnessing Lifestyle" content. Use computer slides or cels to illustrate the lecture.**

STEP 5 (5 min.) **Using the "Evaluate Your Compassion for People" exercise, help the group evaluate their concern for others they encounter day-by-day. Refer to the book *Teaching the Jesus Way: Building a Transformational Teaching Ministry* for more content.**

You can ____________ ____ anyone who has prayed to receive Christ. New Christians need cultivation and nurture, and your friendship and support can be valuable.

You are always looking for ________________________ to:

- celebrate with another Christian;
- enroll someone in Sunday School; and
- encourage other believers in their journey of faith.

Importance of a Witnessing Lifestyle

As Christians, we must ____________________ what we are learning about faith and about the gospel into our everyday life witness. We need to be alert to ______________________ to witness in our daily routine. Remember, Sunday School ministry is a seven-day-a-week process.

A Learner once said, "I took evangelism training so I could witness when the opportunity was presented, and then I learned I was to present the opportunity." This statement accurately describes what life witness is all about.

The Great Commission reminds us we are to witness as we are going. Our witness is to be __________________. Our witness is to be __________________. Our witness is to be a ______________. Our witness is to occur as we intersect the lives of people in daily encounters.

Evaluate Your Compassion for People

Before looking at some settings in which you may have opportunity to share a witness, evaluate the extent to which you are willing to invest yourself in other people. Respond to each statement as "Very Descriptive," "Somewhat Descriptive," or "Not Descriptive" of your concern.

- *Love for God and for people is my primary motivation for reaching out to others.*
- *I am overwhelmed with compassion by the very thought that masses of people in my community have not been reached for Christ.*
- *I am drawn toward ministry to the sorrowing and suffering even when I don't know the people personally.*
- *My caring is expressed and supported by my willingness to act on another person's behalf.*
- *I am willing to reach out and touch even those whom others reject.*[1]

LIFE-WITNESS OPPORTUNITIES

- ❑ Airline travel (opportunities to share with casual acquaintances/new friends)
- ❑ Social events with neighbors, work associates, and so forth
- ❑ Casual contacts with service personnel (waiters, mechanics, clerks)
- ❑ Family gatherings
- ❑ Telephone surveys/opinion polls
- ❑ Parks, beaches, and other recreational facilities
- ❑ Sporting events
- ❑ School events
- ❑ Civic clubs
- ❑ Waiting rooms or offices (doctor, hospital, nursing home, hospice, and so forth)
- ❑ Written communication (mail to family and friends)
- ❑ Prisons or correctional institutions
- ❑ Drug or alcohol rehabilitation centers

Other: ____

[1] Jay Johnston and Ronald K. Brown, *Teaching the Jesus Way: Building a Transformational Teaching Ministry* (Nashville: LifeWay Press, 2000), 112-113.

STEP 6 (5 min.) Say: Place a check mark (√) beside situations in "Life-Witness Opportunities" in which you regularly encounter believers and/or nonbelievers. Next, circle each situation in which you have shared your faith with someone during the past few months.

STUDY IT

STEP 7 (5 min.) Overview Home Study Assignments for Session 13.

- Write—Life witness opportunities, needs discovered in FAITH visits
- Read—*Evangelism Through the Sunday School* assignments and FAITH Tip: "Identifying Your Outreach Networks"
- Journal—Your Journey in Faith

(5 min.) Transition to assemble with FAITH Teams to prepare for home visits.

Visitation Time

DO IT

Lead as much of the visit as you are comfortable doing. Your Team Leader will not expect you to do more than you are willing to do. Potentially, if the opportunity presents itself, you might lead the entire visit, including the ***Invitation.***

(110 min.) DO IT

Celebration Time

SHARE IT

- Reports and testimonies
- Session 13 Evaluation Card
- Participation Card
- Visitation forms updated with results of visits

(30 min.) SHARE IT

Team Learners should share reports.

Home Study Assignments

You have learned the entire FAITH Visit Outline. There is no new memory work. Home Study Assignments continue to be important, and your Team Leader may review you on any assignments and on any memory work that may need review.

You may want to read your session notes again once blanks have been filled in from Teaching Time. A good time to review your notes is before doing Home Study Assignments each week.

Write a brief description of your last life-witness experience:

Describe the last time you let a life-witness opportunity slip by without taking advantage of it.

Make a list of people you have visited during FAITH training (as many as you can recall). Identify specific needs you discovered that call for follow-up.

People	**Actions for Follow-up**

In *Evangelism Through the Sunday School: A Journey of FAITH* by Bobby Welch, read "The Last Call" (p. 163) and the testimony on page 33.

Read the FAITH Tip: "Identifying Your Outreach Networks." Calculate the number of potential contacts you have during each workweek.

FAITH *Tip*

Identifying Your Outreach Networks

One Wednesday a group of 27 Sunday School workers was asked to calculate how many people they had talked with that day. First, they were to record the number of family members with whom they had talked. Next, they were to record the number of people they had talked with at work or at school that day. Next, the number of people they had talked with by phone or by computer. Next, the number of people they had talked with in grocery stores, service stations, restaurants, and so forth. Each worker added each set of numbers. The total for that group was 625.

Bccause 625 represented contacts only for one day," the group was asked to calculate "how many contacts they would make in an average work week of five days. That total came to 3,125. This group of 27 averaged over 3,000 'touches' of some kind during a week. Obviously, many of these contacts or 'touches' were duplicates. Still, it is amazing how many opportunities a group has within a week to network with people.

Lead your class (or encourage a class leader to do so) to calculate its networking potential. Simply ask each member to list the number of people they have some contact with each working day through their conversation, telephone, computer, or business transaction. Add their totals together and multiply by the days of the week. When your class meets each week, consider how much impact participants can have during the coming week. Guide members to participate in their networks of contact the way Christ would were He in their shoes. Pause here and calculate your own network potential in the box provided.

Your Network Potential

Calculating your network potential: Take a typical day of your workweek. Estimate the number of people with whom you had some kind of contact that day. Total the numbers.

____ Family members
____ People at work or school
____ People talked to on phone or by computer
____ People met casually during day (gas station, restaurant, and so forth)
____ People met during recreational activities
____ Others
____ TOTAL

Multiply your total for one day times five (typical workweek)

____ My weekly networking potential

One person can make a difference in the world simply by networking.

Adapted from *The Jesus Touch, Follow Christ's Example: Adult* by Calvin Miller and Keith Wilkinson (Nashville: Convention Press, 1997), 89–90. Out of print.

Your Journey in Faith

Read Matthew 11:28-30. What are some significant ways Jesus has recently ministered to you?

What are some things you have learned about ministry by being in the Sunday School?

What are ministry needs you have discovered during FAITH training that you feel you or members of your class could do?

Prayer Concerns

Answers to Prayer

SESSION 14

Handling Difficulties in a Visit

In this session you will

CHECK IT: engage in Team Time activities, especially practice;

HEAR IT: learn about various types of challenges and distractions that can occur in a visit and principles and approaches for handling;

SEE IT: show the humorous video segment in which distractions disrupt a visit;

STUDY IT: overview Home Study Assignments for Session 14 and begin to pray about the next semester of FAITH training;

DO IT: make visits—as the situation merits, be prepared to share the entire FAITH Visit Outline;

SHARE IT: celebrate

In Advance

- Pray that FAITH Teams and the Sunday School ministry as a whole might see people through Jesus' eyes.
- Familiarize yourself with teaching suggestions and all session content. Use Session 14 computer presentation slides or the overhead transparencies (#63-68) to illustrate the teaching.
- Prepare the room for teaching. Request all needed equipment.
- ***Note:*** There are options on when the video may be used. Preview and cue "Dr. Faith: 'But they won't let me finish!' " either to open the session or to use as Step 4. There is no role play for this session.
- Indicate any special focus to this session's Visitation Time.
- Listen for reports in which Teams handled difficulties well during a visit. Highlight a few such reports during Celebration Time.

(15 min.) CHECK IT
If the computer presentation is used, display the agenda frame for Team Time, as desired. Add other points as needed.

Team Time

CHECK IT

Your Team Leader directs this important time, checking off memory work, reviewing previous sessions and completed assignments, answering questions, and providing guidance to strengthen home visits.

Agenda:
✓ Practice FAITH Visit Outline
✓ Other Home Study Assignments
✓ Session 13 debriefing
✓ Help for strengthening a visit

❑ ***Outline practiced?—check it!***

You have learned the FAITH Visit Outline, so this part of Team Time provides valuable practice. Your Team Leader may ask you to clarify any point in the outline that he or she feels is not yet learned.

FAITH VISIT OUTLINE

❑ *Preparation*

- ❑ **INTRODUCTION**
- ❑ **INTERESTS**
- ❑ **INVOLVEMENT**
  - ❑ **Church Experience/Background**
    - ❑ **Ask about the person's church background.**
    - ❑ **Listen for clues about the person's spiritual involvement.**
  - ❑ **Sunday School Testimony**
    - ❑ **Tell general benefits of Sunday School.**
    - ❑ **Tell a current personal experience.**
  - ❑ **Evangelistic Testimony**
    - ❑ **Tell a little of your pre-conversion experience.**
    - ❑ **Say: "I had a life-changing experience."**
    - ❑ **Tell recent benefits of your conversion.**
- ❑ **INQUIRY**
- ❑ **Key Question: In your personal opinion, what do you understand it takes for a person to go to heaven?**
  - ❑ **Possible answers: Faith, works, unclear, no opinion**
- ❑ **Transition Statement: I'd like to share with you how the Bible answers this question, if it is all right. There is a word that can be used to answer this question: *FAITH (spell out on fingers).***

❑ *Presentation*

❑ F is for FORGIVENESS.

❑ We cannot have eternal life and heaven without God's forgiveness.

❑ *"In Him [meaning Jesus] we have redemption through His blood, the forgiveness of sins"—Ephesians 1:7a, NKJV.*

❑ A is for AVAILABLE.

❑ Forgiveness is available. It is—

❑ AVAILABLE FOR ALL

❑ *"For God so loved the world that He gave His only begotten Son, that whoever believes in Him should not perish but have everlasting life"—John 3:16, NKJV.*

❑ BUT NOT AUTOMATIC

❑ *"Not everyone who says to Me, 'Lord, Lord,' shall enter the kingdom of heaven"—Matthew 7:21a, NKJV.*

❑ I is for IMPOSSIBLE.

❑ It is impossible for God to allow sin into heaven.

❑ GOD IS—

❑ • LOVE

John 3:16, NKJV

❑ • JUST

❑ *"For judgment is without mercy"—James 2:13a, NKJV.*

❑ MAN IS SINFUL

❑ *"For all have sinned and fall short of the glory of God" —Romans 3:23, NKJV.*

❑ Question: But how can a sinful person enter heaven, where God allows no sin?

❑ T is for TURN.

❑ Question: If you were driving down the road and someone asked you to turn, what would he or she be asking you to do? *(change direction)*

❑ *Turn* means repent.

❑ TURN from something—sin and self

❑ *"But unless you repent you will all likewise perish"—Luke 13:3b, NKJV.*

❑ TURN to Someone; trust Christ only

❑ (The Bible tells us that) *"Christ died for our sins according to the Scriptures, and that He was buried, and that He rose again the third day according to the Scriptures"—1 Corinthians 15:3b-4, NKJV.*

- ❑ *"If you confess with your mouth the Lord Jesus and believe in your heart that God has raised Him from the dead, you will be saved"—Romans 10:9, NKJV.*

❑ H is for HEAVEN.

❑ Heaven is eternal life.

❑ HERE

- ❑ ***"I have come that they may have life, and that they may have it more abundantly"—John 10:10b, NKJV.***

❑ HEREAFTER

- ❑ ***"And if I go and prepare a place for you, I will come again and receive you to Myself; that where I am, there you may be also"—John 14:3, NKJV.***

❑ HOW

- **❑ How can a person have God's forgiveness, heaven and eternal life, and Jesus as personal Savior and Lord?**
- **❑ Explain based on leaflet picture, F.A.I.T.H. (Forsaking All I Trust Him), Romans 10:9.**

❑ *Invitation*

❑ INQUIRE

❑ Understanding what we have shared, would you like to receive this forgiveness by trusting in Christ as your personal Savior and Lord?

❑ INVITE

- **❑ Pray to accept Christ.**
- **❑ Pray for commitment/recommitment.**
- **❑ Invite to join Sunday School.**

❑ INSURE

❑ Use *A Step of Faith* to insure decision.

- **❑ Personal Acceptance**
- **❑ Sunday School Enrollment**
- **❑ Public Confession**

❑ ***Other Home Study Assignments completed?—check it!***

There is no new memory work in FAITH training. Continue to practice the FAITH Visit Outline. This also can be a good time to get caught up on any Home Study Assignments not yet completed.

❑ ***Any questions from Session 13?—check it!***

What questions do you have about Session 13? Ask your Team Leader now.

Begin to talk about opportunities you have in daily life to share your faith. As you see ways to share the gospel presentation in these settings, talk about the results with your Team Leader and fellow Learners.

Team Leader: As needed, review any information from Session 13 that will appear on the written review in Session 16.

❑ ***Need help in strengthening a visit?—here's how!***

Have you encountered difficulties in some FAITH visits? Have people raised objections you have not known how to handle? Are there some things you wished you had done differently? This week's Teaching Time will provide additional insights on handling difficulties in order to gain a hearing for the gospel.

By now, you and other Learners, in addition to your Team Leader, should be sharing insights on how to improve visits. Also keep in mind the kinds of valuable evaluation you do in the car immediately after a visit. Make sure the results of visits are clearly summarized so your Team or others can do appropriate follow-up in the future.

(5 min.) Transition to classrooms for instruction on the content of the session.

Teaching Time

HEAR IT

STEP 1 (5 min.) **Overview two general types of difficulties Learners will encounter in a visit.**

STEP 2 (10 min.) **Using "I've Done That" and "I Don't Believe the Bible" content and the computer presentation slides or cels, describe situations and some possible responses. Ask Learners to fill in the blanks while you share.**

Comment as follows: Objections, if they occur at all, may surface at different times in a visit. In fact, additional study on this topic is provided in your second semester of training, *Building Bridges Through FAITH: The Journey Continues.*

For example, the person you are visiting may listen to the entire gospel presentation and then say, "I've done that." In contrast, someone who does not believe the Bible may raise that objection very early in the visit, before the gospel can be presented. The evidences for the Bible that are provided here can guide you in helping the person to reconsider and listen to the gospel presentation.

"I've Done That/I Don't Believe the Bible"

Have you noticed that, even though you have learned how to make a FAITH visit, many of the situations you encounter are less than ideal? Distractions *will* occur. How you handle them is the key; your goal is to gain a hearing for the gospel *despite* problems or difficulties.

Generally, difficulties and distractions fall into two main categories: (1) those posed by questions or concerns about the message you are sharing; and (2) those that disrupt the flow of the visit. Both types of difficulties can crop up any time in a visit, and each creates unique challenges.

"I've Done That"

You can determine from the prospect's answer to the Key Question whether to ______________ by sharing the gospel presentation. Sometimes the person's response may be similar to, "I did what you are talking about" or "I've already done that."

Treat this response much as you would an _____________ response to the Key Question. Gently ask for more information regarding when the individual received God's forgiveness and trusted in Christ only as Savior and Lord. Review whatever portion of the presentation would help.

If after this discussion, the person still indicates he or she already has trusted Christ, celebrate together as believers. Show *A Step of Faith* and introduce the idea of making one's commitment ___________, if that has not been done. Discussion about enrollment in Sunday School and baptism may be needed and is appropriate at this point.

"I Don't Believe the Bible"

It can be difficult to know how to continue if a person says, "I don't believe the Bible." Every part of the gospel presentation grows out of truths of God's Word. If someone does not believe the Bible, how should you continue?

When this response is given, continue by saying: "Some people respond that way, ________________________ *(person's name),* because they have never clearly heard what the Bible has to say about how to go to heaven." In many cases, the presentation can be continued.

If it is determined that more information is needed before you can continue, you may say, "A person would want to consider the ______________ of the Bible." If the person counters with "What evidence?," continue with brief explanations of the following:

(1) There is ________________ evidence for the Bible. The Dead Sea Scrolls, discovered in a Dead Sea cave approximately Spring 1947, contained a scroll of the Old Testament Book of Isaiah. Scientific dating methods reveal this scroll to be more than two thousand years old. Remarkably, it is virtually a word-by-word rendering of the Hebrew text of Isaiah.

(2) Another type of scientific evidence is provided by ____________________. Numerous biblical accounts have been authenticated and proven reliably historical by archaeology. This method supports that what the Bible indicates happened did indeed happen when and where God's Word says. Such discoveries were not made by Christian archaeologist trying to prove the Bible but by people (believers and nonbelievers) doing their jobs. A recent discovery is that of the burial place of Caiaphas, the high priest mentioned in Jesus' trial.

(3) __________________ evidence for the Bible also can be cited. Prophetic revelations permeate both the Old and New Testaments. There are numerous prophetic references to the birth of Jesus. Written hundreds of years before the event, the prophecies in the Bible have been fulfilled in the detail in which they are described. Only supernatural knowledge can account for these outcomes.

(4) No one can argue with your __________________ experience. Tell again how Christ has changed your life and how you draw strength from Him on a daily basis.

How to Respond in Love

When you are in the midst of a visit in which issues or questions are being expressed, take these actions:

________ for the person and for the Team member who is sharing.

__________ ________ with the person. Do not argue the rightness of your belief or antagonize the person. Gently probe for more information that would allow you to share the gospel.

A related principle is to sensitively ____________ to the objection.

_______________ in love.

Some specific responses are to:

- ___________. In some cases, it is appropriate to ask permission to answer a question at a later time. For example, in response to a question that may not be relevant at that point of the presentation, ask permission to answer it later. Encourage the person to remind you later, and then answer the question to the best of your ability.
- Answer ________. If the person's question is relevant and can be

STEP 3
(5 min.)
Using "How to Respond in Love" content, direct Learners to fill in the blanks for ways to handle difficult situations.
How to
Respond in
Love

SEE IT

STEP 4 (10 min.) **Show the video segment "Dr. Faith: But they won't let me finish!" to introduce other kinds of distractions that interrupt a visit.**

***Option:* You might use the video to open the session; follow by saying: You will discover two general types of difficulties—those related to your message and those that disrupt the flow of the visit.**

HEAR IT

STEP 5 (5 min.) **Describe other distractions, using "Other Distractions Can Disrupt" content and the computer presentation slides or overhead cels.**

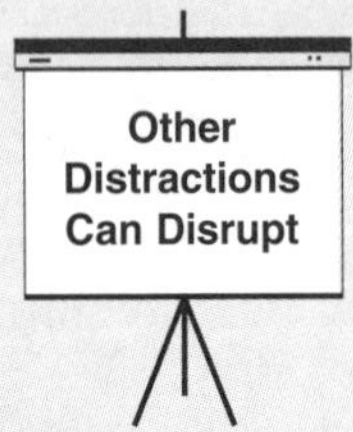

STEP 6 (5 min.) **Conclude by drawing attention to general principles for use in all situations. Ask Learners to take notes based on "General Principles for Handling Difficult Situations" content and media support.**

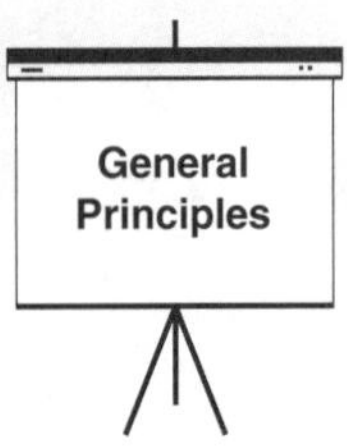

handled at that point in the presentation, go ahead and do so. Make the answer brief and get back to the presentation. Do not get into a debate.

• ___________ ______ ________ __________ the answer. If you cannot answer the person's question, say so. Ask for permission to continue sharing.

You are on holy ground when a person allows you to discuss with them matters of their soul. Your responsibility is to share what God is doing in your life and to offer a short, easy-to-remember explanation of God's good news. Without compromising the truth of Scripture, you are appropriately asking a person to share his or her understanding regarding several spiritual matters. You can explain and clarify without arguing.

Other Distractions Can Disrupt

Other kinds of distractions include interruptions posed by a phone call or the doorbell; stereos or television sets that stay on throughout the visit; and young children, elderly adults, or pets needing attention. And, of course, there's always the distraction or problem yet to be experienced!

These kinds of distractions generally call for a ________ ________.
Team members not presenting the gospel can help. This may mean talking to another family member, dealing with pets, or playing with a child.

Avoid taking a child into a room by yourself. This is especially important if you have no prior experiences with the prospect(s).

A Team effort allows the person hearing the gospel presentation to do so uninterrupted. If possible, however, Team members ________ ____ _______ the person making the gospel presentation.

Remember, ______ may be an interruption to the person you are visiting. For many people today, with the busy schedules they are trying to manage, there is no convenient time to be visited. Your courtesy and sensitivity can be a witness as well as your words.

General Principles for Handling Difficult Situations

• Be ______________ for distractions and challenges. They *will* occur.

• Remember you are on _______________ _________ ________.
You must establish rapport before a person will trust you or hear what you have to say.

• Keep in mind that you represent ___________ and His church. Demonstrating Christlikeness increases the possibility that the person will respect you and your message.

• By being sensitive to what seem to be distractions, you may discover ministry and follow-up _________.

• Sometimes the solution may be to find a _________ _________ ____ ___________. Simply moving to another room in the house may be the solution.

• Be _____________ and clear. You do not need to explain everything there is to know. FAITH is a simple tool to help you and others remember the gospel. Some points will need to be clarified; be prepared to do so as needed or requested.

Now as the good Dr. Faith prescribes, let's practice, practice, practice.

STUDY IT

STEP 7 (5 min.) Overview Home Study Assignments for Session 14.

- Read/write—Responses to Bible study
- Read—*Evangelism Through the Sunday School* assignments and FAITH Tips: "How Jesus Handled Difficult Situations" and "How to Talk About Jesus in a Secular World."
- Journal—Your Journey in Faith

(5 min.) Transition to assemble with FAITH Teams to prepare for home visits.

Visitation Time

DO IT

Lead in as much of the visit as you feel capable of doing. As in previous sessions, your Team Leader will be ready to assume the presentation at any point you feel unable to continue. If you encounter objections you cannot handle, your Team Leader will respond to the concern raised.

(110 min.) DO IT

Celebration Time

SHARE IT

- Reports and testimonies
- Session 14 Evaluation Card
- Participation Card
- Visitation forms updated with results of visits

(30 min.) SHARE IT

Team Learners should take the lead in sharing reports.

Home Study Assignments

You may want to read your session notes again once blanks have been filled in from Teaching Time. A good time to review your notes is before doing Home Study Assignments each week.

Ask God to put on your heart the names of people from your class or department who might be interested in participation in FAITH training. Write any names that come to mind here. Begin to pray for them.

____

____

____

____

Also pray about your involvement in future training.

Read the FAITH Tip: "How Jesus Handled Difficult Situations." Read the following Scripture passages and identify the (1) challenges He encountered and (2) actions He took to handle the situation.

	DISTRACTIONS OR CHALLENGES	**ACTIONS JESUS TOOK TO HANDLE THE CHALLENGE**
John 8:2-11		
	________________	________________
	________________	________________
	________________	________________
	________________	________________
John 4:4-42		
	________________	________________
	________________	________________
	________________	________________
	________________	________________

DISTRACTIONS OR CHALLENGES	**ACTIONS JESUS TOOK TO HANDLE THE CHALLENGE**

Mark 2:1-12

Luke 7:36-50

Other Principles I Discovered:

In *Evangelism Through the Sunday School: A Journey of FAITH* by Bobby Welch read: "Don't Say No!" (pp. 51-53) and "Get a Vision of 'Timothy Training'" (pp. 136-140); and the testimony on page 137.

Read the FAITH Tips: "How Jesus Handled Difficult Situations" and How to Talk About Jesus in a Secular World."

How Jesus Handled Difficult Situations

When you think about Jesus' ministry, you can recall that He encountered many challenging people and situations.

Do you remember when Jesus was teaching in a home? The crowd was so thick that, in order for a group of men to bring their sick friend for healing, they had to dismantle the roof and lower their friend to Jesus. That could have been quite a distraction!

Do you remember when Jesus was teaching a large group in the temple courts and was disrupted by the Pharisees who brought a woman caught in adultery? For many people, this would have been an interruption; for Jesus, it was a valuable and redemptive teaching situation.

Jesus followed certain basic principles in how He approached people and situations—principles we can follow as well.

- Jesus always honored the person as a valuable treasure of God.
- Jesus stayed focused on His message.
- Jesus used every situation as a teachable moment.
- Jesus started with those things He and the person He encountered held in common.
- Jesus graciously led the person toward personal examination.
- Jesus realized that, through God's power and message, people's lives would be changed.
- Jesus entrusted individuals with the message of God's salvation and with the responsibility to share their experience with others.

How to Talk About Jesus in a Secular World

We know that believers live by different standards than do nonbelievers. How can we speak clearly and effectively about Jesus in a secular society?

• Be Blameless

"George Hunter in *How to Reach Secular People* points out that much of what modern secular adults know about Christianity comes from negative impressions they have about television evangelists.

"Believers must accept the fact that their actions must match their words consistently over a period of time before some adults will want to listen.[1] . . .

"Be blameless in your own life. Make your vocal profession of faith in Christ a consistent part of your daily life, along with a demeanor of open concern with right living."

• Be Current

Knowing the language of the persons you are trying to reach will help you communicate. "Be specific with those with no church or religious background."

• Be Ready

"Many adults today—especially younger adults—do not accept traditional authority on face value." Some also may not have thought through the opinions they do hold.

By including in your witness not only the promise of eternal life but also examples of God's presence in your life, "you offer some insights into just how much the Lord means to you in your daily life."

• Be Patient

Many adults will not make quick decisions. They read consumer reports before they make major purchases. They marry later in life because commitment does not come easily. Do not expect these adults to decide quickly about making a life commitment.

Your responsibility is to witness to the truth without compromise. Do not change the message to make it acceptable to your hearers. Jesus is the one and only Son of God—the Savior of all who will make the conscious, personal decision to put their trust in Him.

Worship, work, and witness and let God do what only God can do.[2]

---

[1] George G. Hunter III, *How to Reach Secular People* (Nashville, TN: Abingdon Press, 1992), 23.

Adapted from *The Sunday School Leader*, The Sunday School Board of the Southern Baptist Convention, October 1997, 7–9. Out of print.

Your Journey in Faith

Read Philippians 1:27-30. Describe the most challenging experience you have faced in making a visit. In the form of a prayer, identify requests for Christ to work through challenges like these, as well as praises to the Lord regarding how Christ works for the sake of the gospel.

Read Romans 8:18-39. Imagine Christ Himself giving you these instructions after you have had a particularly challenging encounter with someone, with many frustrating objections and distractions to sharing the gospel. Write your reactions to these instructions.

What are you learning about people you encounter who challenge or reject the message you share?

How do you think Jesus would handle some of the most challenging obstacles and difficulties you have experienced?

Prayer Concerns

Answers to Prayer

SESSION 15

FAITH Growth and Reenlistment

In this session you will

CHECK IT: engage in Team Time activities, especially practice;

HEAR IT: learn ways to enlist from your Sunday School class or department;

STUDY IT: overview next week's plans/Home Study Assignments for Session 16, and write a testimony of what FAITH has meant to you;

DO IT: make visits—at Team Leader's cue and as the situation merits, share full FAITH Visit Outline;

SHARE IT: celebrate.

In Advance

- Prepare Pre-Enlistment Cards or put information on index cards. A sample is printed in this session, and in text file03.txt on the CD-ROM in your *FAITH Training Pack.* Put a card at every place.
- Using the copy "Join Us … on a Journey in FAITH" in this session (pp.233-234) or in text file04.txt, on the CD-ROM (*FAITH Training Pack),* customize an enlistment brochure for your ministry. Distribute copies and walk people through the leaflet at the appropriate time (Step 4).
- Enlist a Team Leader to share benefits of serving in this way.
- Overview teaching suggestions and content. Use either Session 15 overhead cels (#69-70) of the computer presentation slides. Review "Frequently Asked Questions" in the Administrative Guide.
- If dates have been set for the next semester of FAITH, indicate plans.
- Highlight information in this session needed for next week's review. Help Learners know how to prepare.

(15 min.) CHECK IT

If the computer presentation is used, display the agenda frame for Team Time, as desired. Add other points as needed.

Team Time

CHECK IT

Your Team Leader directs this important time, checking off memory work, reviewing previous sessions and completed assignments, answering questions, and providing guidance to strengthen home visits.

Agenda:
✓ FAITH Visit Outline
✓ Other Home Study Assignments
✓ Session 14 debriefing
✓ Help for strengthening a visit

❑ ***Outline memorized?—check it!***

Team Leader: In the adjacent box, check off each word as the Learner recites it correctly. In the space provided for sign-off, indicate your approval by signing your name.

FAITH VISIT OUTLINE

❑ *Preparation*

- ❑ **INTRODUCTION**
- ❑ **INTERESTS**
- ❑ **INVOLVEMENT**
  - ❑ **Church Experience/Background**
    - ❑ **Ask about the person's church background.**
    - ❑ **Listen for clues about the person's spiritual involvement.**
  - ❑ **Sunday School Testimony**
    - ❑ **Tell general benefits of Sunday School.**
    - ❑ **Tell a current personal experience.**
  - ❑ **Evangelistic Testimony**
    - ❑ **Tell a little of your pre-conversion experience.**
    - ❑ **Say: "I had a life-changing experience."**
    - ❑ **Tell recent benefits of your conversion.**
- ❑ **INQUIRY**
- ❑ **Key Question: In your personal opinion, what do you understand it takes for a person to go to heaven?**
  - ❑ **Possible answers: Faith, works, unclear, no opinion**
- ❑ **Transition Statement: I'd like to share with you how the Bible answers this question, if it is all right. There is a word that can be used to answer this question: *FAITH (spell out on fingers).***

❑ *Presentation*

❑ **F is for FORGIVENESS.**

❑ **We cannot have eternal life and heaven without God's forgiveness.**

- ❑ ***"In Him [meaning Jesus] we have redemption through His blood, the forgiveness of sins"—Ephesians 1:7a, NKJV.***

❑ **A is for AVAILABLE.**

❑ **Forgiveness is available. It is—**

❑ **AVAILABLE FOR ALL**

- ❑ ***"For God so loved the world that He gave His only begotten Son, that whoever believes in Him should not perish but have everlasting life"—John 3:16, NKJV.***

❑ **BUT NOT AUTOMATIC**

- ❑ ***"Not everyone who says to Me, 'Lord, Lord,' shall enter the kingdom of heaven"—Matthew 7:21a, NKJV.***

❑ **I is for IMPOSSIBLE.**

❑ **It is impossible for God to allow sin into heaven.**

❑ **GOD IS—**

- ❑ **• LOVE**
  - ❑ ***John 3:16, NKJV***
- ❑ **• JUST**
  - ❑ ***"For judgment is without mercy"—James 2:13a, NKJV.***

❑ **MAN IS SINFUL**

- ❑ ***"For all have sinned and fall short of the glory of God" —Romans 3:23, NKJV.***

❑ **Question: But how can a sinful person enter heaven, where God allows no sin?**

❑ **T is for TURN.**

❑ **Question: If you were driving down the road and someone asked you to turn, what would he or she be asking you to do? *(change direction)***

❑ ***Turn* means repent.**

❑ **TURN from something—sin and self**

- ❑ ***"But unless you repent you will all likewise perish"—Luke 13:3b, NKJV.***

- ❑ **TURN to Someone; trust Christ only**
  - ❑ **(The Bible tells us that) *"Christ died for our sins according to the Scriptures, and that He was buried, and that He rose again the third day according to the Scriptures"—1 Corinthians 15:3b-4, NKJV.***
  - ❑ ***"If you confess with your mouth the Lord Jesus and believe in your heart that God has raised Him from the dead, you will be saved"—Romans 10:9, NKJV.***

- ❑ **H is for HEAVEN.**
- ❑ **Heaven is eternal life.**
- ❑ **HERE**
  - ❑ ***"I have come that they may have life, and that they may have it more abundantly"—John 10:10b, NKJV.***
- ❑ **HEREAFTER**
  - ❑ ***"And if I go and prepare a place for you, I will come again and receive you to Myself; that where I am, there you may be also"—John 14:3, NKJV.***
- ❑ **HOW**
  - ❑ **How can a person have God's forgiveness, heaven and eternal life, and Jesus as personal Savior and Lord?**
  - ❑ **Explain based on leaflet picture, F.A.I.T.H. (Forsaking All I Trust Him), Romans 10:9.**

❑ *Invitation*

- ❑ **INQUIRE**
- ❑ **Understanding what we have shared, would you like to receive this forgiveness by trusting in Christ as your personal Savior and Lord?**
- ❑ **INVITE**
  - ❑ **Pray to accept Christ.**
  - ❑ **Pray for commitment/recommitment.**
  - ❑ **Invite to join Sunday School.**
- ❑ **INSURE**
- ❑ **Use *A Step of Faith* to insure decision.**
  - ❑ **Personal Acceptance**
  - ❑ **Sunday School Enrollment**
  - ❑ **Public Confession**

❑ ***Other Home Study Assignments completed?—check it!***

In reading the FAITH Tip "How Jesus Handled Difficult Situations" and the Scripture passages identifying specific situations He encountered, what principles did you discover for relating to people? For handling "interruptions"? A difficulty, interruption, or distraction may be an opportunity—even a divine appointment—in disguise.

❑ ***Any questions from Session 14?—check it!***

What questions do you have about Session 14? Ask your Team Leader now.

Team Leader: As needed, review any information from Session 14 that will appear on the written review in Session 16. Indicate that other information Learners may need about the reviews may be answered in this session.

❑ ***Need help in strengthening a visit?—here's how!***

In a visit present as much of the FAITH Visit Outline as you feel you can. Remember, you will have the use of *A Step of Faith* to assist you with the ***Invitation.***

Also, remember Philippians 4:13: "I can do everything through him (Christ) who gives me strength" (NIV).

(5 min.) Transition to class-rooms for instruction on the content of the session.

Teaching Time

HEAR IT

STEP 1 (10 min.)

Say: This session is one of the most important of the entire FAITH semester. Any FAITH training ministry is just one semester away from extinction.

Begin by highlighting the importance of pre-enlistment for future growth. Use the computer presentation slides or the overhead cels.

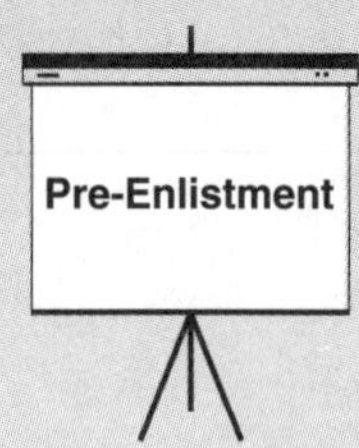

- **Point out the card at every place.**

Say: The Pre-Enlistment Card is not our official enlistment card, but a way to help you focus your thinking on persons who might be open to FAITH enlistment efforts.

You've already been praying for them.

- **On the Pre-Enlistment Card write the names of the two individuals God has placed on your heart.**

Say: If you just cannot think of people who might be the focus of enlistment for next semester, we will have a list of adults who have joined the church since this semester began. They will prove to be some of the most responsive folks to our enlistment efforts.

When enlistment does begin, remember we only enlist members assigned to our Sunday School classes or departments.

NOTICE:
Any FAITH training ministry is just one semester away from extinction.

Our involvement in FAITH enlistment includes three basic steps: pre-enlistment, reenlistment, and enlistment. At the same time we are enlisting individuals personally, public enlistment efforts such as All on the Altar and the FAITH Kickoff Banquet are under way.

Consider the Need for Pre-Enlistment

The effectiveness of our next semester of FAITH training depends on your faithfulness and participation. Have you been praying about your continuing involvement in FAITH? About the participation of other persons from your Sunday School class or department?

FAITH PRE-ENLISTMENT CARD

Name ____________________

Sunday School Department ____________________

List two individuals in your Sunday School class or department for whom you will begin to pray to become FAITH Learners in the next semester of FAITH.

____

____

If someone has not yet come to mind, pray for the Lord to place a name on your heart.

Someone has said, "We need to talk to God about people before we talk to people about God." This is true about our FAITH enlistment process as much as it is about presenting the gospel to a lost person. It is time to begin considering people who might be interested in FAITH training.

The beginning point of our efforts is always prayer. Pray for those members who might benefit and who, in turn, would benefit from our training and our Sunday School ministry.

Activate your prayer partners to "talk to God about people"—about class members who might be future FAITH participants as well as about their own role in the FAITH strategy.

Options for Reenlistment

If Team Leaders fail to reenlist, the equipping ministry comes to an end. Reenlistment is the most important need at this point in the training semester. For every Team Leader who reenlists, two more Team Learners can be trained. Several options are available for reenlistment.

Option 1: First, consider the __________ _____________ option. If possible, those of you who are serving as Team Leaders need to continue serving in this way for the next semester of training. Likewise, everyone who is a Team Learner is needed as a Team Leader during the next cycle of training.

Usually no one feels entirely confident taking this action, but there are those who testify that their spiritual growth is greatly accelerated as they experience the Holy Spirit's leadership in their role as Team Leader.

BENEFITS OF SERVING AS A TEAM LEADER

____

____

____

____

____

Our FAITH ministry cannot grow without Team Leaders continuing to serve. Since every Team has three people, one of whom is a Team Leader, we can only train a number equal to twice the number of Team Leaders who are trained and serving.

Option 2: The second option for reenlistment is to become an _______________ ________ ___________. You will move to the next level of training and be placed with a Team Leader as his or her assistant. In this role you will be introduced to increased responsibility under the direction of your Team Leader. Because you have been through FAITH at least once, you function as an encourager to other Learners. Usually a Team Learner fills out the Team.

Option 3: Third, consider the ________________ option. On occasion someone who completes training as a Team Learner may feel the need to repeat the next semester as a Learner. This option is not encouraged unless you were unable to keep up with assignments and lack confidence in your ability to lead in making a visit using the FAITH Visit Outline. If this is the case, however, simply reenlist as a Team Learner.

STEP 2 (10 min.) **Direct Learners to fill in the blanks while you share options for reenlistment. Use computer slides or overhead cels.**

- **Team Leader**

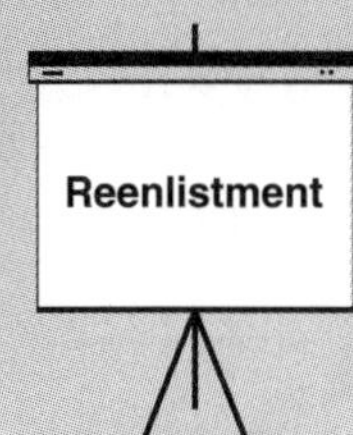

Say: I have asked ________________ to share a brief testimony about his/her experience as a Team Leader. Listen for benefits you feel would help or encourage you.

- **Assistant Team Leader**

- **Learner**

STEP 3 (10 min.) Remind Teams about enlisting for FAITH through Sunday School. Use appropriate media support. Address questions that may come up using "Other Enlistment Considerations" (in advance also review "Frequently Asked Questions About FAITH" in the Administrative Guide.)

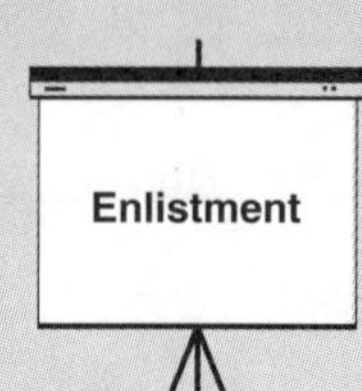

STEP 4 (10 min.) If an enlistment leaflet has been prepared based on "Join Us ... on a Journey in FAITH" copy, walk Learners through the enlistment leaflet now. Explain how it may be used—by Team Leaders to personally contact Learners for their Teams. Distribute copies according to the plans used by your church. Give instructions on when/how it is to be used.

(Copy is at the end of this session and on text file04.txt on the Training Pack CD-ROM.)

STUDY It

STEP 5 (5 min.) Overview Home Study Assignments for Session 15.

- Discuss—Schedule/process for review
- Write—What FAITH has meant to you testimony
- Read—*Evangelism Through the Sunday School* assignments, FAITH Tip: "Why Are We Left Here on Earth?"
- Journal—Your Journey in Faith

Our Process for Enlistment

Remember, we enlist in this manner. Our first goal is to enlist persons from our ______________ ______________ __________. This means that all three members of a Team are from the same class. This can only be done in a coeducational class due to the fact that there must be a woman on each Team.

The second goal is to enlist from our ________________ ____________ ____________________. All three Team members are enlisted from the same department. This would take a combination of men's and women's classes. It also would incorporate most children's and preschool workers.

The third goal is to enlist from our ________-____________ ______________. This approach means all Team members are at least from the same age division. This approach also can include persons who cannot be placed on a Team from the same class or department and can accommodate associate members.

On occasion there are not enough people from the same department or division to make a three-person Team. In those cases, a church staff member or associate member (someone working in another department or age division) is assigned to the Team. Assignments will be made from among members of the respective department(s) or division(s).

Other Enlistment Considerations

You may have questions of your own or discover that questions such as the following come up. Here are some ways to respond.

Question: What about staff members or Sunday School general officers who are not in a class?

Answer: In this case, the other two members of the Team should be from the same class or department. It would be best to use staff or general-officer Teams to strengthen the age divisions with the least representation in the FAITH training program. An example is for a staff member to train two single adults.

Question: What about preschool and children's workers?

Answer: In larger departments it may be possible to get all Team members from the same department. If this is not possible, then form the Team from the same division (Preschool or Children's). Many churches strategically place preschool or children's workers with the appropriate young adult Team members, to better reach the entire family.

Question: What about youth in FAITH training?

Answer: FAITH training works with students as well as adults. Separate materials are available that have a distinctive student focus. Student FAITH works best with older youth, grades 9 and higher.

A Sunday School Moment

When you began FAITH, you were encouraged to know that God would transform both you and our Sunday School ministry.

How is your Sunday School class stronger because of the FAITH strategy or your participation in FAITH? Are members more open to visitors? In what ways is Bible teaching more focused because lost people are attending? Do new members feel the acceptance and nurture of the class? Are prayer and planning evident in everything the class does?

Conclude by asking FAITH participants to think about the questions about their class, in "A Sunday School Moment." Do not call for responses, but dismiss in prayer after a few moments of reflection.

(5 min.) Transition to assemble with FAITH Teams to prepare for home visits.

Visitation Time

DO IT

(110 min.) DO IT

As you have opportunity, take the lead in the entire FAITH Visit Outline. Your Team Leader or other Learner will be ready to assist you.

At some point before the next semester of FAITH, you may be asked to make an enlistment visit. Do not do so until asked, but continue to pray about others who might benefit from involvement in this training. Think about how the benefits you have experienced might help someone else.

Celebration Time

SHARE IT

(30 min.) SHARE IT

- Reports and testimonies
- Session 15 Evaluation Card
- Participation Card
- Visitation forms updated with results of visits

The final checkup of information covered during the past 15 weeks is printed in Session 16. Next week, you will be asked to write from memory answers to the written review. Do not write any answers now on the quiz, but be prepared to do so next week. You may review in advance by referring to the session indicated in parentheses alongside each question.

After the written review you will pair off with another person to recite the FAITH Visit Outline. Your partner will listen and check off all the points you cover. Then you will change roles and listen to your partner recite the outline, checking him or her off as each point is covered.

If you have not already submitted the names of two persons in your class for whom you are praying regarding the next semester of FAITH, turn those names in next week also. Continue to pray about persons you feel would be interested in future semesters of FAITH training.

____

____

Write a brief testimony of what FAITH has meant to you, to turn in during Session 16.

In *Evangelism Through the Sunday School: A Journey of FAITH* by Bobby Welch read "Results You Can Expect" (pp. 62-72) and the introductory article "Sandee's Letter."

As you think about and approach persons who may be interested in FAITH training, do not say no for anyone. Share with them results you have experienced in the FAITH ministry.

Read your final FAITH Tip, "Why Are We Left Here on Earth?," and think about ways God has worked in expected and in unexpected ways throughout FAITH training. Think about: Why did God leave us on earth?

Why Are We Left Here on Earth?

It seems that everywhere Jesus went, He found people needing good news. *Well, sure,* you may be thinking, *if I could heal the blind and raise the dead, I could probably be a more effective witness, too!* Jesus seemed to anticipate our response in John 14:12: "I tell you the truth, anyone who has faith in me will do what I have been doing. He will do even greater things than these, because I am going to the Father" (NIV). Greater things? Yes, Jesus' miracles had to do with the physical: healing diseases, multiplying loaves, even raising the dead.

We, too, can authenticate our message by meeting the physical needs of people. But we cannot fulfill the Great Commission by only having a presence for Christ. We must be willing to share the spiritual power that makes the difference!

Do you struggle with the idea that God can use you in a supernatural way today? Trust God for modern-day miracles. Ask for a fresh vision of His power in your life.

Robert and the Mistaken House

Robert's visitation team had received a guest registration card filled out by a teenage girl requesting a visit. When they arrived at the house, it was dark already. They had difficulty reading the house numbers. They were relieved when a teenage girl answered the door. On hearing they were from First Southern Baptist Church, the teenager invited them in. "Who sent you?" she asked. Robert explained that they were answering her request. "No," she replied, "God sent you. I've never even been to your church." She explained that she was only baby-sitting at this address. She assured them that it was OK to talk because the children were asleep. Their parents wouldn't mind.

"You see," she said, "last night I dreamed about hell. It terrified me; I wanted to know how to escape. I talked to my best friend today at school who said to pray and to ask God to send help. I've been praying all afternoon for God to send someone to tell me how to stay out of hell, and here you are."

Robert suddenly realized that they weren't at the wrong house after all. In fact, they were at the very place God had prepared for them.

Our Call Is to Be Faithful

When God's people are faithful—as you have been to experience FAITH training—to share God's message, then God's Spirit prepares the way in ways you can only begin to imagine. You and your Team probably could recount similar "mistaken visits" or "wrong addresses." Hopefully, you've recalled anew how God works both in the ordinary circumstances of life and in unexpected ways to use you and to prepare other people.

Perhaps our mission becomes clearer if we ask this question: Why are we left here on earth? There's only one thing God would have us do on earth that we can't do in heaven: go, make disciples, baptize, teach—the bearing-fruit aspect of glorifying God.

This semester of FAITH training ends where it began: focused on the Great Commission and our goal to become more effective, committed Great Commission Christians and stronger people of faith.

Don't stop now. You've taken an important step to equip yourself and to learn how to mentor someone else. Continue to go, make disciples, teach, and as you do, you will find people all around you who need the gospel. Share not only your presence but His power and good news.

Adapted from "The Power," in David Self, *Good News for Adults: The Power to Change Lives* (Nashville: Convention Press, 1998), 7, 12. Out of print.

Your Journey in Faith

What benefits have you experienced by following Jesus?

What are some of the most meaningful experiences you have had as a result of participating in FAITH training?

What obstacles have you faced and in what ways have you dealt with those obstacles throughout FAITH training?

Read 2 Timothy 2:1-2. What are ways you feel FAITH training has helped you:
"be strong in the grace that is in Christ Jesus"?

"And the things you have (learned)"?

Prayer Concerns

Answers to Prayer

Join Us . . . on a Journey in FAITH

What Is FAITH Training All About?

FAITH training is designed to:

- equip our members to effectively share the gospel; and
- strengthen and build our Sunday School.

Our first goal is accomplished as Learners develop a clear understanding of the FAITH Visit Outline. The second goal is accomplished as Teams are formed from within the same Sunday School class, department, or division.

Teams visit prospects for their class and department. They try to enroll those prospects who are not involved in any church's Bible study and who agree to be enrolled. Teams also minister to their class members.

Why Do We Do FAITH Training?

The Bible is clear about our responsibility to witness. The following verses are just a few indicating this all-important command: Matthew 28:19-20; Mark 1:17; Mark 16:15; Luke 24:47-48; John 20:21; Acts 1:8; Acts 8:4. In the New Testament *witness* means being a verbal witness, one person telling another the good news of the gospel.

In FAITH training, which we have based on 2 Timothy 2:1-2, we can multiply ourselves as active witnesses. The good news of salvation which we have received, we are to pass on to others and equip them to pass it on as well. FAITH helps us multiply our witness.

Why do we have FAITH training? Because the Bible commands us to do what FAITH provides.

What Benefits Do We Receive?

- Spiritual growth
- Joy in service
- Rewards in heaven
- Sunday School growth
- Souls saved
- People baptized

How Do We Do FAITH?

When and Where?

Our FAITH Training Dates: ______________________________

We meet each __________ at _____ a.m./p.m. for Teaching Time that lasts about an hour. After this time, we visit until about ______ a.m./p.m. Our schedule for several training groups of FAITH is:

Day ____________________________ Time ____________

Day ____________________________ Time ____________

Location(s): ____________________________

FAITH training is not done on Sunday mornings during Sunday School. This is the time for our ongoing Bible study.

How?

Each week for 16 weeks of training, we will meet at the church for classroom training. In Teaching Time, we use FAITH resources to learn how to make ministry and evangelistic visits. You will be on a three-person Team who visits prospects and members of your Sunday School class or department. I will be your Team Leader.

After the class session each week, we will visit prospects for our class. I will present the gospel to those who need and express interest in hearing, and you watch and listen to what we call the FAITH Visit Outline. We also will make ministry visits to our class members as the need arises. We usually visit for about an hour and a half.

We then return to the church for what we call Celebration Time. This is when Teams report the results of their visits.

During the week, at your own time and pace, you have Home Study Assignments to supplement what you are learning in the classroom and from visits. This personal time will help you journal your experience and focus on ways God is helping you in your journey of faith.

Who?

This question brings us back to YOU. It will be a pleasure and a privilege to have you on my Team. I will do my best to be a good Team Leader and to help you any way I can to make your experience a good one.

There is a place for you to sign if you will agree to be my FAITH Learner.

(Sign and detach):

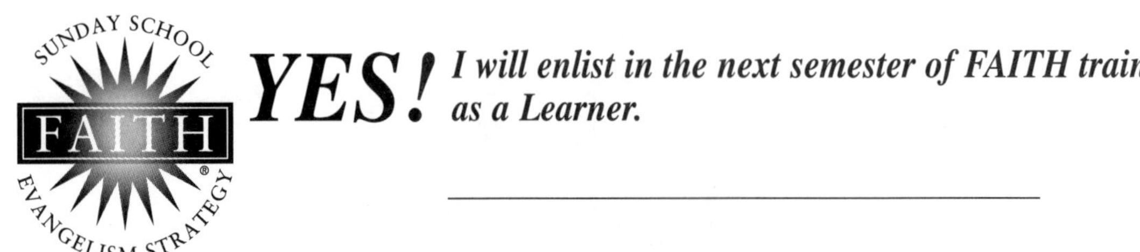

SUNDAY SCHOOL
FAITH
EVANGELISM STRATEGY
YES! I will enlist in the next semester of FAITH training as a Learner.

Dear Learner:

You're at the Finish Line! Congratulations!

In the very first Training Clinic (called the Originator Clinic) at First Baptist Church, Daytona Beach, Florida, when all 650 clinicians had gotten to this point in their training I shouted out, "Congratulations! You're at the finish line!" They too shouted and applauded their accomplishment!

That was just as it should have been because they, like you, had reached a tremendous milestone in their spiritual growth in FAITH. However, those dear souls did not stop there; they made another commitment to go home to their churches and do it again and encourage others to do the same.

My heartfelt prayer is that you will do the same: reenroll for the next semester and go back to your Sunday School and enroll at least two people to start in FAITH. Please do not drop the ball now, but let the Lord use you to pass FAITH training on to others.

When just one person drops out of FAITH, Satan is happy: fewer people are being saved and others are not growing in Christ as much as they might otherwise. You, your pastor, your staff, and your class and other Sunday School members need to help keep FAITH going. You will continue to grow personally as you continue in FAITH.

The next level of training is going to be most exciting and helpful. You'll learn how to go on winning and discipling your world in your lifetime!

Truthfully, it took me until the end of the second semester before I really felt comfortable with all aspects of the FAITH Visit Outline. I needed to keep on, and I pray you will keep on in FAITH, too. Remember, FAITH keeps going out through us to the world around us!

God bless you in your exciting and continuing journey in future levels of FAITH.

Please write a prayer for yourself and your Team here.

____

____

With You in His Certain FAITH Victory!

Bobby

Bobby

SESSION 16

Celebrating FAITH: Final Checkup

In this session you will

CHECK IT: take verbal/written reviews to evaluate your learning over the past 16 weeks;

DO IT: visit according to the plans of your church;

SHARE IT: celebrate accomplishments or announce plans for a FAITH Festival in which such celebration will occur.

In Advance

- Be prepared to explain correct answers to the written review.
- Identify the process for recognizing Learners and for certifying Team Leaders, based on information in the FAITH Administrative Guide. See your FAITH Director.
- Announce plans for the FAITH Festival.
- Announce dates for the next semester of training, and give Learners any instructions about enlistment contacts to be made.
- Share any special plans for Visitation Time.

Teaching Time

STEP 1 (20 min.) Give instructions for the written review.

Say:

The first thing you will do tonight is to take the written review in your FAITH Journal. You will have 20 minutes.

After the review you will grade your own work as I give the answers. Items have different point values because they may have several parts to the answer. Subtract the number you missed from the highest possible score (56 points).

Allow persons time to take the review. Indicate answers.

Congratulations!

You have accomplished 16 weeks of faithful participation in FAITH Sunday School evangelism training. Hopefully, you have seen results in your life and in the life of our church.

FAITH WRITTEN REVIEW

My Score: _______

____ **(Session 1, *point value 1*)** *1.* **In what ways does 2 Timothy 2:1-2 express the purpose of FAITH training?**

____ **(Session 1 FAITH Tip, *point value 3*)** *2.* **Matthew 28:19-20 is one passage that calls for believers to witness to others. What are three other verses overviewed in our training that explain the responsibility and privilege we have in sharing our faith with others?**

____ **(Session 1, *point value 1*)** *3.* **What are distinctives of FAITH Teams?**

____ **(Session 1, *point value 2*)** *4.* **Who are Teams assigned to visit?**

____ **(Session 1, *point value 1*)** *5.* **What are purposes for visits?**

____ (Session 1, *point value 5)* *6.* **What is the primary responsibility of each of the following FAITH leaders? Match the letter statement (right column) with the person who has that FAITH responsibility (left column).**

__ **FAITH Director**	**A. Leads in making visits and in training two Team members to make visits**
__ **FAITH Group Leader**	**B. Coordinates FAITH with the work of the Sunday School**
__ **FAITH Team Leader**	**C. Participates to learn how to share a gospel presentation in evangelistic visits and how to make ministry visits representing the Sunday School**
__ **FAITH Learner**	**D. Coordinates the work of 5-6 FAITH Teams with the work of the Sunday School**
__ **FAITH Assistant Team Leader**	**E. Repeats training with the intention of helping the Team Leader/encouraging Learners**

____ (Session 1, *point value 4*) *7.* **List four items in the visitation folder used by each Team each week *(answer may include resources your church provides).***

____ (Session 2, *point value 1)* *8.* **Explain what you would say during the INTRODUCTION of a visit.**

____ (Session 2, *point value 1)* *9.* **What are some INTERESTS you have talked about or heard someone discuss during your visits?**

____ **(Sessions 1 and 2, *point value 1*)** ***10.*** **What are benefits of sharing a Sunday School testimony?**

____ **(Session 1, *point value 1*)** ***11.*** **What are appropriate topics to share in a Sunday School testimony?**

____ **(Session 3, *point value 3*)** ***12.*** **What outline are you to follow in sharing your evangelistic testimony?**

____ **(Sessions 2-5, *point value 1*)** ***13.*** **What is the Key Question?**

____ **(Session 2, *point value 4*)** ***14.*** **What are ways a person might respond to the Key Question? How are you to respond to each?**

Person's Answer to Key Question	***FAITH Team Response***
A ___________ Answer	______________________
A ___________ Answer	______________________
An ___________ Answer	______________________
A ___ - ________ Answer	______________________

____ *(Sessions 5-10 point value 5)*

15. **Write the transition or explanation statement that follows each letter in the FAITH acronym.**

F is for FORGIVENESS:

____

A is for AVAILABLE:

____

I is for IMPOSSIBLE

____

T is for TURN:

____

H is for HEAVEN:

____

____ **(Sessions 6-10,** ***point value 11)***

16. **Match the corresponding word in the acronym with the supportive verse(s).**

F (FORGIVENESS) __	**A. Luke 13:3*b***
	B. Romans 3:23
A (AVAILABLE) __, __	**C. John 10:10*b***
	D. Matthew 7:21*a*
I (IMPOSSIBLE) __, __, __	**E. Ephesians 1:7*a***
	F. James 2:13*a*
T (TURN) __, __, __	**G. 1 Corinthians 15:3*b*-4**
	H. John 14:3
H (HEAVEN) __, __	**I. John 3:16**
	J. Romans 10:9

____ **(Sessions 2-11,** ***point value 1)***

17. **What is one appropriate way you have seen *A Step of Faith* used?**

____ (Sessions 10-11, *point value 1)*

18. **After showing the leaflet, you explain that F.A.I.T.H. also has this meaning:**

____ (Sessions 10-11, *point value 1)*

19. **What question do you ask to inquire whether a person wants to accept Jesus as Savior?**

____ (Sessions 10-11, *point value 1)*

20. **What elements are included in a prayer to receive Christ?**

____ (Sessions 10-11, *point value 1)*

21. **What elements are included in a commitment prayer?**

____ (Session 11, *point value 1)*

22. **In addition to inviting someone to accept Christ, what do you want to invite a person to do during a visit?**

____ **(Sessions 2-11,** ***point value 4)***

23. **Briefly explain appropriate actions to take during a visit if you find out a person you are to visit is:**

- *Already a Christian* ______________________

____

____

____

- *Not involved in Sunday School/ Bible study* ______________________

____

____

____

- *Giving some answer other than a faith response to the Key Question* ______________________

____

____

____

- *Not at home or declines to accept Christ at this time* ______________________

____

____

____ **(Session 15,** ***point value 1)***

24. **Why are Team members encouraged to reenlist in FAITH training?**

STEP 2 (20 min.) Explain the process for the verbal review.

Say:

Next you will recite the FAITH Visit Outline to another person. He or she will listen and mark your Journal as you cover each item. Each item counts one point; the highest possible score is 67. Subtract the number you missed from this total to get your score.

Change places and be the listener for your partner.

VERBAL REVIEW

My Score: _______

FAITH VISIT OUTLINE

____ *Preparation*

____ INTRODUCTION
____ INTERESTS
____ INVOLVEMENT
  ____ Church Experience/Background
    ____ Ask about the person's church background.
    ____ Listen for clues about the person's spiritual involvement.
  ____ Sunday School Testimony
    ____ Tell general benefits of Sunday School.
    ____ Tell a current personal experience.
  ____ Evangelistic Testimony
    ____ Tell a little of your pre-conversion experience.
    ____ Say: "I had a life-changing experience."
    ____ Tell recent benefits of your conversion.
____ INQUIRY
____ Key Question: In your personal opinion, what do you understand it takes for a person to go to heaven?
  ____ Possible answers: Faith, works, unclear, no opinion
____ Transition Statement: I'd like to share with you how the Bible answers this question, if it is all right. There is a word that can be used to answer this question: *FAITH (spell out on fingers).*

____ *Presentation*

____ F is for FORGIVENESS.
____ We cannot have eternal life and heaven without God's forgiveness.
  ____ *"In Him [meaning Jesus] we have redemption through His blood, the forgiveness of sins"—Ephesians 1:7a, NKJV.*

____ **A is for AVAILABLE.**

____ **Forgiveness is available. It is—**

____ **AVAILABLE FOR ALL**

____ ***"For God so loved the world that He gave His only begotten Son, that whoever believes in Him should not perish but have everlasting life"—John 3:16, NKJV.***

____ **BUT NOT AUTOMATIC**

____ ***"Not everyone who says to Me, 'Lord, Lord,' shall enter the kingdom of heaven"—Matthew 7:21a, NKJV.***

____ **I is for IMPOSSIBLE.**

____ **It is impossible for God to allow sin into heaven.**

____ **GOD IS—**

____ **• LOVE**

____ ***John 3:16, NKJV***

____ **• JUST**

____ ***"For judgment is without mercy"—James 2:13a, NKJV.***

____ **MAN IS SINFUL**

____ ***"For all have sinned and fall short of the glory of God"—Romans 3:23, NKJV.***

____ **Question: But how can a sinful person enter heaven, where God allows no sin?**

____ **T is for TURN.**

____ **Question: If you were driving down the road and someone asked you to turn, what would he or she be asking you to do? *(change direction)***

____ ***Turn* means repent.**

____ **TURN from something—sin and self**

____ ***"But unless you repent you will all likewise perish"—Luke 13:3b, NKJV.***

____ **TURN to Someone; trust Christ only**

____ **(The Bible tells us that) *"Christ died for our sins according to the Scriptures, and that He was buried, and that He rose again the third day according to the Scriptures"—1 Corinthians 15:3b-4, NKJV.***

____ ***"If you confess with your mouth the Lord Jesus and believe in your heart that God has raised Him from the dead, you will be saved"—Romans 10:9, NKJV.***

STEP 3 (5 min.) Make any concluding announcements. Indicate whether Teams will make visits tonight and on what schedule.

Reminder: Have you turned in names for prayer and possible enlistment for the next semester of FAITH training? Announce the dates.

Have you turned in a written testimony of what FAITH means to you?

____ **H is for HEAVEN.**
____ **Heaven is eternal life.**
____ **HERE**
    ____ ***"I have come that they may have life, and that they may have it more abundantly"—John 10:10b, NKJV.***
____ **HEREAFTER**
    ____ ***"And if I go and prepare a place for you, I will come again and receive you to Myself; that where I am, there you may be also"—John 14:3, NKJV.***
____ **HOW**
  ____ **How can a person have God's forgiveness, heaven and eternal life, and Jesus as personal Savior and Lord?**
  ____ **Explain based on leaflet picture, F.A.I.T.H. (Forsaking All I Trust Him), Romans 10:9.**

____ *Invitation*

____ **INQUIRE**
____ **Understanding what we have shared, would you like to receive this forgiveness by trusting in Christ as your personal Savior and Lord?**
____ **INVITE**
    ____ **Pray to accept Christ.**
    ____ **Pray for commitment/recommitment.**
    ____ **Invite to join Sunday School.**
____ **INSURE**
____ **Use *A Step of Faith to* insure decision.**
    ____ **Personal Acceptance**
    ____ **Sunday School Enrollment**
    ____ **Public Confession**

Your Journey in Faith

Read Acts 11:21-24. One of the next steps of faith may be for you to help train people from other churches regarding evangelism and ministry visits. Read Acts 11:25-26. Remember that Saul (at this point in the Scriptures) was still known more for being against the church than for having started his journey of faith in Jesus.

What are ways you would be willing to be used by God to train persons (in similar fashion as Barnabas trained Saul)?

____

____

____

____

____

Read Luke 15:1-10. In what ways do you better relate to this passage after completing this semester of FAITH than before you received training?

____

____

____

____

____

____

____

Write verses from three or four psalms that help you describe what FAITH training has meant to you.

____

____

____

____

____

____

____

____

____

____

____

____

____

____

Prayer Concerns

Answers to Prayer

Team Leader Supplement

Helps for Leading Your Team in FAITH

Welcome to your important responsibility as a FAITH Team Leader. Matthew 28:18-20 describes the focus of your job as a Christian. Second Timothy 2:1-2 expresses the application of the Great Commission as the purpose of FAITH and particularly of your job as a Team Leader.

As a Team Leader, your responsibility is to apply these biblical directives by mentoring and encouraging persons as they grow as Great Commission Christians. You will personally train a Team of Learners from your Sunday School department or class to make visits to members and prospects. Part of that training includes being prepared (when appropriate) to share the gospel presentation that is such a vital part of the FAITH Visit Outline. You also will help your Team learn appropriate visitation techniques and approaches for relating to persons during a visit.

Your job as Team Leader began when you completed your training in FAITH and when you committed yourself to be used of God to train others. You took an important step of faith when you initially participated in training.

You are continuing your journey of faith with this new step of commitment. God will honor your obedience and trust.

Take a few moments to list, in the space provided, information about each person on your Team. Use this information throughout training to help you know how to pray for, encourage, and support each Team member.

Note space to write down the names of other persons in FAITH training who would benefit from your prayers. Recall and share with your Learners that other persons in Sunday School are lending their support through prayer.

Learners

Name:__________

Address:__________

Phone/Email:__________

Notes:__________

Name:__________

Address:__________

Phone/Email:__________

Notes:__________

Facilitator

Name:__________

Address:__________

Phone/Email:__________

Notes:__________

Other FAITH Leaders (Group Leaders/Director/Pastor)

Suggestions for Success as a Team Leader

• Participate in advanced training designed to strengthen your work as a Team Leader (FAITH Advanced and FAITH Discipleship).

• Be thoroughly familiar with FAITH resources and assignments.

• Encourage Learners as they recite the assigned portion during each session's Team Time.

• Personally contact Team members during the week, particularly after any absence. Update your Group Leader on any issues related to improving the work of the Team.

• Work with Learners outside of class time as needed.

• Be able to answer any questions about church expectations for FAITH, which may include—

enlisting a prayer partner;

being on time and participating fully in the sessions;

calling the church office (indicate the person to call) to indicate absences (describe the kinds of absences that are excused)

memorizing the FAITH Visit Outline and sharing it during Team Time;

completing Home Study Assignments; and

submitting in writing a Sunday School testimony, an evangelistic testimony, and regular evaluations.

• Be able to explain the different parts of the FAITH Participation Card (how to complete, visitation information needed, copies to complete, and so forth).

• Help Learners feel comfortable during visits. Do not force anyone to share more than he or she is knowledgeable about at the time. Work with Team members to help them feel comfortable as you cue them to participate and as they indicate a need for assistance.

• Communicate a healthy sense of expectation of Learners; inspect their work and carefully show them ways to improve without being judgmental.

• Recognize that Team members are busy laypersons, with other responsibilities and demands on their time.

• Assume that everyone has the same motivation and desire as you do to be obedient to God and to serve Him through His church.

Be a Good Role Model

• Always be ready to share the gospel presentation based on the word *FAITH.*

• Be on time for Team Time, and lead your group to return promptly for Celebration Time reports.

• Use travel time wisely to discuss assignments, approaches, and ways to handle different parts of the visit. After the visit, debrief what happened, consider what could have been done differently, and discuss who will handle reports.

• Keep up-to-date on your journal and other Home Study Assignments.

• Be prepared to discuss assignments with Team members.

• Follow the outline in making the visit, but know when to adjust any part of the visit. After leaving the home, explain to Learners why you made a change.

• Demonstrate use of items in the visitation folder or packet of information.

• Model appropriate follow-up actions and lead the Team to do so as well. For example, fill out cards; work with Sunday School class(es) to plan and conduct follow-up actions; write notes to persons who received a visit; and take other actions.

• Demonstrate positive, God-honoring attitudes.

• Be faithful in other church and Sunday School responsibilities.

• Practice evangelism and ministry as a lifestyle.

Your Roles as a FAITH Team Leader

Your responsibilities, as described in Session 1 of FAITH training (pp. 1-22) and the FAITH Administrative Guide, include many different, important roles.

Your Role During the Week

• Overview the upcoming session material. Do the same assignments Learners are expected to do.

• Review Home Study Assignments and be prepared to explain and discuss work with Team members.

• Work with Team members as needed to help them learn and apply various aspects of the FAITH Visit Outline.

• Pray for Team members and for persons to be visited.

• Communicate with the FAITH Director or your Group Leader any issues that impact visits and Team members.

• Participate in weekly Sunday School leadership meetings as appropriate to your church-elected position.

Your Role During Team Time

Team Time is officially the time you have with Team members before Teaching Time. This 15-minute segment begins with Session 2. During this important time:

• Lead Learners to recite all assigned memory work.

• "Sign off" on each session's memory work by writing your initials or name in the Team Time section of each member's Journal.

• Practice designated portions of the FAITH Visit Outline to facilitate learning. (If your church uses this FAITH resource), provide Learners with a *FAITH Visit Outline Card* so they can conveniently keep it in purse or pocket. The FAITH Visit Outline audiocassette is another option.

• Overview Home Study Assignments in addition to the memory work. Make sure Learners have written or shared responses as appropriate.

• Discuss previous visits and ways to strengthen visits.

• Reinforce concepts taught in previous sessions.

• Help Team members be prepared to successfully complete the verbal and written reviews, to be taken in Session 16. Routinely review questions from any Home Study Assignment they have had up to that point in the study. Particularly review memory work concepts.

• Encourage Team members as they seek to learn and apply the FAITH Visit Outline. Particularly help members where they seem to be weak.

Team Time also includes time you spend with Learners in the car en route to and from visits. Always lead your Team to pray in the car before leaving the church. Travel time can be valuable for:

• making assignments (who will share what during the visit);

• practicing parts of the presentation;

• discussing ways to strengthen and follow up on visits made; and

• considering ways to handle different parts of the visit.

After a visit, debrief what happened, consider what could have been done differently, and discuss who will handle reports during Celebration Time.

Your Role During Teaching Time

During most sessions, you will be participating in advanced training with others who have completed the first semester of training. Learn how to lead a visit in a variety of situations. Learn how to strengthen your opportunities for training others. During some sessions, you may be asked to work directly with your Team in practicing aspects of the FAITH visit.

Your Role During Visitation Time

Your leadership is key to effective visits, as you will be activating Team members at the point at which they are comfortable sharing and for which they have received training. Your objective is to give Team members opportunities to:

• *Observe someone share the FAITH presentation.*

• *Experience someone inviting a person to make life-changing commitments.*—Potentially, Learners can see someone accept Christ as Savior, enroll in Sunday School, and agree to make a public declaration of faith.

• *Share their Sunday School testimonies.*

• *Briefly share their evangelistic testimonies.*

• *Take the lead in various aspects of a visit.*—Ultimately, your objective is to lead Team members to be able to take the lead in making a visit. Use travel time constructively. Answer questions Learners may have, or let them share or practice.

In approaching the house, be sure the woman on your Team is clearly visible from the door. This will avoid the appearance of a group of men visiting at a home where that might be a concern.

You are modeling all aspects of the visit, particularly during the first few FAITH

Qualities Needed by People Who Visit

✓Compassion

✓Desire to help

✓Willingness to be involved

✓Ability to listen

✓Accepting of others

✓Confidentiality

✓Emotional stability

✓Spiritual stability

Be aware of and knowledgeable about:

- Insurance/liability issues;
- What to do in case of an accident;
- Rights of homeowners in your community;
- Process for accounting for everyone after visits;
- Matters of discretion and propriety, both for Teams and for individuals being visited (never take a child into a room alone; never leave a woman alone with only one man)
- Community restrictions or bylaws

sessions. It will be important to lead Team members to take the lead in the part(s) of the visit they already have learned during training. Let the Team member know how and when you might "cue" him to share. Always be ready to help model any given parts of the visit under the Holy Spirit's leadership. Follow the outline in making the visit; know when to adjust any part of the visit. Explain why any change was made.

Discuss use of items in Learners' visitation folders. If items are left in a home, make sure Team members understand why. Depending on the situation each week, you may be taking some information about an upcoming special event in your church; if so, highlight during the visit some activities planned for the event. Make sure correct information is recorded on the visitation assignments, the Opinion Poll, and/or the Commitment Card from *A Step of Faith.*

Use consideration and common sense as you make FAITH visits. Some issues of propriety already have been addressed by how FAITH Teams are organized.

Avoid taking your Team into any unsafe situation. A house marked by "Beware of Dog" or "No Trespassing" signs may not be appropriate to approach, especially at night. A staff member may need to make the initial contact. Sometimes daytime scheduling is all that is needed for a better scenario.

Some situations may call for a telephone call to schedule an appointment in advance. While you most desire face-to-face contact with the prospect, this step may be needed in some situations. Few people will refuse the church an opportunity for a contact, especially if they have filled out information that indicates a call is acceptable. Such a call actually may help ensure the best possible visit!

Gated communities are becoming increasingly common. In addition, some complexes do not want groups approaching or soliciting residents and so have instituted guidelines the church should respect. Sometimes guidelines include restrictions on leaving written material in the door. Even if guidelines are not clearcut, avoid leaving anything visible that might create security problems. Again, courtesy may be an issue when safety is not.

Once a Team is admitted into a gated community, such permission usually implies admission into the home. However, it may be wise to ask again. Once inside, do not be so eager to share that you pressure someone into listening or into making a decision. Be courteous and respectful of the person—and his or her right to listen or to refuse.

Your church may want some way of accounting for everyone after Visitation Time each week. If your Team finishes a visit late and will miss Celebration Time, w[ill] someone be staying at the church until all Teams have returned? Be knowledgeable about whatever guidelines your church suggests to make sure all Teams are accounted for each week. In addition to safety, this issue affects child-care workers.

Before beginning FAITH, review with your FAITH Director the church's insurance and liability guidelines, as well as appropriate community restrictions. At the same time you seek to provide the safest possible experience, do not ignore the Holy Spirit's prompting if He is leading you to continue in some situations.

Your Role During Celebration Time

• For each session, make sure Team members complete the Participation Card in their Journals and complete and turn in an Evaluation Card.

• Turn in to the FAITH Director Visit Assignment Cards and/or Commitment Cards with complete, up-to-date information recorded.

• Encourage Team members to be prepared to share results from visit(s) made, particularly when someone gave a testimony or shared the gospel or when a prospect makes a commitment. It is important for Team members to share ways they observed the Holy Spirit working in the lives of persons being visited as well as in their own lives.

How to Complete the FAITH Participation Card

Each session be prepared to lead your Team to record all numerical information about visits during Celebration Time. This information is compiled on the Report Board as a summary of all Team results. As you are compiling your Team's report, also check Visit Assignment Cards and Opinion Poll surveys to see whether totals match information on individual forms. Each Learner also is keeping a record of weekly results on the copy in *A Journey in FAITH: Journal* (p. xiii).

CLASS PARTICIPATION

Weekly attendance, completion of Home Study Assignments, and recitation of the appropriate part of the FAITH Visit Outline can be indicated by a check mark.

Other categories reflect visits made and so call for numbers—either of attempts/visits made or of persons hearing/responding to some part of the visit.

VISITATION

No. of Tries—Number of homes your Team actually attempted to visit.

No. Visits—Number of homes in which some information was provided

No. People Talked with—Number of persons you talked with, whether they allowed you to continue or not.

FAITH Participation Card

Name ______________________________ Semester dates ______________

Address ______________________________ Phone ______________

Sunday School class/department ______________________ Teacher ______________

Other Team members ______________________________

Check one: ❑ FAITH Team Leader ❑ FAITH Assistant Team Leader ❑ FAITH Team Learner

	1	2	3	4	5	6	7	8	9	10	11	12	13	14	15	16	Totals
Class Participation *Place a check to indicate completion for the appropriate session.*																	
Present																	
Home study done																	
Outline recited																	
Visitation *Indicate a number for the following areas.*																	
Number of tries																	
Number of visits																	
Number of people talked with																	
Type of Visit *(Assignments)*																	
Evangelistic																	
Ministry																	
Baptism																	
Follow-up																	
Opinion Poll																	
Gospel Presented																	
Profession																	
Assurance																	
No decision																	
For practice																	
Gospel Not Presented																	
Already Christian																	
No admission																	
Sunday School Enrollment																	
Attempted																	
Enrolled																	
Baptism Explained																	
Committed																	
No decision																	
Life Witness																	
Profession																	
Assurance																	
No decision																	

TYPE OF VISIT

Evangelistic—Number of visits made in which one or more persons did not know Christ as Savior (may or may not be assigned visit).

Ministry—Number of visits made in which one or more Sunday School members were addressed.

Follow-up—Number of visits made in which one or more persons recently contacted made some commitment (conversion, enrollment, public declaration).

Opinion Poll—Number of visits made in which the Opinion Poll was used as the primary instrument for beginning the visit. When you are allowed to share the gospel presentation using the Opinion Poll, indicate as an evangelistic visit.

GOSPEL PRESENTED

Profession—Number of persons who prayed to receive Christ as a result of the visit (whether an assigned visit or an Opinion Poll contact).

Assurance—Number of persons already trusting Christ who heard the gospel presentation and acknowledged their assurance/reassurance of heaven.

No Decision—Number of persons who heard the gospel presentation and rejected the gospel or chose not to pray to receive Christ.

For Practice—Number of persons already trusting Christ who agreed to hear the gospel presentation as practice for a Team member.

GOSPEL NOT PRESENTED

Already Christian—Number of persons who answered the Key Question with a faith answer and the FAITH gospel presentation was not shared.

No Admission—Number of visits attempted in which the person would not permit the Team to share (assigned visit or Opinion Poll).

SUNDAY SCHOOL ENROLLMENT

Attempted—Number of persons not already enrolled in Sunday School who were invited to enroll in our Sunday School sometime before concluding the visit.

Enrolled—Number of persons who agreed to enroll in our Sunday School and who provided information to be used for enrollment purposes.

LIFE WITNESS

Profession—Number of persons who prayed to receive Christ during the week as a result of a Team member's sharing the gospel presentation.

Assurance—Number of persons already Christian who heard the gospel presentation from a Team member during the week and acknowledged assurance/reassurance of heaven.

No Decision—Number of persons who heard the presentation from a Team member during the week and either rejected or chose not to pray to receive Christ.

Use the Evaluation Card to Improve FAITH

Your FAITH Director or Facilitator, working with Group Leaders, assume the responsibility of duplicating and distributing enough copies of the Evaluation Card

FAITH Evaluation Card

Session ___

Instructions: Circle the number that best represents your evaluation of participation and the assistance you received during each segment of the session *(1=poor, 10=excellent).* Write any comments, particularly those that would indicate where you feel something could be strengthened.

1. TEAM TIME

Usefulness of Time	1	2	3	4	5	6	7	8	9	10
Helpfulness of Team Leader	1	2	3	4	5	6	7	8	9	10

Comments: ____________________

____

____

____

2. TEACHING TIME

Value of Session	1	2	3	4	5	6	7	8	9	10
Helpfulness of Facilitator	1	2	3	4	5	6	7	8	9	10
Amount of Practice Time	1	2	3	4	5	6	7	8	9	10

Comments:

____

____

____

3. VISITATION TIME

Correct information on Visit Assignment Cards? ❑ Yes ❑ No

Who led in making visit? ____________________

Describe highlights and concerns in visit(s) ____________________

____

____

____

Recommendations for follow-up: ____________________

____

____

____

4. CELEBRATION TIME

Value of Session	1	2	3	4	5	6	7	8	9	10

Comments: ____________________

____

____

____

for each participant for each session of FAITH.

The Evaluation Card is designed to get input from Team members regarding their experience each session. This information is shared with you and other Team Leaders, the Facilitator, the FAITH Director, and FAITH Group Leaders. In Group Leader Meetings and other settings, such as at the end of a semester of FAITH, these leaders use the information to strengthen participation and to enhance FAITH training opportunities.

As you work with your Learners encourage them to indicate any significant help or lack of help they might be receiving—both from you and from the FAITH Facilitator and from the experiences and resources provided. This feedback should not be threatening but an opportunity to grow and to improve.

Clarify the use of the card for Team members as needed. For all sessions but Orientation and Session 12, the form provides opportunity to specify aspects of Team Time, Teaching Time, Visitation Time, and Celebration Time that helped or hindered Learners in learning and practicing FAITH. Orientation does not have these four segments of time, and Session 12 is exclusively Team Time (practice).

Emphasize the follow-up section of the card. In this section Team members indicate any potential follow-up opportunities discovered during visits. This important information is used by the FAITH Director and Group Leaders in making follow-up assignments to FAITH Teams and to Sunday School classes or departments.

Be Supportive of Your Team at Challenging Times

You can especially encourage Learners during the most challenging aspects of FAITH training. These assignments generally give Learners a sense of pressure:

Sessions 3-4 Writing an evangelistic testimony that does not "tell all" or answer the Key Question

Session 5 Being asked/prepared to take the lead in the ***Preparation*** portion of a visit

Sessions 6-11 Recognizing that memory work and Home Study Assignments are at their maximum and call for a significant amount of time

Session 11 Being prepared to take the lead in sharing the entire gospel presentation

Session 16 Taking verbal and written reviews.

By being sensitive to the pressures many Learners feel, you can be better prepared to recognize signals of dropout. Think about ways you could encourage Learners on your Team if any of these symptoms begin to surface:

- unexcused absence;
- tardiness;
- getting behind in memory assignments;

• expression of dissatisfaction with some aspect of the training experience;

• resistance to taking part in visitation; and

• leaving before Celebration Time.

Of course, these symptoms also can indicate areas of improvement that are needed somewhere in the FAITH ministry. Along with Group Leaders and your FAITH Director, be sensitive to ways training needs to be strengthened.

Help Learners Develop and Share Their Evangelistic Testimony

Every believer's journey of faith is unique. Your job is not to make every testimony alike but to help Learners share their testimonies in a concise and meaningful way. Many believers have never shared their testimonies with someone else. Many believers have never shared their evangelistic testimonies without telling someone the answer to the Key Question.

Your job is to help your Learners feel comfortable enough through written and verbal practice to share their testimonies so someone will want to know what has made a difference in their lives. Review the contents of Session 3 as you seek to help Learners with their evangelistic testimonies.

If a Learner had a childhood conversion, the evangelistic testimony may not match up as closely to the evangelistic testimony of someone who came to know Christ as an adult. Learners may need help recalling early experiences that helped them see their need for Christ. Based on the three-point outline being used, more benefits of assurance may be recalled than pre-conversion experiences. However, all Christians should be able to recall events and experiences that led them to realize their need for Christ and specific life-changing experience(s) that helped them make the decision to follow Him.

For Learners whose evangelistic testimony is characterized by childhood conversion, use these statements as needed to help them articulate and recall their Pre-Conversion Experience.

I became aware of my need for salvation when . . .

I did not understand . . .

I talked with this person(s) about my questions or concerns . . .

Bible verses or ideas that helped me . . .

In all situations, your evaluation can help Learners keep the main part of their salvation story and eliminate trivial or unnecessary details for this time in a FAITH visit. (Remember the Session 3 video segment, "Dr. Faith: The Testimony!")

NOTE: During Home Study Assignments for Sessions 3 and 4, Learners are assigned to practice writing their testimonies on separate sheets of paper and to submit them for evaluation. In Session 4 Team Time, use the criteria given in Session 3 to offer suggestions to strengthen the testimonies.

A Session 4 Home Study Assignment gives Learners space to record their evangelistic testimonies in their Journals—not necessarily for memorization, but for recall of significant aspects of their personal journeys (as was done with Sunday School testimonies). In some cases, churches will want Learners to submit an "official" version of their testimonies, which could be used during future enlistment campaigns and other special evangelistic opportunities of the church. In this case, submit written testimonies to the FAITH Director who will work with the church staff in compiling and using these at appropriate times.

Translate "Churchy" Language into Everyday Language

Church members have a strong tendency to use the "language of the kingdom," assuming other persons have the same understanding or connotation we have. This language is particularly obvious when we share about spiritual matters with unchurched persons. Notice how easy it is for many churched people to use words or phrases such as "walk the aisle," "redeemed," "sinful," "through His blood," "grace," and "conversion" without giving a simple explanation. It is a good exercise to be able to restate words, to make sure you are not dependent on certain language to communicate.

The FAITH Visit Outline provides opportunity to share many significant theological truths in simple, easy-to-understand terms with adults, youth, and older children. Many persons are quite familiar with the key terms and their corresponding images: *Forgiveness, Available to All, Impossible for God to Allow Sin . . . , Turn,* and *Heaven.*

On the other hand, many people you encounter will either have no background to help them comprehend the impact of the gospel on their lives or they may have preconceived misconceptions of faith in Christ. Others will need some of the words or concepts "translated" for them. Be particularly sensitive to situations in which you may need to briefly explain something in the presentation.

For example, in visiting a nine-year-old, one Team member realized immediately that the child related to FORGIVENESS and AVAILABLE FOR ALL by merely emphasizing the importance of God's love for her when John 3:16 was shared. Also, when it was time to share the illustration of "turning" a car, the Team member altered the illustration by asking, "When you are riding with your Dad in the car and you tell him to turn, what do you want him to do?" That kind of intuitive thinking is how you will help your Learners be effectively trained.

Many people who might have some trouble relating to words we use will "see" the gospel through the picture on the front of *A Step of Faith.*

Always be sensitive to the fact that kingdom language is somewhat foreign to many people today. At the same time, remember that the Holy Spirit will be working through you to help individuals understand the simplicity and the life-changing implications of the good news of faith in Christ.

Evangelistic Testimony Outline

(1) Pre-Conversion Experience

When conversion was as a child, recall that time by using these and other questions:

I became aware of my need for salvation when . . .

I did not understand . . .

I talked with this person(s) about my questions or concerns . . .

Bible verses or ideas that helped me . . .

(2) Conversion Experience: "I had a life-changing experience"

(3) Recent Benefits of Conversion (includes assurance of salvation)

Opinion Poll for Ministry Development Questions

1. In your opinion, do people attend church now as often as they did 5 years ago? *(yes/no)*

2. For what reasons do you think people attend church?

3. To what group(s) do you think the church needs to give more attention? *(Senior Adults, Median Adults, Young Adults, Singles, College Students, Youth, Children, Preschoolers, Other—be specific)*

4. In your opinion, is it important for people to read the Bible? *(yes/no)* Why or why not?

5. In your personal opinion, what do you understand it takes for a person to go to heaven? *(depending on response)* Could we have a few more moments to share with you how the Bible answers the last question?

If You Need Evangelism and Ministry Opportunities, Use the Opinion Poll

The Opinion Poll is designed to briefly interview someone who likely has no connection with ministries of your church. This tool is designed to be used when you are in a community where you do not have information on or input from residents. On some occasions, a Team may have made or attempted visits from all their assignments and have time before returning for Celebration Time.

Use the Opinion Poll to survey persons about their awareness and receptivity to ministries of your church. This may give you opportunity to share any or all aspects of the FAITH Visit Outline (Sunday School testimony, evangelistic testimony, the gospel presentation, invitation to enroll in Sunday School). Information collected from persons interviewed is to be returned to the FAITH Director, who works with Sunday School leaders in determining follow-up actions to take.

When using the Opinion Poll, use the following suggestions:

- As you meet someone, greet him and immediately introduce your Team (first name only) and your church.
- State the purpose of this brief survey: to be more responsive to the needs of persons in the community. Ask for permission to get person's opinion about the five questions.
- Record information about the person and his opinions/openness to ministries. One person on the Team may ask questions while another records responses on the card.

If permission is given to share ". . . how the Bible answers the (key) question," thank the person and share the gospel presentation.

If a person is not willing to participate, graciously thank him or her. Always remember to "keep the door open" for future ministry or evangelism opportunities. You may be able to leave information about your church, especially about ministries the person indicated were important personally.

Based on the answers you receive, make the following responses as appropriate:

If someone answers the Key Question with a faith response, say something like, "That's wonderful, ———— *(person's name).* I'm so glad you also trust Christ as your Savior and Lord. Are you attending a local church anywhere?" If not, invite the person to your church and give directions. Seek to enroll the individual in Sunday School by using *A Step of Faith.* If already participating in a local church, encourage the person.

If he or she answers the Key Question with a works answer, ask for permission to share how the Bible answers the question by sharing the gospel presentation. Get appropriate information for follow-up. If a person makes a commitment, record responses on the perforated Commitment panel of *A Step of Faith.*

If Opinion Poll visits indicate areas of church ministry that can be strengthened or highlighted, be sure to share such information with Group Leaders and the FAITH Director. Persons in the community may be desiring what your church has to offer.

Follow-up information to request from an Opinion Poll prospect:
- Name
- Address
- Approximate age
- Religious background
- Openness to future visits
- Whether gospel presentation was made/response

If the Person Is Undecided, Consider Leaving *Exploring Faith*

By now you should be familiar with the process of leading a person to saving faith by using *A Step of Faith.* This leaflet is used if a person hears the FAITH gospel presentation and prays to receive salvation by accepting Jesus Christ as Savior and Lord. It also is used to record commitments by persons you are visiting (accept Christ, enroll in Sunday School, plan to publicly declare Jesus as Savior).

You will encounter some persons who hear the gospel and either reject it or are not ready to make this commitment. Provide the tract *Exploring Faith* for persons you feel would benefit with a resource to further explain or remind them of the FAITH gospel presentation. *Exploring Faith* reinforces what you have shared and can remind the person of what was said. It also may be left at residences when no one is at home.

Be sensitive to the fact that some persons need additional time to think about the implications of the FAITH gospel presentation. If someone rejects the gospel after hearing the brief presentation, offer a copy of this tract. Briefly point out the information inside. Write your name and phone number on the back of the leaflet, and give it to the person as a reminder of the visit.

Many persons, as influenced by the Holy Spirit, will read *Exploring Faith* alone after the Team has departed. Pray for and be prepared to follow up at a later time with persons to whom you have given this tract.

What If These Situations Occur?

Learners will be approaching FAITH training with questions. They will be counting on you for support, guidance, and encouragement. Here are some of the more common situations Learners will encounter.

What If Your Assigned Person Is Not at Home?

Many times the individual you are assigned to visit is not at home. In this day of busy schedules, that is understandable. Maximize the time you spend in traveling to the person's home by preparing to leave information for the person. It may be helpful to write a short note (indicating your name, phone number, and purpose) and attach it to appropriate church resource(s) that you can leave at the door. Or consider leaving a copy of the *Exploring Faith* tract. Any items left should not be visible from the street. Indicate results on your FAITH Visit Assignment Card so a future visit can be assigned.

Many times the Lord will have planned for you to go to a particular community to discover and contact "unassigned" names. This may include using the Opinion Poll with neighboring homes or visiting with a family member of someone assigned. Always be sensitive to divine appointments.

What If the Person You Visit Is Already a Christian?

One of the most wonderful opportunities any Christian has is to celebrate what Christ means to him with another believer. FAITH visitation assignments will give you and your Team many opportunities to visit fellow believers.

One purpose in visiting is to help people grow in their journey of faith. On many occasions you will be assigned to visit a Christian already active in your church, perhaps to make a ministry contact.

In other cases (such as in an Opinion Poll contact), you will find out that the person is already a believer and is active in another local congregation. When you discover that a person you are visiting is a believer in Christ as their Savior, you can do the following actions as led by the Lord:

• Share Sunday School testimonies (including invitation to enroll in Sunday School if not enrolled or encouragement to attend if not participating).

• Encourage each other by discussing ways Christ is working in your lives.

• Some Teams will find opportunity for a Learner to "practice" the FAITH Visit Outline with someone he knows to be a believer. Teams also can share the gospel presentation as a means of giving other believers a tool *they* can use to share their faith.

• People can discuss how they have experienced God's forgiveness and how they have learned that God's forgiveness is available to everyone but is not automatic. Christians can dialogue about how they realized it was impossible to have eternal life on our own because of sin and how they decided to turn from sin and self to Christ alone. Believers can share benefits of assurance of heaven.

• Believers can discuss ways to represent Christ's love to others and can pray together.

• Believers can encourage each other in their journeys of faith in Christ.

• The person being visited may have helpful information about the church's ministries or prospects. As appropriate share this feedback with church leadership.

What If the Person Does Not Give Permission to Continue?
What If He or She Says No?

It would be wonderful if everyone you encountered gave permission for you to share the FAITH gospel presentation and would accept Jesus as Savior with no further questions. Unfortunately, this will not happen. You job is not to force anyone to hear and accept the gospel, but to be available to the Holy Spirit as He works in the lives of believers today.

The tendency is for many people to want someone they do not know to leave them alone. Your job is to help them feel comfortable with you during sometimes awkward encounters. You also are to leave the door open for future ministry and evangelism opportunities.

Notice that, throughout the FAITH Visit Outline, there are opportunities to ask a person several opinion questions. You are asking for permission to share with the person. If a person does not give you permission to continue:

• *Thank the person.*—If appropriate, ask whether something was shared that the person does not understand.

• *Ask permission to leave one or more resources from the church.*

• *Ask how you can pray for, support, or encourage the person and/or members of his family.*

• *Look for opportunities for follow-up.*—Always seek to leave the door open for further ministry and evangelism opportunities.

Ways to Strengthen a Visit

Use FAITH Tips and the following visitation tips, plus experiences you and others have had, to indicate ways to strengthen a visit. Each week's Team Time agenda suggests an opportunity to strengthen visits.

Remember that you always have the option and responsibility to make ministry visits. In some cases the priority may be to make a Sunday School visit to chronic nonattenders, absentees, people facing critical needs such as surgery; persons experiencing special times (new baby); new enrollees; someone who has joined the church but not yet the Sunday School. In some cases, there may be the opportunity to enroll the person or family member(s) in Sunday School.

If You're Visiting to Enroll Someone in Sunday School

• Follow your church's policy on enrolling people in Sunday School. In general, open enrollment means inviting anyone who is not attending Bible study somewhere else to join your Sunday School. No attendance requirements are necessary. Only drop names if the person dies, joins another church, moves out of the ministry area of the church, or asks to be removed.

• Always be ready, even beyond a home visit, to enroll someone in Bible study.

• Be aware of special studies, Bible study groups, and other entry-point ministries that might appeal to the unchurched.

• Be prepared to describe benefits of your class or department by sharing your Sunday School testimony.

• Use the Response Card information in *A Step of Faith* to record and submit information about the person(s) being enrolled.

Adapted from "Making an Enrollment Visit," E. S. (Andy) Anderson in *Going . . . One on One: A Comprehensive Guide for Making Personal Visits* (Nashville: Convention Press, 1994), 110-14. Out of print.

• Have appropriate information and supplies, including something to leave with the person.

VISITATION TIP

If You're Visiting a Chronic Absentee

First, review information in Session 4 (pp. 53-66) for making a Sunday School ministry visit. The following information can enhance that session and help your Team be prepared for possible dynamics when visiting chronic absentees.

Effective ministry to chronic absentees (members who are absent for more than several months) begins with a commitment to reach out to members before they become absentees and to absentees before they become apathetic.

Factors contributing to chronic absenteeism become part of a continuing cycle: hurt (misunderstandings, being left out of the group, unfulfilled expectations); anger (hurt not taken seriously can turn into anger!); resentment (attitude hardens, frequently becoming defensive); and apathy (indifference, from which it is difficult to reclaim a person).

Team members can be more effective in this situation by knowing some basic conflict resolution skills:

• Expect some anger on the part of the person and don't try to circumvent or ignore it.

• Deal with the person's feelings by asking questions and allowing the absentee to vent anger.

• Don't defend or criticize others.

• Ask what it would take for the absentee to feel comfortable again in Bible study.

• Emphasize the role of forgiveness in the Christian life.

• Affirm the absentee's worth and importance to the class or department. Suggest attending another class if that would make the person feel more comfortable.

• As always, provide members with as much information as is available so they can make an effective visit.

Adapted from "Making a Visit to a Chronic Absentee," R. Wayne Jones in *Going ... One on One: A Comprehensive Guide for Making Personal Visits* (Nashville: Convention Press, 1994), 101–4. Out of print. For more information, check Session 4.

VISITATION TIP

If You're Visiting Bus Ministry Families

If your church has prospects through a bus ministry, there may be times when FAITH visits include these families. If so:

• Know the routes and their schedules.

• Be aware of any special church/bus ministry plans.

Adapted from "How to Visit a Child," by Jerri Trammel and "Bus Ministry" by Tom Lee in *Going ... One on One: A Comprehensive Guide for Making Personal Visits* (Nashville: Convention Press, 1994), 251, 259–60. Out of print.

• Encourage parents of younger children to ride the buses with their children.

• Know about home needs that may have surfaced in earlier bus visits and ways other ministries of the church may be involved.

• Know how to speak to a child; such home visits likely will include children. Use words and concepts the child can understand. Listen to the child. Attempt to get on his eye level. If he is on the floor, your best communication will happen when you are on the floor, too. Anytime you give special attention to a child, you help him realize he is special!

• Observe the home atmosphere. Notice how the child relates to his parents/siblings. If discipline is needed during the visit, let the parents handle it.

VISITATION TIP

If You're Visiting in Conjunction with a Church Project or Event

Often special church events are planned to coincide with Christmas, Easter, or special community events. These events—revival, choir program, Vacation Bible School—all have tremendous outreach appeal. Occasionally FAITH visits may include contacts before or after a church project.

• Be sufficiently informed about the project. Assess your own commitment to the project, and determine benefits for being involved in it.

• If visits precede a church project, take along appropriate promotional material and share details about the project with Learners in advance—and with prospects during a visit.

• After some events (revival, stewardship emphasis, or earlier FAITH visit) people may be particularly open to a witnessing visit. Make sure sufficient copies of *A Step of Faith* or *Exploring Faith* tracts are available for such visits.

• Be aware of differences of opinion about the value of a project. One person in the home may be eager to respond while another may be reluctant. Also be sensitive to other pressing needs in the home. Team members may need to redirect the focus of the visit.

• Gather/share accurate family or personal information. Team members need to know what level of response has already been made by the person or family who is being visited.

• These skills are especially helpful in a visit to follow up a church project: listening skills, conversational skills, first-hand knowledge of the project, ability to guide toward a response, evangelistic witnessing skills, basic Bible knowledge.

Adapted from "Making a Visit to Follow up a Church Project," Bernard W. Spooner in *Going ... One on One: A Comprehensive Guide for Making Personal Visits* (Nashville: Convention Press, 1994), 133–37. Out of print.

Adapted from "Making a Visit to a Newcomer" by Alan Tungett in *Going ... One on One: A Comprehensive Guide for Making Personal Visits* (Nashville: Convention Press, 1994), 117–20. Out of print.

If You're Visiting Newcomers to the Community

Newcomers are people in transition. Newcomers to a community search for products and services that relate to their needs and desires. They seek to discover the best places to shop, activities in which to be involved, and opportunities to satisfy their interests.

Church can provide a sense of belonging, a means to a relationship with God, and a focus on the meaning of life and its purpose. Finding a point of commonality and responding to needs and hurts are key to reaching newcomers (see 1 Cor. 9:22).

Some means used to secure names include community newcomer services, local records of new homeowners, birth records, utility-company records, residential realtors, rental-storage companies, and even "list brokers."

Some churches use a process to screen newcomer lists. This screening may be assigned to teams of church members who contact newcomers by telephone. Using a prepared script, these callers help determine the newcomers who are interested in receiving additional materials or who desire a personal contact. Additional materials from the church may include a letter from the pastor inviting the newcomer to the church. A visit to the home is the logical next step.

• Be sensitive about timing for a visit (during the Super Bowl or after 9:00 p.m. are not good times). Accomplish the purpose of your visit without staying too long.

• Visit promptly after receiving newcomer information so information is accurate.

[a] Include children and other family members in the conversation.

• Go in a listening mode. Be sensitive to needs expressed, including for salvation and church membership. If the opportunity allows, share FAITH; otherwise, plan for timely follow-up.

Plan appropriately to reach this target group and experience the joy of serving newcomers.

Adapted from "Making a Visit in the Workplace" by Lowell Lawson in *Going ... One on One: A Comprehensive Guide for Making Personal Visits* (Nashville: Convention Press: 1994), 153–55. Out of print.

If You're Visiting in the Workplace

If someone gives you permission to share FAITH in the work setting, observe these guidelines (and others, if dictated by the situation):

• Visit at a convenient time for the individual. Break periods and lunch hours are preferable. If you don't work with the person, schedule an appointment.

• Respect the rules of the workplace.

• Make the visit brief.

• Plan follow-up for a more relaxed setting, such as a home or restaurant.

• Allow time for the individual to talk about his work.

• Don't interrupt the ongoing work. The primary purpose of the workplace is to conduct business.

• Don't ignore supervisory channels. Every worker is accountable to his or her supervisor.

If You're Visiting When a Child Is in the Home

The focus of most FAITH visits will be adults or youth. In some situations, older children may be in the room when the gospel presentation is shared with their parents/caregivers. If the child indicates openness or interest, or a parent indicates that the child has questions, seek to clarify and answer any questions the child may have. Another visit may be appropriate to talk with the child. You may want a children's worker to accompany you.

In talking with the child, use terms and concepts he or she can understand. Literally get down on his level. In seeking to clarify whether the child has understood what was shared earlier, ask questions that cannot be answered with a yes or no. Try to get the child to restate what he understands.

Never manipulate or pressure; this applies to adults and youth, but especially to highly impressionable children.

Adapted from "How to Visit a Child,' by Jerri Trammel in *Going ... One on One: A Comprehensive Guide for Making Personal Visits* (Nashville: Convention Press, 1994), 250–51. Out of print.

If You're Making a Follow-up Visit

Part of what you have learned, and your Team members will be learning, is how to make an effective follow-up visit. When a decision is made by someone your FAITH Team visits, your Team will make the follow-up visit. Other church leaders may visit also.

A follow-up visit is to a person in response to a decision made or a need identified. Examples of follow-up visits include but are not limited to:

• *Encouraging a person to consider baptism and church membership following a decision to accept Christ as Savior.*—Assist the person in determining ways to put actions to the decision made.

• *Explaining basic church practices and ministries following a decision to enroll in Sunday School and/or decision to accept Christ.*

• *Explaining aspects of publicly declaring faith in Christ for those who did not have opportunity to attend worship.*

• *Explaining benefits of participating in Sunday School if they have not yet attended.*

• *Providing information about church ministries or events.*

• *Providing ministry after discovery of a need or concern.*

• *Being prepared to share appropriate information with other Sunday School members.*—Sometimes other members or leaders need to do additional follow-up and help assimilate the person into the life of the church.

When making a follow-up visit, determine whether an appointment is appropriate. Introduce your Team as from the church; identify the Team members who came by earlier. Remind the person of the purpose of your visit. "You made a very exciting decision last week when we were here, and we want to see how you're doing. As we mentioned, we'll all be in the same Sunday School class. What questions do you have since we last talked?"

Spend time as appropriate getting (re)acquainted with the person. Spend most of the time addressing the purpose of your visit. Provide names and phone numbers of other people in the class or church who can provide assistance. Be sure to pray with and for the person before leaving.

Evaluating a FAITH Visit

After each visit you will have opportunity to lead your Team to share written evaluation for the session. Lead Team members to use the Evaluation Card for that session to record comments. Emphasize the need to share comments regarding aspects of Team Time and Teaching Time, as well as of visits themselves. Group Leaders will be interested in knowing ways to improve the sessions as well as in knowing Learners' specific observations follow-up that is needed. It is up to Team members to offer evaluations after each session.

Team members can evaluate visits by discussing responses to questions and concerns such as but not limited to the following:

(1) In what ways did you notice the intervention of the Holy Spirit in this person's situation?

(2) What situations caused discomfort for the person being visited or for the Team making the visit? What are ways to diminish such discomfort in the future?

(3) Did the Team press for a decision when the person really was not ready to respond? If so, how can Team members be more sensitive to some people's receptivity to spiritual things?

(4) What opportunities for follow-up were discovered?

(5) Did the Team overlook an obvious opportunity to share, to deal with a ministry need, or to follow up on a concern or issue previously discovered?

(6) What difficult situations surfaced during the visit? What are ways to more effectively deal with difficult situations in future visits?

(7) What could Team members do to strengthen their participation in future visits?

The Journey Continues with BUILDING BRIDGES

You are to be congratulated for having completed A Journey in FAITH, the first basic course in FAITH training. To finish this course reflects a serious commitment and willingness to be obedient.

You should notice evidences of your own personal growth, of numeric and spiritual growth in your Sunday School class/department, of growth among fellow Team members, and of a mounting awareness within your church of the lostness of people without Christ. You should see more evidences of a desire to carry out Christ's Great Commission.

Just as you continue to grow and mature as a Christian, so does FAITH have additional opportunities for you to grow in your commitment and in opportunities to share your faith. The second 16-session course of FAITH training (Basic 2) is entitled *Building Bridges Through FAITH: The Journey Continues.*

You will learn how to:

- (if a Team Leader) lead a Team through FAITH
- make a follow-up visit to help a new believer become involved in first steps of growth and discipleship
- talk to someone about baptism using a baptism tract
- learn ways your Sunday School class/department can reach out to and can involve the unchurched in your community
- learn how to be more effective in ministering to your class/department members
- use an Opinion Poll for discovering evangelistic prospects
- handle the various new and different situations that come up in a visit
- be better able to share your faith in daily life
- share your faith with other family members
- become more effective in using the FAITH Visit Outline.

You may be participating as a FAITH Team Leader or as an Assistant Team Leader; if so, you should receive the help you need to recognize and carry out your responsibility to mentor and encourage someone else. If you are repeating this training as a Learner, you will find your Journey in FAITH study enriched by new truths, understandings, and experiences.

As FAITH enlistment efforts begin, be ready to say, "Yes, I want to help build bridges to people through FAITH." God will bless and honor that commitment.

Answers to Written Review

1. **In what ways does 2 Timothy 2:1-2 express the purpose of FAITH training?**
   (Answer should include concepts such as the following: Believers are called to grow/be strong in grace and to equip others to share their faith.)
2. **Matthew 28:19-20 is one passage that calls for believers to witness to others. What are three other verses overviewed in our training that explain the responsibility and privilege we have in sharing our faith with others?**
   (Answer: Mark 16:15; Luke 24:47-48; John 20:21; Acts 1:8)
3. **What are distinctives of FAITH Teams?**
   (Answer: Three persons on a Team; each team includes both male and female members; comprised of persons from the same Sunday School class or department)
4. **Who are Teams assigned to visit?**
   (Answer: Evangelistic prospects; church visitors; Sunday School members and prospects needing ministry, contact, or follow-up; persons responding to the Opinion Poll)
5. **What are purposes for visits?**
   (Answer: Share gospel or seek to insure person's salvation experience; provide ministry or follow-up from earlier visit; enroll in Sunday School; get information through Opinion Poll)
6. **What is the primary responsibility of each of the following FAITH leaders?**
   (Answers: FAITH Director, B; FAITH Group Leader, D; FAITH Team Leader, A; FAITH Learner, C; FAITH Assistant Team Leader, E)
7. **List four items in the visitation folder used by each Team each week *(answer may include resources your church provides).***
   (Possible Answers: Visitation assignments, Sunday School materials, map of community, A Step of Faith; *information about the church/Sunday School; Sunday School directory; also may include* Exploring Faith if used by your Teams)
8. **Explain what you would say during the INTRODUCTION of a visit.**
   (Answers should include: Introduce self/persons on Team; get acquainted with person being contacted; indicate the church you represent; clarify purpose of visit)
9. **What are some INTERESTS you have talked about or heard someone discuss during your visits?**
   (Answer will differ but likely will center around family, work, hobbies)
10. **What are benefits of sharing a Sunday School testimony?**
    (Answers include: Help put persons at ease and establish rapport; assess spiritual interests and needs; open up opportunity to enroll someone in Sunday

...le transition to evangelistic testimony; create follow-up opportu- ... Sunday School leaders)*

11. ...at are appropriate topics to share in a Sunday School testimony?**
(Answers include benefits or a personal experience such as: Friends/Support; Help in Times of Need; Opportunities to Learn and Apply God's Word; Growth as a Christian; Other Benefits)

12. **What outline are you to follow in sharing your evangelistic testimony?**
(Answer: Pre-Conversion: Tell a little of pre-conversion experience; Conversion: Say "I had a life-changing experience"; Benefits of Conversion: Tell recent benefits of your conversion)

13. **What is the Key Question?**
(Answer: In your personal opinion, what do you understand it takes for a person to go to heaven?)

14. **What are ways a person might respond to the Key Question? How are you to respond to each?**
(Answers: (1) A faith answer—affirm and ask the person how received God's forgiveness; (2) A works answer—indicate common response and ask permission to share how the Bible answers that question; (3) An unclear answer—seek clarification; (4) A no-opinion answer—respond as if to a works answer.)

15. **Write the transition or explanation statement that follows each letter in the FAITH acronym.**
(Answers:
F is for Forgiveness: *We cannot have eternal life and heaven without God's forgiveness.)*
A is for Available: *Forgiveness is available.*
I is for Impossible: *It is impossible for God to allow sin into heaven.*
T is for Turn: (after the explanatory question) *Turn means repent.*
H is for Heaven: *Heaven is eternal life.)*

16. **Match the corresponding word in the acronym with the supportive verse(s).**
(Answers: Forgiveness, E; Available, I, D, ; Impossible, I, F, B; Turn, A, G, J; Heaven, C, H)

17. **What is one appropriate way you have seen *A Step of Faith* used?**
(Answer should include: use of picture)

18. **After showing the leaflet, you explain that F.A.I.T.H. also has this meaning:**
(Answer: Forsaking All I Trust Him).

19. **What question do you ask to inquire whether a person wants to accept Jesus as Savior?**
(Answer: Understanding what we have shared, would you like to receive this forgiveness by trusting Christ as your personal Savior and Lord?)

20. **What elements are included in a prayer to receive Chris**

(Answer: Person should acknowledge personal sin; express bel

died on the cross and rose from the grave for him/her; request Jesus

him/her of sin and to save soul)

21. **What elements are included in a commitment prayer?**

(Answer: Person should express gratitude to Jesus for saving me; agree that he/she is not ashamed of Jesus; identify specific ways/commitments to grow in his/her journey of faith)

22. **In addition to inviting someone to accept Christ, what do you want to invite a person to do during a visit?**

(Answers: enroll/participate in Sunday School; take a public stand)

23. **Briefly explain appropriate actions to take during a visit if you find out a person you are to visit is:**

- Already a Christian
  (*Celebrate journey of faith together; could allow Team to practice presentation)*
- Not involved in Sunday School/Bible study
  (*Invite to enroll in Bible study)*
- Giving some answer other than a faith
  (*Ask for more information and for a* response *to the Key Question clarification of answer; move into FAITH gospel presentation when appropriate)*
- Not at home or declines to accept Christ at this time
  (Leave behind a copy of Exploring Faith*/ask permission to leave a copy and for the person to read at his/her leisure)*

24. **Why are Team members encouraged to reenlist in FAITH training?**

(Answer: So FAITH ministry can continue; needs ongoing involvement of Team Leaders and Learners)